Decent Homes for All

The United Kingdom is in the throes ... prices, new housing developments, a ... and a drastically changed demograp... this ...try is facing at the present time. *Decent Homes for All* ...ount of h... ...e planning system, historically and in recent times, has shaped and impacted upon the delivery of new housing in the UK. The book focuses on housing supply, on the quality and form of residential development, on affordability, and on the changing nature of planning itself. It examines the antecedents and evolution of the modern housing debate, and addresses a number of fundamental questions about the current 'housing crisis':

- Why have we moved away from state housing provision?
- How might the current crisis in housing affordability be addressed through planning policy?
- Why has recent debate broadened to encompass the idea of 'sustainable communities'?
- How will we deliver quality, affordable housing in the future?
- And what role should the evolving planning system play in delivering decent homes?

Decent Homes for All provides students, planners and researchers with an accessible and comprehensive narrative of the evolving relationship between planning policy and housing provision, showing how we have arrived at our present situation, and examining how current issues might evolve in the years ahead.

Nick Gallent is Reader in Housing and Planning at University College London's Bartlett School of Planning. He has previously lectured in UK housing policy at the University of Manchester and been a researcher at Cardiff University's Centre for Housing Management and Development. His principal research interests are in the areas of planning for affordable housing, the housing and planning policy relationship, and planning in the rural–urban fringe and in the countryside.

Mark Tewdwr-Jones is Professor of Spatial Planning and Governance and Director of Research at University College London's Bartlett School of Planning. His research interests are related to planning, politics, community planning, and urban and regional development. He is currently involved in a number of research projects, including work on European spatial planning, the scope and relevance of local planning, and the relationship b...

Housing, Planning and Design Series

Editors: Nick Gallent and Mark Tewdwr-Jones,
UCL Bartlett School of Planning

This series of books explores the interface between housing policy and practice, and spatial planning. Various facets of this interface are explored, including the role of planning in supporting housing policies in the countryside, the pivotal role that planning plays in raising housing supply, affordability and quality, and the link between planning/housing policies and broader areas of concern including homelessness, the use of private dwellings, regeneration, market renewal and environmental impact. The series positions housing and planning debates within the broader built environment agenda, engaging in a critical analysis of different issues at a time when many planning systems are being modernised and prepared for the challenges facing twenty-first century society.

Decent Homes for All
Nick Gallent and
Mark Tewdwr-Jones

**Planning and Housing in the
Rapidly Urbanising World**
Paul Jenkins, Harry Smith
and Ya Ping Wang

**International Perspectives on
Rural Homelessness**
Edited by Paul Cloke and
Paul Milbourne

**Housing in the European
Countryside**
Rural pressure and policy in
Western Europe
Edited by Nick Gallent,
Mark Shucksmith and
Mark Tewdwr-Jones

Private Dwelling
Contemplating the use of housing
Peter King

Housing Development
Andrew Golland and Ron Blake

Forthcoming:

**Sustainability and New Housing
Development**
Alina Congreve

**Housing Market 'Renewal'
in the City of Culture**
Chris Allen and Rionach Casey

Decent Homes for All

Planning's evolving role in
housing provision

Nick Gallent and Mark Tewdwr-Jones

Routledge
Taylor & Francis Group

LONDON AND NEW YORK

First published 2007
by Routledge
2 Park Square, Milton Park, Abingdon, Oxon OX14 4RN

Simultaneously published in the USA and Canada
by Routledge
270 Madison Ave, New York, NY 10016

*Routledge is an imprint of the Taylor & Francis Group,
an informa business*

© 2007 Nick Gallent and Mark Tewdwr-Jones

Typeset in Galliard by
Florence Production Ltd, Stoodleigh, Devon

Printed and bound in Great Britain by
TJ International Ltd, Padstow, Cornwall

British Library Cataloguing in Publication Data
A catalogue record for this book is available from the British Library

Library of Congress Cataloging in Publication Data
Gallent, Nick.
   Decent homes for all: planning's evolving role in housing
   provision/Nick Gallent and Mark Tewdwr-Jones.
      p. cm. – (Housing, planning, and design series)
   Includes bibliographical references and index.
   1. Housing policy – Great Britain.   2. City planning –
   Great Britain.   I. Tewdwr-Jones, Mark.   II. Title.
   HD7333.A3G35 2007
   363.5′5610941–dc22

ISBN10: 0–415–27446–X (hbk)
ISBN10: 0–415–27447–8 (pbk)
ISBN10: 0–203–64256–2 (ebk)

ISBN13: 978–0–415–27446–3 (hbk)
ISBN13: 978–0–415–27447–0 (pbk)
ISBN13: 978–0–203–64256–6 (ebk)

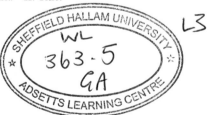

Contents

Preface and acknowledgements

Decent Homes for All is an account of how the planning system, historically and in recent times, has shaped and impacted upon the delivery of new housing. The book focuses on housing supply, on the quality and form of residential development, on affordability and sustainability, and on the changing nature of planning itself. It examines the antecedents and evolution of modern housing debate, and addresses major contemporary questions: why is the planning system currently in a state of transition? Why have we moved away from state housing provision? How might the current crisis in housing affordability be addressed through planning policy? Why has recent debate broadened to encompass the idea of sustainable communities? How will we deliver quality, affordable housing in the future? And what role should the planning system play in delivering decent homes in the years ahead? These questions, and others, are addressed within a narrative structure: we show how planning's evolution has run parallel with shifting concerns over public and private housing provision in the United Kingdom. The story we offer assumes some basic knowledge, on the part of the reader, of the purpose and scope of planning in the UK and also some general awareness of housing issues. But for those readers unfamiliar with the detail of these issues, *Decent Homes for All* provides a narrative of the evolving relationship between planning policy and housing provision, showing how we arrived at our present situation, and examining how current issues might evolve in the future.

This narrative begins in the nineteenth century where we explore the urban problems confronting an emergent planning profession (Chapter 2). Our account of 'historical development' begins in the mid-nineteenth century and ends with the arrival of the 1947 Town and Country Planning Act: it is not intended to be an exhaustive account of planning's evolution (there are already a great number of these available – see Cherry, 1974; Hall, 1996; Ward, 2004) but is intended to illustrate that modern debates – over housing supply, state versus private action, liveability and sustainability – have deep roots. The second chapter explores these roots, before jumping forward in time to consider the eclipse of state housing provision by privatisation from the 1980s onward

(Chapter 3). Much of the planned housing provision during the twentieth century was delivered by the public sector in the form of council housing and, according to Ravetz (2001), represented a 'social experiment' on an unprecedented scale. The apparent end of this experiment – marked by the sale of council housing in the 1980s under the direction of the New Right, and an overall decline in housing supply – is examined in Chapter 3. The consequent dominance of private provision in the UK has resulted in a great burden of responsibility being placed on public planning, which must strive to ensure affordability and quality in new housing development.

Chapters 2 and 3 provide the historical context of this book: the platform from which to gain a clearer perspective on recent and emerging debates. But the line between the historical and the contemporary is not the only line we draw. The arrival of the government's Sustainable Communities Plan in 2003 and subsequently the Barker Review of Housing Supply and a new planning act in 2004 provide another critical juncture. Chapters 4, 5 and 6 examine the house building, housing quality and density, land release, regional and strategic housing and affordability debates that prompted the Barker Review and the planning reforms of 2004. Hence there is a 'before' and 'after' structure in Chapters 4 to 9. Chapter 4 establishes the broad parameters of pre-2004 debate; Chapter 5 looks at how planning has intervened in housing development to achieve higher design standards, the efficient use of land, and affordability (through planning obligations); Chapter 6 then looks at these same issues within the context of regional, strategic and local case studies, illustrating how the national issues find expression in local stories. The book's later chapters – 7, 8 and 9 – then provide analyses of what are considered to be the major issues of our time: the question of future housing supply (a question now framed by the Barker Review of 2004 – Chapter 7), the positioning of housing issues with the concept of 'sustainable communities' (Chapter 8), and the prospects for delivering 'decent homes for all' – a title that we hope captures both the need for the right number and the right quality of homes – through the government's much-lauded 'step change' in planning and the current departure from a strictly 'land-use' to a broader 'spatial' planning model (Chapter 9).

In the face of massive household growth – driven by fundamental social changes, migration patterns, a growing economy and rising salaries – arguably the biggest challenge for planning is how and where to direct new house building. At the same time, it is also being called upon to prescribe the form of new housing built through the local processes of development planning and development regulation. But can the system really deliver decent homes for all, or are we on the brink of the biggest housing crisis yet to face the UK? The primary purpose of the book, which is also the focus of its conclusion, is to ask how effectively planning has delivered decent homes for all or whether, in an age of private house building, its principal success has been in serving the needs of a well-housed majority by creating scarcity and driving the large increases in property values that have been experienced in recent years. Can planning vent the current crisis of mathematics and facilitate sufficient house building in the twenty-first century? Or will it fall at this hurdle to the detriment not only of the poorly housed but of an entire generation whose future can only be assured through access to decent homes? It is our hope that this book will have wide appeal and offer an accessible, and also detailed, introduction to these important debates. It is mainly aimed at students of planning, housing and related disciplines who already have some basic knowledge of UK planning but who wish to explore the relationship between planning and housing and how this relationship has evolved. As an account of these issues offered by researchers who have been working in the area of planning and housing for more than a decade, we hope that it will also prove challenging and provoke further debate.

Numerous friends and colleagues have contributed to this book in one way or another. Special thanks are extended to Marco Bianconi who co-authored Chapter 2. We are also grateful to Johan Andersson for his help with updating the earlier drafts, and to the office staff at UCL Bartlett School of Planning – Carol Fitzpatrick, Lisa Fernand, Judith Hillmore and Laura Male – whose support in all matters administrative enable the rest of us to spend more time engaged in research and writing. Thanks are also extended to Caroline Mallinder and Michelle Green (Taylor & Francis) for their guidance in the early stages of preparing this book. Kate McDevitt took over as our main contact at Taylor & Francis in 2005 and because of her encouragement and patience we were finally, after some mid-term setbacks, able to bring this project to completion. Nick would also like to thank Manuela who agreed to make 1 July 2006 the real deadline for the completion of this book. The photographs contained herein were all (with the exception of Plate 12: the Hertfordshire countryside) taken by the authors, during research projects and less formal outings between 1993 and 2006. But despite all the assistance we received, the views (and errors, if they remain) contained in the book are entirely our own.

Nick Gallent
Mark Tewdwr-Jones
London, June 2006

List of abbreviations

AAP	Area Action Plan
ADP	Approved Development Programme
AONB	Area of Outstanding Natural Beauty
CABE	Commission for Architecture and the Built Environment
CASE	Campaign Against the Stevenage Expansion
CIH	Chartered Institute of Housing
CP	Communities Plan
CPA	Comprehensive Performance Assessment
CPD	Continuing Professional Development
CPP	Community Planning Partnership (Scotland)
CPRE	Campaign to Protect Rural England
CRC	Commission for Rural Communities
CUV	current use value
DCLG	Department for Communities and Local Government
DEFRA	Department for the Environment, Food and Rural Affairs
DETR	Department of the Environment, Transport and the Regions
DoE	Department of the Environment
dph	dwellings per hectare
DSN	Development Start Notice
DTLR	Department for Transport, Local Government and the Regions
EERA	East of England Regional Assembly
EIP	Examination in Public
ERM	Environmental Resources Management
ESDP	European Spatial Development Perspective
GAD	Government Actuary's Department
GDP	Gross Domestic Product
GIA	General Improvement Area
GO	Government Office
GONW	Government Office for the North West
GRF	Grant Redemption Fund
GVA	Gross Value Added

HAA	Housing Action Area
HAG	Housing Association Grant
HAT	Housing Action Trust
HBF	House Builders Federation
HDG	Hostel Deficit Grant
HFC	Homes for Change
HFW	Homes for Work
HIP	Housing Investment Programme
HMRI	Housing Market Renewal Initiative
HNI	Housing Needs Index
IDeA	Improvement and Development Agency
IPPR	Institute for Public Policy Research
JUDP	Joint Unitary Development Plan
LAA	Local Area Agreement
LDF	Local Development Framework
LDSPB	Lake District Special Planning Board
LEF	Local Economic Forum (Scotland)
LFS	Labour Force Survey
LPA	Local Planning Authority
LSP	Local Strategic Partnership
MAFF	Ministry for Agriculture, Food and Fisheries
NHBC	National House Building Council
NHF	National Housing Federation
NIMBY	Not In My Back Yard
ODPM	Office of the Deputy Prime Minister
ONS	Office for National Statistics
PCNPA	Pembrokeshire Coast National Park Authority
PDL	Previously Developed Land
PGS	Planning Gain Supplement
PPG	Planning Policy Guidance
PPS	Planning Policy Statement
PV	planning value
RA	Regional Assembly
RDG	Revenue Deficit Grant
RPE	Regional Planning Executive
RPG	Regional Planning Guidance
RSL	Registered Social Landlord
RSPB	Royal Society for the Protection of Birds
RSS	Regional Spatial Strategy
RTB	Right to Buy

RTPI	Royal Town Planning Institute
(S)CS	(Sustainable) Community Strategy
SHG	Social Housing Grant
SPG	Supplementary Planning Guidance
UDP	Unitary Development Plan
UTF	Urban Task Force
VDS	Village Design Statement
VPG	Voluntary Purchase Grant
VST	voluntary stock transfer

Chapter 1
Introduction

Decent homes for all

Decent Homes for All looks at the role of the planning system in the provision of the right quantity of homes, of an appropriate quality, in the right locations. It considers – by examining areas of interface in the past and present, and by looking at a range of historical and contemporary issues – whether planning is evolving into the right mechanism for increasing access to 'decent homes': namely, whether the procedures, remit and objectives of land-use – and 'spatial' – planning are fit for purpose. The book also examines planning's changing role in housing provision and in the light of recent legislation (in the form of the Planning and Compulsory Purchase Act 2004) asks what role planning will play in the years ahead. It is the government's objective to promote 'decent homes for all' (DETR, 2000c; ODPM, 2005j): it is our intention to consider planning's role in meeting this objective historically, today, and in the years to come. The aims of this opening chapter are to:

- Introduce the main strands of current housing-planning debate in Britain and set out the key themes to be considered in later chapters; it is our intention to reveal the broad parameters of the current housing dilemmas in this chapter and then to consider some of the historical 'antecedents' (in the next two chapters), its current form and aspects (in Chapters 4, 5 and 6) and latest debates (in Chapters 7, 8 and 9).
- Set out the overall structure of the book and the objectives of different sections and chapters.

In a recent examination of the housing-planning question and its political context, Murdoch and Abram (2002) suggest that the planning for housing debate in England (how many homes should be built, of what type and where) is shaped by the tension between developmental (pro-house building and general housing provision) and environmental interests (anti-development in many instances); the former pushing for additional house building and the latter seeking to place strict limits on such building. The same tension has been evident in historic and contemporary housing and planning policy: while the housing agenda has been one of targeted growth (the current call for 'decent homes for all' is only the most recent of a long line of government targets for supplying new or better homes), planning's role has been to ensure any and all development is balanced with other policy goals. This includes environmental protection. And if the planning agenda swings too far in favour of protection – as a result of changing policy emphasis nationally, and the way the system is implemented locally – then an inherent contradiction may emerge within policy, characterised by a desire to provide housing, but at the same time, limit provision where it is often most needed: frequently in the countryside (where the environmental costs of development are judged to be greater) or around urban demand hot-spots (where the priority is often to 'contain' urban encroachment away from 'green-field sites'). A compromise may emerge from an approach that aims towards 'sustainable development', which can be viewed – as Murdoch and Abram point out – as an attempt to strike a balance between developmental and environmental agendas. In other words, sustainability is about seeking compromise where there might otherwise be contradiction: how this compromise is achieved is an inevitable focus of this book.

The structure of *Decent Homes for All* was highlighted briefly in the Preface. We begin by examining some of the 'antecedents' of recent and current debate, in the more distant and more immediate past. We then establish the 'parameters' of recent debate (focusing on the status quo before the arrival of the 2004 planning Act and the Barker Review of Housing Supply) before detailing this debate and then moving to consider the latest developments in policy (particular planning policy and the emergence of strategic 'spatial planning') that may – or may not – move housing delivery onto a different track in the years ahead. The remainder of this introductory chapter is divided into two parts. In the first half, we begin by introducing recent planning-housing debate and some of the problems behind government's call for 'decent homes for all'. In the second half, we introduce the major themes to be examined in the rest of the book.

A 'manufactured' crisis?

> The overall aim of the government's housing policy is to offer everyone the opportunity of a decent home and so promote social cohesion, well-being and self-dependence.
>
> (Armstrong, 1999: 122)

In 2001, the Labour government formally set itself the target of ensuring that all *social housing tenants* have access to a 'decent home' by 2010 (DTLR, 2001c);

this target was re-iterated more recently within the context of the government's Sustainable Communities Plan (ODPM, 2003a: 13). The decent homes target was one of several stated objectives aimed at tackling deprivation in some of England's poorest neighbourhoods (DTLR, 2001b). The focus of this book is on Britain's wider housing problems, affecting both current and future generations of people occupying all types of housing across all forms of tenure: the idea of delivering decent homes for all includes the need to deliver both adequate quality and quantity of accommodation for the country's population and captures the full spectrum of housing concerns. Government also possesses this wider agenda, and the need for universal access to a decent home is a prime objective of the ODPM's (Office of the Deputy Prime Minister, now the Department for Communities and Local Government or DCLG) 2005 instalment of the Communities Plan (CP) (ODPM, 2005j: 2). More generally, housing debate in England since the arrival of the Labour administration in 1997 has become dominated by 'will they – won't they' speculation: will they – that is, the government – ensure improved standards in the public and voluntary sectors, moving beyond weaknesses and limitations inherited from the Conservative era? Will they create a planning system that can deliver a sufficient quantity and quality of new homes in the context of their 'modernising agenda' and via ongoing reforms of the planning system (instituted through the 2004 Planning and Compulsory Purchase Act)? And will they move beyond the housing mistakes and problems that have hounded governments for a century?

Governments regularly commit themselves to ambitious (albeit sometimes ambiguous) targets. In 1919, Lloyd George wooed the electorate with the promise of 'homes fit for heroes' (though he never used these exact words). In 1964, Richard Crossman – Labour's Housing Minister – pledged to build half a million extra council homes by 1970 (a rather more tangible target). Such promises usually mark a recognition of the depth of contemporary housing problems. In 1919, it was the absolute shortage of quality housing and the proliferation of slum conditions. In 1964, it was the acute slow-down in council provision – relative to a growth in need – presided over by the previous Conservative administration. Today, it is:

- The recent decline in new house building and the problem of housing affordability and hence access.
- The dwindling supply of affordable (and particularly council) housing, which is a product of two decades of the 'Right to Buy' policy and of recent abuses of that right (Regan, 2002). Government acknowledges in the CP that 'For every social home added to the stock in the last few years, at least two have been sold under the Right to Buy' (ODPM, 2003a: 28).

- The insufficient supply of new housing association ('Registered Social Landlords' or RSLs since the 1996 Housing Act) homes as a result of falling grant rates and the inadequacies of the planning system in generating land or developer subsidy for affordable homes.
- Projections of massive household growth during the next 20 years and the expectation that we are facing the deepest crisis in housing supply for a hundred years – given that demand is projected to outstrip supply by a ratio of almost two to one (that is, households forming against houses built – see Table 1.1).
- Views that the planning system has slowed the supply of new homes in all sectors by constraining land release and prioritising environmental over developmental interests.
- A belief that the market should dictate, to a greater extent than is currently the case, the quantity and location of new housing.
- A recognised need to connect housing provision with the need for sustainable development within durable communities.

In its recent response to the Barker Review of Housing Supply (Barker, 2004) – which examined the role of the planning system in supplying new homes to meet demand – the ODPM noted that:

- The country (i.e. England) faces 'growing housing demand with an increasing number of people living alone relative to previous decades and others marrying later in life. Single person households, according to ODPM's latest household projections, will account for 67 per cent of household growth between 2001 and 2021.'
- 'By 2026 only three out of ten of today's ten year olds will be able to afford to buy a home when they have families of their own if we stick with current building rates.'
- 'Average deposits for first time buyers have gone up from £5,000 in 1996 to £34,000 in the first half of 2005. In 1980 only 4 per cent of first time buyers relied on gifts or loans from friends or relatives to help with finding a deposit. That figure has now shot up to 23 per cent.'
- 'Social housing waiting lists are also affected by lack of new housing across the board. The long-term impact on low income households with pressures on social housing waiting lists, overcrowding and homelessness could be considerable if we don't act.'
- 'There are currently 150,000 fewer workers than jobs in the south-east and this number could treble if we continue building at current rates – a sign that the mismatch between supply and demand could seriously damage local economies if left unchecked' (ODPM, 2005c: 2).

The planning system is viewed as a key player in this current crisis; and while past pledges have focused on direct supply responses, the current response (in relation to the general housing question) has been to reform the processes of delivering new homes: in other words, to look at the planning system and the part it plays in helping or hindering new housing supply. The planning system has been seen as the single most significant barrier to new house building (HBF, 2002) with its lack of speed, efficiency and transparency blamed for the under-supply of new homes (Carmona *et al.*, 2003; see also Carmona *et al.* 2001). The Planning Green Paper (DTLR, 2001c) sought to address this problem through a comprehensive streamlining of planning processes, advocating a move from complex unitary development plans to simpler local development frameworks, abolishing structure plans, establishing delivery contracts and targets on large strategic sites, and a host of other measures designed to more effectively 'grasp development opportunities' and beat the housing backlog. A key criticism has been that the planning system has retrenched into statutory duty, emphasising the need to regulate growth (through development control), but neglecting the need to set a positive growth agenda. It has been hijacked by environmental inter-ests – or because of its local political nature, pays excessive attention to Not In My Back Yard (NIMBY) elements – and the pendulum has swung too far away from developmental interests. Such is the view of the House Builders Federation (HBF, 2002), which argues that the bureaucracy of planning is a hindrance to both business and house buyers, and is central to the problems listed in its 2002 report *Building a Crisis* (ibid., see Box 1.1). For many, planning's failure to lis-ten to the market, is central to the current housing crisis (see Chapter 7).

Hence any casual observer could be forgiven for attributing Britain's housing problems – and particularly the widening mismatch between homes being built and households forming (see Table 1.1) – to shortcomings in the planning system alone and the way in which the planning process seems to be so easily thwarted by anti-development pressures. It is certainly the case that building constraint has manufactured part of the current crisis in housing supply. 'Hometrack.co.uk', for example, estimated that house prices would rise by 20 per cent during 2002 (that is, between December 2001 and December 2002), which they did according to many lenders and analysts. This level of price infla-tion is not unprecedented and relatively higher rates were reached at the end of the 1980s, when slump followed boom and the market collapsed. But today, the combination of low interest rates (a response to weaknesses in the manufacturing sector and perhaps a desire to seek greater convergence with our European neigh-bours) and a stronger service sector placing inflationary pressure on wage levels have combined with low house building rates to push up housing demand at a time when supply constraints (particularly those caused by planning) are acute.

Box 1.1 Housing facts from the House Builders Federation

Population, households and dwellings

- The UK population grew by 0.25 per cent per year (145,700 pa) from 1981 to 1991 and 0.37 per cent per year (215,800 pa) from 1991 to 2000.
- The number of households in Great Britain grew by 1.0 per cent per year from 1981 to 1991 (220,000 pa) and 0.9 per cent (220,400) from 1991 to 2000.
- The proportion of Britain's population living in urban areas (90 per cent) is the second highest in Europe and the sixth highest worldwide (excluding several city and small island states).
- To accommodate expected household growth, it has been estimated that the urban area of England will increase from 10.6 per cent in 1991 to 11.9 per cent by 2016. Consequently, urban expansion takes 0.05 per cent of England's land area each year, or 1 per cent every 50 years. Typically, housing accounts for 70 per cent of land in urban areas.

Land, planning and new homes

- Housing completions in Great Britain in 2001 (162,000) fell to their lowest for 54 years. Excluding the war years and their immediate aftermath (1940–7) completions were at their lowest since 1924.
- The UK housing stock expanded by between 0.7 per cent and 0.8 per cent per year over the last decade. At current demolition rates, new homes built today will have to last 1,400 years before it is their turn for demolition.
- From 1985 to 1998, the UK invested a smaller proportion of Gross Domestic Product (GDP) in housing (3.3 per cent) than any other major industrialised nation – a record the UK has held for decades.

Source: HBF, 2002

In 2001, for example, the House Builders Federation (HBF) noted that new house building was now at its lowest rate since 1924 (excluding the war years 1939–1945). More buyers, with greater disposable income were competing for fewer homes in a market where, because of interest rates, borrowing against a new home had never been more affordable. According to the Campaign to Protect Rural England (CPRE), the apparent fall in the rate of house building in recent years is central to wider public concern over housing issues:

> a number of recent factors have contributed to the renewed interest in Government housing policy, and planning for housing in particular. Among other things, the latest

housing completions figures (which show that housing output is at its lowest level since 1924) have been used by a number of interested bodies to predict a crisis in homelessness and [. . .] conflate a number of issues. Among these issues are: affordability of market housing for key workers, in London and the South East especially; levels of affordable housing provision more generally; homelessness and use of temporary accommodation; the effects of revised PPG3 Housing (2000); Green Belt policy; and the brownfield–greenfield debate.

(House of Commons , 2002a: 222)

However, the CPRE contends that the simple link made between completion rates and a range of housing stresses – including homelessness – is unproven and a number of other factors relating to the use of homes – under-occupancy and empty dwellings (Empty Homes Agency, 2002) – are equally significant contributors to the country's persistent housing dilemma. Whatever the truth, the issue of household growth is no longer merely a civil service or academic concern, but has captured the public imagination and made planning itself and the entire housing question suddenly newsworthy. There is an acute awareness of the pressure to build new homes and great interest in exactly where these homes should be built. London is acknowledged to be a hot-spot of demand, where 'key workers' – nurses, policemen, teachers and others – are being priced out of the housing market (Hamnett, 2001; ODPM, 2002b; see also ODPM, 2003a). In the countryside too, there is public recognition of an apparent housing crisis, with a dysfunctional market favouring wealthier people from cities and leading to the exclusion of young local first-time buyers (DEFRA, 2006: 65). All these issues are of course linked and it is perhaps ironic (but also predictable) that as awareness of Britain's housing problem grows, objections to new development are also on the increase. In the face of crisis, there is a palpable fear that planners and the house building industry will get it wrong and that swathes of English countryside will be drowned beneath a sea of bricks and mortar (see, for instance, Prescott, 2002). The apparent mismatch between supply and demand was set out in a study for the Joseph Rowntree Foundation in 2002 (see Table 1.1). This analysis can be updated using the latest household projections for England for the period 2003 to 2026, issued by the ODPM in March 2006. These are shown in Table 1.2. While Holmans – a key figure in the projections debate in the UK – suggested that an additional 4.5 million households would form in the earlier 20-year period up to 2016, official figures published by Government project growth in excess of 4.8 million.

Emerging from this general picture of the current housing situation, are two overriding concerns: the first is that of 'sustainability', particularly in relation to the apparent scale of future household growth and required house

Table 1.1 Newly arising demand and need for new housing, 1996 to 2016

	Owner occupied and market rented	Affordable housing	All tenures
Net increase in households	2,904,000	643,000	3,547,000
Increase in secondary residences	100,000	0	100,000
Net increase in vacant dwellings	124,000	41,000	165,000
Adjustment for sales to sitting tenants	−785,000	+785,000	0
Net increase in housing stock	**2,343,000**	**1,469,000**	**3,812,000**
New provision to offset demolitions and other losses	540,000	200,000	740,000
New provision demanded and needed			
(i) Numbers	**2,883,000**	**1,669,000**	**4,552,000**
(ii) Proportion	**63%**	**37%**	**100%**
(Figures calculated by Holmans)			

IMPLICATIONS: THE NATIONAL DILEMMA

Required housing
- 4.5 million new homes needed (1996 to 2016)
- this equates with a building rate of 225,000 dwellings per annum
- of which 141,750 are market and 83,250 are affordable/social

Housing projected on basis of recent building rates
- building rate in the 1990s was 146,000 homes per annum
- of which123,000 are market and 23,000 are affordable/social

At current rates, 2.92 million dwellings added by 2016, resulting in undersupply of:
- 372,000 market homes
- 1,205,000 affordable/social housing units

Source: Holmans (2001) and Barlow *et al.* (2002)

building (Box 1.2). In response to the Barker Review's (2004) call for additional house building in order to achieve greater levels of affordability (by addressing undersupply – see Chapter 7), government has focused its attention on the environmental implications of growth. Central to the current sustainability debate is the question of how to accommodate future household growth and satisfy housing demand without compromising wider environmental, social and economic objectives. Essentially, how can the planning system deliver a compromise between developmental and environmental interests? As always, the CPRE

Table 1.2 Projected household growth in England 2003 to 2026

Region	Number of households 2003	Number of households 2021	Number of households 2026	Average annual change 2003–2026
North-east	1,088,000	1,194,000	1,211,000	5,300
North-west	2,847,000	3,290,000	3,378,000	21,900
Yorkshire and the Humber	2,104,000	2,437,000	2,511,000	17,700
East Midlands	1,782,000	2,146,000	2,230,000	19,500
West Midlands	2,193,000	2,526,000	2,602,000	17,800
East	2,286,000	2,797,000	2,926,000	27,800
London	3,093,000	3,756,000	3,926,000	36,200
South-east	3,348,000	4,013,000	4,184,000	36,300
South-west	2,137,000	2,622,000	2,745,000	26,400
England	**20,904,000**	**24,781,000**	**25,713,000**	**209,000**

Source: ODPM (2006c)

has been quick off the mark in pointing to the environmental costs of viewing the latest household projections 'as instructions for the number of new homes that have to be built in England over the next 20 years' (CPRE, 2006) arguing that 'If these projections were translated into new homes built, that would represent more than 16 square miles of countryside disappearing under new housing estates each year' accompanied by a consequential 'increase in climate changing greenhouse gas emissions, in road traffic and pollution and in consumption of finite natural resources such as water and minerals' (CPRE, 2006). Planning must address such concerns while facilitating new housing delivery in response to the latest projections.

The second core concern is that of 'affordability', given that an undersupply of more than 1 million affordable units is projected by 2016 (see Table 1.1), and probably more by 2026 (Table 1.2). When past governments set targets for future house building they did so in a context dominated by public sector provision. Thus when Lloyd George pledged homes fit for heroes or Crossman promised more council homes, affordability was perhaps less of an issue. The homes being discussed were for rent and provided by the public sector. But today, the context is radically different. Eighty per cent of all house building is undertaken by speculative builders (Hooper and Nicol, 1999) and local authorities have added little to their existing stock (which has in fact diminished rapidly – see Chapter 3) for two decades. Thus, in the context of mass private provision, planning has become a critical tool for ensuring affordability and wider social access to housing. Affordability is, in part, about how planning intervenes in local housing schemes and it is also, increasingly, about reading the market and ensuring that some equilibrium is achieved between supply and demand. These key concerns are briefly introduced below.

Sustainability

Planning policy is a key juncture between developmental and environmental interests and policy has become increasingly influenced by ideas linked to sustainability and the need for environmental safeguards: government policy reveals that the planning system is to play a key role in achieving sustainable development (Box 1.2; see also, detailed discussion in Chapter 8). The problem is that environmental priorities may conflict to some degree with meeting housing needs and demands, creating and sustaining inherent contradictions. For example, releasing more land in an attempt to boost housing supply and thereby reduce prices and increase affordability (see discussion from p. 16 onwards) may mean opening up more land for development in the countryside or the outward extension of existing settlements. Such moves often court strong local opposition and the planning system finds itself trying to mediate between national priorities (such as government's objective to ensure general access to a decent home or meeting

---

Box 1.2 Planning and sustainable development

Planning should facilitate and promote sustainable and inclusive patterns of urban and rural development by:

- making suitable land available for development in line with economic, social and environmental objectives to improve people's quality of life;
- contributing to sustainable economic development;
- protecting and enhancing the natural and historic environment, the quality and character of the countryside, and existing communities;
- ensuring high quality development through good and inclusive design, and the efficient use of resources; and,
- ensuring that development supports existing communities and contributes to the creation of safe, sustainable, liveable and mixed communities with good access to jobs and key services for all members of the community.

Source: ODPM, 2005h: para. 5

regional housing demand – in the future, national and regional affordability targets may be added to this list – see Chapter 7) and local concerns, ostensibly the protection of community assets (the rural landscape, farming, sense of community, etc.) but also the reality of self interest (development constraint and scarcity contribute to equity growth and the wealth of existing homeowners).

Conflicts centre not only on new housing provision per se, but also on the type of housing provided and the type of land-used for development. Approaches deemed to be sustainable will emphasise higher building densities and more concentrated development within existing urban areas (see Chapter 5), preferably on previously used land and in locations that increase the likelihood of reducing private car use (Bramley and Watkins, 1996; Williams, 2000: 35; ODPM, 2005c). But higher densities can conjure images of the high-rise failures of the 1960s; the eradication of urban communities and their replacement with soulless and unsociable tower blocks. One problem with the housing density debate is that it is heavily polarised: opponents fear higher densities will lead to low quality developments and supporters often see the promotion of higher densities merely as an antidote to sprawl. There is a tendency to focus on *possible* (and unlikely) outcomes, and not on the underlying rationale of higher densities, or the fact that the density (and housing design) debates are merely components of a new emphasis on demand management, which is another product of the move to a sustainability agenda.

A 'management' approach to planning in recent years is largely a result of government wanting to be seen to have a pre-emptive strategy in place, while also countering the accusation that it merely 'reacts' to housing pressure. Hence, its stated aim is now to 'plan, monitor and manage' rather than 'predict and provide' (DETR, 2000c), and also to arrive at tailored solutions to development pressure. Past Labour governments have been considered the enemies of the countryside, and it has been the current government's intention to shake off this image by embracing a planning agenda that addresses the fears of 'middle England'. 'Management' suggests that demand is not absolute but can be dealt with in ways other than through the direct provision of new homes; this, of course, is difficult to achieve, but government is able to claim that it will manage *land release* in such a way as to favour re-use over the use of greenfield sites. Hence the planning-housing agenda (and the need to reach compromise) is predominantly concerned with how land is used, resulting in policies seeking urban consolidation and renewal with the redevelopment of existing 'brownfield' sites. Indeed in the final version of Planning Policy Guidance Note 3 (PPG 3 – issued March 2000, but superseded by Planning Policy Statement 3 (PPS) in 2006), the Government clarified its commitment to 'maximising the re-use of previously developed land and empty properties'. To this end, PPG3 stated that by 2008, 60 per cent of all new housing should be provided on previously developed land and through conversions of existing buildings (DETR, 2000a). However, severe difficulty has been anticipated in meeting this aim. In research for the Town and Country Planning Association (Breheny and Hall, 1996), it was found that in virtually all of the metropolitan areas there was the view that 'easy' brownfield sites had already been developed. The remaining sites were those with major problems – contamination, poor access, weak demand, high costs – and would require high levels of subsidy if they were to be reclaimed (Breheny and Hall, 1996). Yet, this reality did not prevent the government from claiming in 2002 that it has reached its target 6 years early, with 61 per cent of housing completions now occurring on previously developed land. But bearing in mind that new house building had now (almost) fallen to an all-time-low (see p. 6), the factor resulting in this early 'success' was not government's prudent use of the planning system, but the system's insistence that most greenfield sites should be closed to development. There has been no rush to develop brownfield land, but the proportion of sites categorised as such has risen relative to the absolute decline in new build. The arguments for both the increased use of brownfield land and the sustained use of greenfield sites have been usefully summarised by Balchin and Rhoden (2002, see Box 1.3).

The reality would appear to be that house builders are facing a scarcity of 'easier to develop' greenfield sites given that an environmental agenda seems to have stolen centre stage. It may be that they will adapt to this change in the land market, and over the long term, the movement to re-use sites will not be a problem. However, there is some suggestion of a current bottleneck, with developers reticent about committing to brownfield development and clinging to the hope that further large greenfields will be made available for house building: a hope that has been increased by the 2004 Barker Review of Housing Supply and the possibility of market-led strategic land releases (see Chapter 7). But even before 'Barker' – who argued for greater market responsiveness of the release of housing land – a 2002 Ministerial Statement (Prescott, 2002) on planning (the precursor to the 2003 Communities Plan) confirmed the continuing need to release large strategic greenfield housing sites (as well as finding further brownfield sites) in the south of England:

> Two years ago, I asked for reports to be prepared on potential growth in the Thames Gateway, Ashford, the Milton Keynes area and the London-Stansted-Cambridge area. These studies are [. . .] nearing completion and show how economic development will increase the number of homes we need. Over the coming months, taking account of these studies, I will work with regional and local partners [. . .] to establish where, at what scale, and how quickly growth can be achieved. Overall we estimate that 200,000 new homes could be created in the growth areas.

Box 1.3 Brownfield and greenfield development

The use of derelict **brownfield** land will:

- Enhance the environment since derelict areas in British towns and cities would be cleared, and the countryside would be better preserved.
- Reduce the volume of commuting and lower exhaust emissions.
- Protect the green belt since urban encroachment into rural areas would be reduced.
- Result in more vibrant cities since – with densities being raised, for example, to Parisian levels of around 20,000/km^2, compared to only 8,000/km^2 in London – more capital would be invested in both private and public services.

Supporters of **greenfield** development point out:

- Brownfield sites are not distributed evenly across England. Most derelict urban land is in the north and in the midlands, whereas most new housing that will be required is in the South and East. Counties with the highest projected demand – Somerset, Berkshire and Suffolk – have little or no developable brownfield land.
- Most new housing units developed in the inner city would be unaffordable to new households, and even if they became affordable (possibly as an outcome of subsidised regeneration), many new households would prefer a detached house in the country to a flat in the city for the same price.
- There are over 700,000 empty houses in England, mainly in cities, which if occupied would reduce the need to develop new housing in the inner cities.
- The inner city environment needs protecting just as much as the rural environment [. . .] and many inner city residents might place a great priority on space, peace and quiet, and traffic-free areas than on its antithesis: high-density 'town cramming'.
- The urban poor might be the principal victims of brownfield development since they would be squeezed into the worst sites and into the worst housing.
- The costs of site preparation in greenfield areas are comparatively low (there is little contaminated land).
- House building in the countryside is often highly profitable – because of land banking and land speculation – and thus there is little need for supply-side subsidies (as there is for much brownfield development), although there are calls on public expenditure for infrastructure development, notwithstanding the tendency for many developers to offer financially constrained local authorities facilities such as new schools, leisure centres and swimming pools in return for planning permission ('planning gain').

Source: Balchin and Rhoden, 2002: 57–59

Yet the general move away from releasing greenfields and towards prioritising land re-use has raised a number of technical and financial questions; and these questions fuel concerns over housing supply. For instance, brownfield sites are extremely diverse in type, are often in fragmented ownership and may be costly to develop because of possible contamination or the need to demolish – and thereafter remove – existing buildings (Barlow, 1999). The added cost burden of developing brownfield sites figured prominently in housing debate towards the end of the 1990s, with the UTF (Urban Task Force, 1999) calling on government to provide incentives for house builders to increase the volume of provision on such sites. The UTF argued strongly that VAT should be harmonised on brown- and greenfield sites, making brownfield development a more attractive proposition. So far, government has not acted on this advice, which might seem peculiar given the number of commentators arguing that reducing construction costs is the only plausible means of increasing brownfield output (Hooper and Nicol, 1999), though clearly house builders, for their part, will also need to explore technical means of bringing down construction costs (Barlow, 1999).

Sustainable development – which we examine in more detail later on and especially in Chapter 8 – offers a way of thinking that seeks to balance these 'developmental' agendas and concerns with environmental considerations. In some respects, the collection of chapters contained in this book reveal that the developmental agenda grew out of nineteenth-century urbanism and dominated planning debate at least until the 1950s (see Chapter 2). After this time, a series of planning failures gradually paved the way for a new environmental agenda that only slowly took shape over the next half century. Arguably, its ascendancy arrived in the 1990s and it was at this time that the need to achieve a better balance between these apparently opposing priorities gained most urgency, given the failure of planning to deal with dramatic growth pressures. Sustainability has offered a means of rationalising these pressures, recognising the legitimacy of both and seeking a compromise. In the arena of housing, it has meant striving towards social goals but not at the expense of resource depletion. Countless policy notes and circulars have sought to clarify the meaning of sustainability with regards to new housing provision, and the last PPG3 on Housing set out five key messages for local planning authorities: these are listed in Table 1.3.

Although PPG3 (DETR, 2000a) remained 'in force' at the time of writing, in late 2005 and early 2006, government consulted on the replacement of existing planning guidance on housing (and *Circular 6/98: Planning and Affordable Housing*) with a new 'Planning Policy Statement', that will accord with the changes in the planning system instituted by the Planning and Compulsory Purchase Act 2004 (see Chapter 8), and the government's wider

Table 1.3 Sustainable housing development

Development that is linked to public transport	The location of new housing must allow for the maximum use of public transport, and reduce the need to travel by private car. It must reduce the volume of commuting; possibly by prioritising brownfield development (see also Box 1.3).
Mixed-use development	The promotion of mixed-use development should enable people to live close to places of employment and also close to key services. Planning should move away from allocating land for mono-use, which creates an artificial separation of land-uses and promotes long-distance daily movements.
A greener residential environment	A push towards higher densities (see below and also Box 1.3) should not mean a loss of urban green space. The more efficient use of urban land needs to balance with the need to maintain a high quality urban environment in which people want to live. Urban communities value their green space.
A greater emphasis on quality and designing places for people	Housing quality issues have, in recent years, been secondary to issues of quantity. But the more efficient and sustainable use of land means that a greater emphasis needs to be placed on housing and residential quality if the mistakes of the past are to be avoided. Higher densities, for example, need to be balanced with better standards of construction and good design.
The most effective use of land	Fundamental to achieving more sustainable housing development is the effective use of land. This means building well-designed homes at higher densities and using such mechanisms as the 'sequential approach' to ensure that maximum use is made of previously developed land before development of greenfield sites is permitted.

Source: DETR, 2000a

thinking on the role of regional planning and development frameworks in the way housing is planned for, especially at a sub-regional level, and through these new policy frameworks. The consultation draft of PPS3 reinforces the messages set out in Table 1.3 – that planning should ensure 'balance' between housing types, between supply and demand within housing markets, and in terms of community mix. It also reiterates the objective of 'ensuring that everyone has the opportunity of living in a decent home' (ODPM, 2005j: 8). Not surprisingly, there is no backing away from the objective of sustainable residential development; rather the need for sustainability is emphasised, as is the need to deliver housing in the context of 'sustainable communities' and this is an issue that we return to in Chapter 8. Some of PPS3's more radical departures from the PPG3 approach, link to housing affordability and are examined in the next section.

Affordability

Affordable housing does not sit outside of the sustainability agenda – the planning for and provision of affordable homes is an integral part of the wider housing debate, but merits separate mention owing to the huge changes that have occurred in the way that non-market housing is provided in Britain in recent years. Two initial points need to be made:

- First, the relationship between planning and housing, and the difficulty in managing developmental and environmental pressures, may generate a policy-induced need for affordable housing. Planning control hikes up land values and hence property prices, making homes unaffordable for those on lower incomes. Planning may therefore be seen as a cause of unaffordable housing. Balchin and Rhoden (2002) point out, for example, that 'most new housing units developed in the inner city would be unaffordable to new households' (ibid., 58), and therefore recent constraints on new development and an emphasis on land recycling can accentuate affordability concerns.

- Second, planning has become integral to the provision of additional affordable housing, and is part of the solution. As government has withdrawn from direct provision of subsidised rented homes (see Chapter 3), there has been a need to look for new ways of delivering affordable housing, and this can be achieved through the planning system.

There is clearly great irony here, with planning both the cause of and solution to a shortage in affordable homes. The general constraints noted earlier, largely stemming from the emergence of an environmental agenda, have acted to limit overall housing supply, which has created a shortage of new housing in the face of growing demand. At the same time, the availability of rented housing fell off rapidly after 1980 with the introduction of the 'Right to Buy' (see Chapter 3) obliging local councils to sell their rented stock to sitting tenants. The equation seems to be a simple one: housing demand has continued to grow, particularly in the light of social trends that have resulted in smaller households and more people leaving parental homes at a younger age; the supply of cheaper social rented housing has dwindled; new market housing has become scarcer as a result of planning constraint, and also physical constraint – Britain, after all, has a limited land mass and one of the highest population densities in Europe (if England is taken alone, it has a higher population density than any other European country. If the whole of the UK is considered instead, the Netherlands has the greatest population density in Europe; www.environment-agency.gov.uk;

accessed 30 October 2002) – and the affordability of homes for those on the lowest incomes has tailed off. The problem for policy makers has therefore been twofold: to deal with the general supply issue, balancing the wider developmental and environmental agendas, and thereafter (or simultaneously) to ensure that the cost profile of homes matches the income profile of potential occupants. In other words, general supply and affordability are the most pressing housing concerns at the current time, and planning would appear to be the critical sticking point, squeezing the absolute supply of new homes and, at the same time, making them less affordable. This is an issue considered in length in Chapter 7 where the relationship between planning, housing supply and the market is examined.

With regard to the role of planning in governing housing supply and affordability, one theory suggests that in a completely (planning-) 'free' market, suppliers (the house builders) would build to the full range of market require-ments, delivering products to suit all income levels. Unfettered by public sector planning, the market could provide for all: such is the anarchic anti-planning ideal. But would this really happen? Surely, house builders would want to ensure long-term profitability: they would want to create scarcity in order to push up land prices and raise income from development. In reality, they would not simply buy up swathes of land and erect houses to meet demand: rather, they would buy land to halt development and thereafter build at a controlled rate for maximum profit. We would retain a planning system, but it would be a priva-tised system administered by big business rather than a nationalised system administered democratically. Regarding housing provision and housing afford-ability, the activity of planning is inevitable, though in the world as it exists, constraint policies meet the needs of an environmental rather than a business agenda.

However, the result of even 'democratic constraint' is, to a varying extent in different local areas, that housing assumes a scarcity value, and competition for a finite housing resource causes an elevation of house prices. The market cannot (or would not) provide for all households, either under current condi-tions or if the planning system were to be abandoned. Hence there is a need for policy makers to deal with general supply issues and – to some extent sepa-rately – the issue of affordability. This is the current situation, or the 'status quo' examined in Chapter 7 and contrasted with a reinvigorated system – proposed by government – that is more market responsive. In the previous section of this chapter, we noted the recent (ODPM, 2005a) publication of revised plan-ning guidance on housing. This establishes the current position on housing affordability and the market and suggests that future determination of housing provision and distribution should reflect 'government's overall ambition for affordability' (ibid., 10), drawing on sub-regional market and land-availability assessments (which the new statement advises on). A call to more clearly understand the characteristics of regional and sub-regional markets – while displaying greater concern for infrastructure provision – perhaps reflects a shift in attitude in relation to housing and planning. The new round of planning policy statements, some of which are discussed in later chapters, are much more market driven and aimed at rectifying past market discrepancies.

The introduction to government's consultation on PPS3 – the newest statement on housing at the time of writing – begins with a narrative of market failure: household formation has increased, but house-building levels have fallen (ibid., 1). The aim of planning should be to help rectify this failure and smooth the way for future growth. The link between planning and government's growth agenda – expressed in the Sustainable Communities Plan (ODPM, 2003a) – is made explicit mid-way through the new housing statement (ibid., 11). As noted above, the new PPS3 repackages many of the basic messages set out in PPG3, but with greater emphasis on framing policy within a regional agenda, and tying housing concerns to other local strategies. There is a great deal of what critics might call 'spin' in the new planning policy statements, but there is a also a concern for selling the idea of a (spatial) planning system that integrates policy areas and thinks across different tiers of planning and areas of responsibility (see Chapter 9). The market – as context – figures more strongly in the consultation of PPS3. The idea of market viability finds its way into guidance on land allocation (ibid., 12), and the same issue is hinted at in relation to the allocation of brownfield sites. The ways in which the planning system might promote or procure affordable housing – by setting targets regionally and discussing finance allocations with the Housing Corporation, or by levering planning gain locally – is also set in the context of site viability, and the operation of the housing market. Indeed, a market operating efficiently may need less intervention of the type set in PPS3's companion guide on affordable housing. But still, mechanisms for procuring affordable housing through planning, or making planning 'exceptions' in rural areas, will still be available if PPS3 is eventually published in a form similar to that which was consulted on in early 2006.

Affordability – whether addressed through local planning intervention or at a systemic level – is a major concern of this book. There is a substantial unmet and growing need for affordable housing in many urban and rural areas (Barlow *et al.*, 2002). De facto restrictions on greenfield development noted above, and government's reticence towards releasing large strategic sites, are likely to exacerbate this problem. The shortfall between the supply and the need for affordable housing is perhaps indicative of the fact that neither registered social landlords nor the private sector have been able to meet demand (TCPA, 2000). Across the UK the shortfall in the supply of affordable housing is generally agreed to be in the order of 60,000 dwellings per annum (see Barlow *et al.*, 2002 and Table 1.1). This shortfall is examined in greater detail in later chapters (especially in the context of the 2004 Barker Review), though for the moment it is worth emphasising that planning has been called upon to play an ever larger role in the provision of affordable homes though the use of planning obligations. The most recent planning statement on housing (the draft of PPS3 outlined above) reiterates that affordable housing is a material consideration when assessing planning applications and that planning should 'ensure that a wide choice of housing types is available, for both affordable and market housing, to meet the needs of all members of the community' (ODPM, 2005a: 8). Obligations – used as the basis for requiring developers to include 'affordable units' in new market housing schemes – is one of two mechanisms (see Chapter 5) whereby the planning system can be used to ensure that the cost profile of new housing matches society's needs, as opposed to the needs of a building industry whose primary objective is merely to maximise profit. However, the question of housing affordability seems to be broadening out at the present time, and this is reflected in those parts of the new PPS3 described above. A concern over the use of the planning system to 'procure' affordable homes by generating land-subsidy (again, discussed in Chapter 5) is today being balanced, and perhaps even overshadowed, by a debate over the way general land release should follow 'market signals' and hence respond to local crises of affordability by releasing additional land for house building. This broader 'supply' issue is examined at length in Chapter 7.

The two main issues – sustainable and sufficient supply alongside affordability (a product of adequate supply plus planning intervention) – introduced above, dominate current housing-planning debate. The means by which the planning system shapes general housing development, mediating between developmental and environmental agendas seeking a compromise is paramount. But if planning were merely about efficient land release, then there would be little to distinguish it from a world of big business corporate planning hypothesised above. Planning has and always has had a social dimension: this is most visible at the present time in the area of affordable housing – and the desire to deliver decent homes in the setting of sustainable communities (see Chapter 8) – with the system seeking to balance land-use objectives with specific social concerns. The chapters that follow broadly review the role of planning in housing provision, tracing how this role has changed and revealing why and how the current emphasis on sustainability and affordability has evolved.

Structure of the book

Systemic development

Britain's planning system has evolved in tandem with housing policy, both of which find their roots in the nineteenth century and a period of accelerated evolution in urban governance. Various writers have sought to explain the antecedents of Britain's current planning system: notable among these is Cherry (1974; 1978) who attributes much of what we know today as 'planning' to ideas of Victorian utopianism. The same utopian vision is also used to explain the way in which housing policy has developed during the last 150 years (Malpass and Murie, 1999: 26–30; Ravetz, 2001; Holmes, 2006). But added to the notion of utopianism – that drew inspiration from Christian charity and the philanthropic tradition of Victorian industry – are the very tangible changes in the way that Britain was governed during the latter part of the nineteenth century. Ideas of a planned society free from disease and decently housed, fell prey during much of the nineteenth century, to the lack of structured local control over housing and planning matters. The root of this problem was the absence of any integrated local governance that could take up challenges and arrive at coherent answers. The move from local Boards with specific remits to local councils with broad powers to deal with planning and housing matters was central to structured housing and planning policy.

The actual strength of the bond between planning and housing has been noted by Ravetz (2001: 2), who highlights the association of

> utopian socialism and communitarianism with the land question and nascent town planning, and the linking of these to the idea of state-provided working-class housing.

In the next chapter, we begin our narrative of planning's role in housing provision by looking at some of the historical antecedents to current planning–housing debate: those processes and drivers that have culminated in current debates and have shaped our perception of the role of planning in relation to housing. Broader historical issues are introduced in Chapter 2 while the following chapter concentrates on the relationship between public and private housing provision during the last 25 years. Chapter 3 considers mass public housing provision's fall from grace after the election of the first Thatcher government in 1979, which seemed intent on dismantling both the welfare state (whose most tangible asset was council housing) and planning's central role in housing provision. This chapter examines how the successive Conservative administrations 'eclipsed' council housing, promoted a philosophy of privatism and presided over an evolving private sector housing crisis, despite the ascendancy of a developmental culture.

Housing and the pre-2004 planning system

The general shape of the recent planning problem with regards to housing provision was highlighted earlier, and is the central issue examined in the book's middle chapters (4, 5 and 6). In broad terms, planning has been called upon to mediate between developmental and environmental agendas, creating the conditions in which sufficient housing will be provided, and which also matches the needs of different types of household distinguished by income and wealth. In recent times, the planning system has facilitated the delivery of an insufficient quantity of new homes in the right locations, and therefore contributed to a crisis of affordability. This has resulted in calls for a new direction in planning policy and for planning to re-invent its role in housing provision. The recent Review of housing supply in England (Barker, 2004), by the Treasury, addresses this central concern. It has similarly been suggested that a planning system borne of the post-war period is unable to cope with the huge social changes being experienced in contemporary Britain (Cullingworth, 1996). These include a significant growth in household numbers (18.5 per cent since 1980; Balchin and Rhoden, 2002: 3), driven in the 1990s not by absolute population increase but by emergent social trends (leading to a rise in single-person households) and a culture of the 'household' no longer based on the idea of the nuclear family.

The aim of the book's middle chapters is to 'problematise' housing and planning debate in the years immediately prior to the 2004 Planning Act: to set out its key parameters. Chapter 4 embarks on this process by establishing key themes in policy and critique, flagging up critical issues surrounding planning and housing. It also looks at the changing policy context. Chapter 5 then examines some of these issues more closely, dealing with questions of housing design, density and the role of planning in delivering affordable housing (a key area of policy debate since the late 1980s). This chapter is concerned with planning's role as an intervening force in the delivery of housing by the private sector. The following chapter (6) aims to 'spatialise' this context and debate, focusing on the regional housing agenda (and the process of regional planning for housing), strategic concerns at a more local level, and challenges specific to more rural areas. It deals with the housing figures and their movement through to development planning, with housing development on a strategic scale, and with housing in the countryside. The countryside, and particularly, smaller rural communities have witnessed burgeoning housing pressure in recent years. A combination of lower rural wage levels and urban–rural migration have led some commentators to point to a 'dysfunctional' rural housing market where only the most affluent (and frequently ex-urban) households are able to access homes. In the light of rural and urban pressures, attention then refocuses on planning's role in ameliorating these problems, and with the way in which planning is being 'reinvented' (or at least revamped) in order to respond to current pressures.

Looking ahead at planning's evolving role in housing provision

At no other time during the last fifty years has government or society been more concerned with the operation and future of the planning system: planning has become a central theme of government policy, inextricably linked to the delivery of sufficient homes in the right locations. The problems facing the pre-2004 system were expressed in the following terms:

> some fifty years after it was first put in place, the planning system is showing its age. What was once an innovative emphasis on consultation has now become a set of inflexible, legalistic and bureaucratic procedures. A system that was intended to promote development now blocks it. Business complains that the speed of decisions is undermining productivity and competitiveness. People feel that they are not sufficiently involved in the decisions that affect their lives.
>
> (Stephen Byers, Forward to the Planning Green Paper,
> DTLR, 2001c)

In the last chapters of this book (7, 8 and 9), we focus on emergent debates and planning's future role in housing provision. Three key issues are addressed. The first is the housing supply question and the argument that policy should concentrate on 'making up for' historic undersupply. This draws inspiration from the recent Barker Review (2004) of housing supply in England, which has prompted broader debate over housing's links with the macro-economy, affordability, the operation of the housing market, and the impacts of growth. Government's preferred option for dealing with future housing demand is set out in the 2003 Communities Plan. In Chapter 8, we look at the idea of 'sustainable communities' (the creation of which is the central concern of the CP) and consider whether these offer an appropriate framework for addressing persistent housing supply concerns. This is followed by a further analysis of the changing nature of planning, and the departure from a largely land-use planning model to one that embraces wider 'spatial' concerns. Chapter 9 really provides the context for bringing this book to a close in the final, tenth, chapter which considers whether the current or a future government can adequately address the UK's

Plate 1 New red-brick housing in England, of the type that often galvanises public opinion against new house building (Stratford-upon-Avon, 2001)

housing problems given the present trajectory of planning reform, particularly its emergent leaning towards greater market responsiveness.

Indeed, the government hopes to achieve 'decent homes for all' through new directions in both housing and planning policy. In this book, we review the role that planning – past, present and future – has and will play in trying to meet this aim. We do not believe that housing problems will vanish in the near future and therefore end this book (in Chapter 10) by considering just how far planning can and might contribute to alleviating the current housing crisis in the coming years. One of the key problems of the more recent past has been the unsustainable nature of house building – putting the wrong homes in the wrong locations. Britain's population is therefore accustomed to apparently 'poor planning' and this legacy means that opposition to future development has been heightened. The key challenge over the next few years is to demonstrate the virtues of good inclusive planning and good design and thereby reduce opposition to new housing provision (see Plate 1). Making the planning system more inclusive, as the government now realise (ODPM, 2002b) would be a key step forward. However, it has recently been argued that in some places, existing homeowners will oppose new development proposals irrespective of their nature and quality. How do we overcome this attitude towards development and create an acceptance of the need to prioritise community over individual interest? This would appear to be one of the greatest hurdles confronting planning for housing at the beginning of the twenty-first century. The communitarian and utopian visions of the nineteenth century have been replaced with a desire to juggle environmental and developmental interests, guaranteeing a more sustainable future. At the same time, the rhetoric of social democracy and equality of opportunity have supposedly replaced the polarisation of left and right politics (Giddens, 1998). But will this mean 'decent homes for all', or just for the fortunate majority? Chapter 10 rounds on this central question, concluding a book that we hope will provide a useful introduction to and analysis of planning's role in housing provision.

Chapter 2
The co-evolution of housing and planning

This chapter was co-authored by Marco Bianconi,
UCL Bartlett School of Planning

> It is only in the last few years that there has been any idea that the regulation of [. . .] living conditions for the benefit of the poor, as well as the rich, is one of the duties of a modern State, just as much as the provision of pure food and water. It must necessarily be difficult to fit fresh regulations in accordance with new ideals to the old manners and customs, but this is a difficulty which confronts all progress.
>
> (Nettlefold, 1914: 1)

Introduction

Current housing debates are rooted in a long period of historical development, which has produced a particular array of challenges, presided over by a unique planning response. This chapter charts those problems evident in urban areas in the nineteenth century that gave rise to the desire for state intervention to solve a range of social problems generally, and severe housing conditions in particular. Our aim is to set out the historic antecedents of contemporary housing–planning debate, focusing particularly on England, but also examining a pattern of rapid industrialisation and urbanisation that has determined the general shape of housing and urban problems across much of Western Europe.

The rapid transformation of the UK from a largely agrarian to a predominantly urban society on the back of the Industrial Revolution had three negative consequences. The primary consequence was poor quality, unsanitary housing. Secondary consequences were (a) declining environmental conditions (and 'reduced liveability' in modern parlance) and (b) worsening public health in many if not all of the UK's larger towns and cities. The demand for labour in the new industries of the nineteenth century resulted in cheap housing being built quickly and with little attention paid to the principles of good planning or sound sanitation. Development was driven by business interests whose primary concern was for satisfying labour demand at the lowest possible cost. The result was worsening housing conditions throughout much of the nineteenth century, with subsequent public health, social and political implications (and tensions). But for much of the century, the belief that individuals were responsible for their own situations, contributed to a general reluctance to intervene. There was also a popular belief, held by the ruling classes that the 'proletariat' were generally unclean and would remain unclean, and unhealthy, even if government were to intervene in 'private' housing matters. Poor housing did not create the conditions of poor living, poor health and immorality. Rather, the former was viewed as a function of the latter. But this position became increasingly untenable as the century wore on. Reports and surveys prepared by religious leaders, journalists and philanthropists brought the plight of the urban masses to a larger audience. Although it was some time before the state accepted the need to even consider public health issues or the introduction of legislation to improve housing conditions, it was during the nineteenth century that the seeds of modern housing and planning debate were sown. Having taken root by the turn of the century, it took another 50 years before debates over the physical condition of cities, and housing, shaped what we have until very recently considered to be the 'modern' planning system. This chapter is concerned with this early evolution of planning and housing debate from the mid-nineteenth century to the creation of the modern planning system in 1947. It examines the evolution of planning, and its links to housing provision during this historical period and addresses four key questions:

1   What were the conditions and problems faced by residents of British towns and cities in the nineteenth century?
2   How did government – and others, including business interests – react to the various reports and studies cataloguing housing conditions within these urban areas?
3   What initial role was 'planning' expected to perform in overcoming housing – and subsequent social and environmental health problems – identified at the time?
4   And, in conclusion, how did this role continue to evolve during the earlier years of the twentieth century?

Urban housing in the nineteenth century

Living in the slums

Our first question concerns the parameters of nineteenth-century housing and urban problems: essentially, high development densities coupled with a lack of sanitation and poor housing resulted in the frequent outbreaks of disease and localised social unrest. Britain's industrial age was characterised by an unprecedented expansion of towns and cities driven by the rapid migration of a previously rural population to the new employment opportunities springing up across the country. At the beginning of the nineteenth century, the urban population of England and Wales was a little over a third (9 million) of the total population: by 1901, this proportion had risen to 77 per cent, or just over 25 million of 32.6 million. This was a period of rapid growth for many of England's major cities: London doubled its population in the first 50 years of the nineteenth century (from 1 to 2 million); Liverpool's population total rose from 82,000 to 375,000 and Manchester's from 75,000 to 300,000 during the same period. Back in London, the 1901 census revealed that Stepney, Bethnal Green, Finsbury, Shoreditch and Southwark had population densities in excess of 150 persons per acre (reaching a peak of 182 persons per acre in some neighbourhoods: see Hall *et al.*, 1973: 76; Cherry, 1996: 26). Total population was growing and people were being squeezed tightly into these new centres of industry. At the same time, the amount of new housing being built was failing to keep pace with this growth: the consequence was severe overcrowding. In London, entire families were often crammed into a single room. A study by the Statistical Society in Marylebone (Central London) in 1848 reported that within 205 surveyed houses, 859 separate families were occupying 845 rooms (Statistical

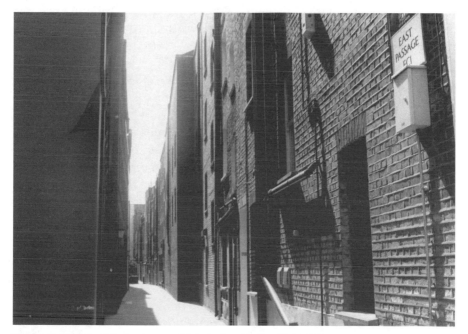

Plate 2 The narrow, dark streetscape of Victorian London (East End, 2005)

Society, 1848). Such problems were not unique to the United Kingdom, but were being experienced across continental Europe. In Paris, for example, by 1891 more than 2.4 million people were living in the historic core at a density twice that of the London County Council area (Hall, 1996: 31). European cities were growing at the expense of an economically marginalised and politically weak underclass.

Competition for space in the nineteenth-century city was intense. In central areas, offices and shopping districts serving an affluent middle class came to occupy prime locations. Beyond this centre, the working classes were packed in adjacent to the new industries, often living in high-density tenement blocks. But at least London's population benefited from some basic controls over construction standards enacted by Parliament in the late eighteenth century (i.e. the Building Act 1774). Outside the capital, there were no such controls. Sewage often accumulated in streets as few houses enjoyed the luxury of a toilet or clean running water. Terraced housing came to dominate many inner cities, sometimes inserted into existing open spaces, depleting the previous greenery and openness of urban areas. This form of development deprived children of play-areas, creating a dark and depressing cityscape often devoid of sunlight. Dwellings themselves were frequently blackened by industrial smog: if any windows were present, it was often difficult for light to penetrate dirt and grime. In the Midlands and much of the north of England, 'back-to-back' housing was common, though less prevalent in Scotland where multi-storey tenement blocks were the norm (Ward, 2004). Cellar dwellings – a feature of earlier times – remained common in the nineteenth century. But they were now old and their physical condition had deteriorated, becoming overcrowded, dirty, dank pits.

Migrants moving to the cities for the first time often found themselves sub-letting small rooms or space from principal tenants. Alternatively, accommodation could sometimes be found in purpose-built or converted lodging houses. In London, and elsewhere, 'common lodging houses' offered single rooms for rent to entire families: 80,000 people lived in these houses in London. They were well known for their unsanitary conditions and the police often attributed spiralling crime rates to occupants of the lodging houses. Among the middle and upper classes, cellar dwellings and lodging houses were viewed as nests of crime, disease and depravity: they were home to society's 'low life' and offended higher Victorian morals.

Despite the apparent employment opportunities to which many migrants flocked, extreme poverty was central to the burgeoning urban crisis of the nineteenth century. Not everyone was fortunate enough to find work: unemployment and low wages meant that many were forced into poverty and appalling housing. For most of the century, urban rents increased exponentially while wages remained low: restricting the working classes to a breadline existence. A key problem was the concentration of housing demand in central locations. People needed to live close to jobs as they could neither afford rail fares to and from the suburbs, nor endure a 4-hour walk home after a gruelling 12-hour shift (Dilke, 1885: 17–19; Mearns, 1885: 69). High demand for accommodation and relative scarcity resulted in constant rent inflation. This situation was exacerbated by unscrupulous landlords and property managers. The granting of 'short-end' leases on agreed terms meant that rents could be raised very quickly with families forced to suffer the increases or risk losing their homes. This financial pressure was compounded by the frequent outbreaks of disease that often prevented people from working, sometimes permanently. In the slum conditions of the nineteenth century, typhus and cholera were rampant, quickly passing from house to house and from room to room, thriving among an undernourished populace living in unventilated dwellings. Illness, alcohol-dependency and prostitution often followed on from poverty and despondency. But while localised death and deprivation could be ignored, two serious cholera epidemics in 1831–1833 and in 1848–1849 together with two less virulent outbreaks in 1853–1854 and 1866–1867 alerted the middle class to the risk of maintaining a passive attitude towards the problems of the inner-city slums. Mortality rates in many towns reached a zenith by the middle of the century (Sutcliffe, 1981: 49) and at the same time, the problems facing the less fortunate members of society became an issue of popular writing and reporting across Western Europe. In 1841 a young Friedrich Engels recorded the conditions he observed in Manchester:

> One penetrates into this chaos of small one-storied, one-room huts, in most of which there is no artificial floor [. . .] In such a hole, scarcely 5 feet long by 6 feet broad, I found two beds, [. . .] in several others I found absolutely nothing, while the door stood open, and the inhabitants leaned
>
> (Engels, 1969 [1841]: 84)

> More than one family lived in a single damp cellar, in whose pestilent atmosphere twelve or sixteen persons were crowded together. To these and other sources of disease must be added that pigs were kept [. . .]. We must add that many families, who had but one room for themselves, receive boarders and lodgers in it, that such lodgers of both sexes by no means rarely slept in the same bed with the married couple
>
> (ibid. 98)

Within the industrial towns of mid nineteenth century Britain, this was not an unusual sight. An article by the journalist George Sims, published in *Pictorial World* in June 1883, reported:

> Scene after scene is the same. Rags, dirt, filth, wretchedness, the same figures, the same faces, the same old story of one room unfit for habitation yet inhabited by eight or nine people, the same complaint of a ruinous rent absorbing three-fourths of the toiler's weekly wage, the same shameful neglect by the owner of the property of all sanitary precautions, rotten floors, oozing walls, broken windows, crazy staircases, tileless roofs
>
> (Sims, 1889: 45)

The nineteenth century was characterised by a housing and social crisis of unprecedented magnitude. Some groups were able to break out of the poverty trap. Following an economic crisis in the mid-1880s real incomes began to rise, allowing a lower middle class, comprising skilled workers in regular employment, to form and subsequently secure better housing on the back of higher incomes (Ward, 2004: 14). At the same time, the introduction of a Cheap Trains Act in 1883 allowed these same groups to escape the slums by migrating to London's newly established outer ring of less dense and better quality housing (Cherry, 1979: 309–10). However, conditions for the vast majority remained unchanged. Casual employment and low pay locked people into poverty, creating a crisis that seemed persistent and intractable. Poverty was not a new feature of life in Britain, but in previous centuries it had been distributed across the countryside (Hall, 1996: 45) and largely invisible to the urban elite. But now it was concentrated and highly visible and threatened the comfortable existence of the rich and powerful. Concentration exposed the misery of the poor, but it was not merely compassion that prompted political action. There was also a palpable fear that the huddled masses would not tolerate their poverty ad infinitum.

A fear of the mob

The middle classes abhorred the conditions they witnessed in many urban areas: no-one wishes to be reminded of poverty and suffering on a daily basis, and cities were in danger of becoming significantly less attractive places. There was an aesthetic reason for action: but more important was the fear that the impoverished classes might rise up against their wealthy neighbours, securing by revolution what they could not gain via an elite political system. This, in itself, was sufficient justification to take an interest in the conditions of the working classes.

The nineteenth century had already witnessed a number of potentially revolutionary uprisings in some urban areas linked to poor housing conditions, industrialisation (and the threat it posed to traditional jobs) and a lack of political representation. The Chartist movement was particularly important with

Thomas Carlyle describing Chartism as 'bitter discontent grown fierce and mad, that crystallized middle-class fears of a conjecture of political radicals and urban underclass' (Carlyle, 1840: 2). Ten years later, Thomas Beames linked the growth of slum conditions to the fragility of the existing social order, arguing the 'rook-eries [the slums] are among the seeds of revolution; that taken in connection with other evils, [. . .] poison the minds of the working class against the powers that be, thus leading to convulsions' (Beames, 1850: 198). Britain had no revo-lutionary tradition. The Civil War 200 years before had resulted in no significant change to the political status quo; a situation that contrasted markedly with other European states where bloody revolution in the mid-nineteenth century commonly led to significant political upheavals at a price paid by the ruling classes. Could Britain face such a revolution, ending the comfortable existence of the rich and the aristocratic?

Localised uprisings in which gangs took to the streets to demonstrate against the inequities imposed upon them by landlords and managers had never evolved into a coordinated national insurrection. These had always been dealt with, often brutally, by local militia and the perpetrators faced harsh penalties including deportation or hanging. Indeed, petty theft was often viewed as just cause for a public execution and those challenging state authority could expect to meet the same fate. The state's capacity to maintain law and order was increased after 1829 with the creation, by Sir Robert Peel, of the country's first official and permanent police force in London. But generally, authorities lacked any real capacity to deal with minor disturbances, local riots or insurrection, especially within the rapidly growing cities. In many smaller towns – and in the countryside – a system of 'local watches' and 'constables' dating back to the Tudor period retained responsibility for local policing and appeared increasingly inadequate.

Urban conditions provided a potential catalyst for revolution, but only on the back of a more established problem: that of political representation. As cities grew and their boundaries changed it was not uncommon for urban areas to be represented by an often aristocratic parliamentary member, in a constituency that had previously been largely rural. In the worst-case scenarios, the member – incensed by the squalor of his own constituency – would have simply moved, but retained his parliamentary seat. Throughout much of the nineteenth century, British governments were dominated by aristocrats and major landowners who fiercely defended the interests of the gentry. The highest positions in govern-ment were occupied by Dukes, Marquesses and Earls, often sitting in the House of Lords rather than the Commons. Of the 20 Prime Ministers who held office between 1801 and 1900, 12 were members of the House of Lords. In 1885, the newly elected Prime Minister for the Conservatives was an aristocrat, Robert Arthur Talbot Gascoyne-Cecil, third Marquess of Salisbury, a descendent of the first Lord Salisbury who was son of Lord Burghley, a minister to Elizabeth I. The Cecil family's place in Parliament was guaranteed, not through the democratic process but through hereditary appointment. Ten members of the third Marquess' 1886 Cabinet either sat in the House of Lords, were peers or were the sons of peers.

Although the appointments may not necessarily have been bad, it seems likely that such politicians were ill-equipped to appreciate the severe problems confronting urban areas or the plight of the working classes during this time. These political figures were drawn from a privileged landed class and had little connection within the emergent industrial towns and cities other than through landownership mediated through distant agents. The physical and social distance between the poor and their representatives contributed to a significant delay in government's reaction to urban problems, generated by a lack of awareness and concern that became a source of growing tension and fury.

The sense of community was an early victim of deteriorating urban conditions in nineteenth-century industrial towns. Previously 'balanced communities' became fractured along class and income lines: they became increasingly segregated. As the poor descended into misery, bourgeois society became ever-more anxious, fearing the mob and its capacity to bring about radical social and political change. The urban poor came to be seen as savage, uneducated criminals: they were a separate race, uncultured, immoral and almost sub-human. An urban 'underclass' had been born: a 'dangerous class' – comprising criminals, paupers and those within reach of contagion – that threatened stability. Marx and Engels saw this 'dangerous class' as something distinct from the wider proletariat, referring to it as 'the social scum: that passively rotting mass thrown off by the lowest layers of the old society' (Marx and Engels, 1998 [1848]: 48). Mary Carpenter, elaborating upon the theme of moral contagion and decay, suggested that 'the honest poor, forced to live cheek by jowl in squalor with the criminals, paupers and beggars, could not help but suffer social demoralisation and thus sink into crime and depravity' (Carpenter, 1864: 54). But membership of this underclass, or dangerous class, was uncertain. Were the criminals and beggars a corrupting force, or were they simply part of the hitherto honest poor corrupted by desperation? It became useful, as the century wore on and a desire to intervene grew, to distinguish between a 'deserving' and an 'undeserving' poor, with the former becoming the subject of a growing number of measures designed to lift people – at least a small distance – above their existing poverty. As the horror of the nineteenth-century industrial city was slowly acknowledged, the first moves towards urban improvement emerged.

Official and non-official reactions

So how did government – and others, including business interests and social philanthropists – react to the various reports and studies cataloguing housing
conditions and the poverty that had, by the middle of the nineteenth century,
become endemic to urban areas? The first half of the century was characterised
by a general inclination towards minimum state intervention in issues of social
welfare. Although the daily experiences of the professional classes – especially
doctors and businessmen – working in or close to the slums pointed to an
inability of market process to solve the Victorian housing crisis, lawmakers
remained reluctant to introduce permissive or interventionist legislation, prefer-
ring instead to look to private landlords for solutions. However, the squalor
reported in the press steered public opinion towards the idea that something had
to be done: and once this idea took firm root the next question was exactly what
action should be taken. A major barrier to official local action for much of the
nineteenth century was the lack of coordinated local government. Local authorities – multi-function bodies with broad powers and remits – did not arrive on
the scene until the 1880s. This meant that 'local services' were overseen by an
array of local boards – brought together within municipal councils from 1835 –
each with a different agenda and usually rather limited powers. These were
frequently bureaucratic, slow to act, inefficient, parochial and, worst still, corrupt.
There was no confidence, at the level of national government, in the ability of
local boards to deal with the scale of the housing crisis. But more importantly,
the wealthy electorate resisted the higher tax levels that would be needed to fund
a bolder programme of state intervention. Sometimes, a simple monetary agenda
was cloaked behind a liberal 'anti-state' rhetoric, which continued to argue in
favour of private solutions to private problems. The liberal rhetoric had many
supporters: Lord Shaftesbury, for example, a fervent supporter of social reform
argued against state intervention in working-class housing:

> it will in fact be an official proclamation that, without any efforts of their own, a certain
> portion of people shall enter into the enjoyment of many good things, altogether at
> the expense of others.
>
> (Shaftesbury, *The Mischief of State Aid*
> (December 1883); quoted in Jones, 1976: 228)

Liberalism did not extend to 'charity' or, rather, it did not believe that the
state should engage in the act of charity at the expense of the taxpayer. This was
not to say that private philanthropy should not be directed towards the relief
of the poor. Charitable (voluntary) giving by the wealthy and by aristocrats to

support the establishment of educational facilities or hospitals had long been a source of public welfare. It had become a tradition among the rich to shower the poor with alms, an act often motivated by religious belief or, more specifically, that this was a likely route to Heaven. But much of the philanthropy that took root in the nineteenth century was grounded in real social concern, coupled with concern over future economic growth (an unhealthy workforce was less likely to be a productive workforce) and underlying revolutionary sentiments. In this context, philanthropic effort expanded and diversified. By the end of the 1860s, it was estimated that official poor relief in London was costing the Treasury £2 million per annum; private charity accounted for a further £7 million of expenditure. Jones (1976: 244–245) has revealed that at this time London's philanthropists were spending almost as much on social welfare as the government was spending on the Navy. A small but growing number of social reformers, philanthropists and enlightened employers (motivated, in part, by the productivity argument noted above) had instigated a range of initiatives, some of which survived into the twentieth century and beyond, intended to provide decent homes for the working classes.

The nature of philanthropic efforts

Perhaps the best-known philanthropic efforts of the nineteenth century involved the establishment of trusts and other not-for-profit bodies whose mission was to provide new homes for working-class tenants. Sometimes, these tenants worked for the philanthropist in question, but this was not always the case. The 1840s marked the beginning of a wave of trust and society formation. Lord Shaftesbury's pioneering 'Society for Improving the Condition of the Labouring Classes' (1844), with the Queen as Patron and the Prince Consort as President, was the first among many bodies formed in the latter half of the century. In much the same way as modern housing schemes are held up as 'exemplars' or experiments in good design (see Chapter 5), the Society's 'model dwellings' (designed by the architect Henry Roberts) were lauded as a positive and possible answer to the problems facing the urban poor. Tenement blocks with good sanitary facilities were built at high density, illustrating that it was possible to provide relatively cheap housing on expensive urban land, without promoting overcrowding and combating the dismal conditions, which were – in 1844–1845 – being catalogued by Edwin Chadwick.

Another body with a similar mission – and which has survived to this day – was the Peabody Trust, founded in 1862 with a donation from George Peabody, an American who had made his fortune as a merchant in England. Having decided to 'help the poor of London', by 1867 the Trust had provided over 5,000 new dwellings (Holmes, 2006: 4). Several other 'housing societies' or trusts sprang up in the years that followed, including Sidney Waterlow's Improved Dwellings Company, the Guinness Trust and the Samuel Lewis Trust (ibid., 4). Funding for the housing produced by these bodies was raised by borrowing from investors willing to accept a return of between just 4 and 5 per cent. This became known as 'five per cent philanthropy'; despite being an uncertain and unstable source of funding (the majority of investors remained committed to profit maximisation), the aim was to show – as in the case of Lord Shaftesbury's Society – that it was possible to provide profitable, decent housing for working-class families. With this aim in mind, the various trusts established in this period met with some, albeit limited, success. While the Peabody Trust was able to provide a superior quality of housing for a wider cross section of the working classes, it was not able to reach those in greatest need (Whelan, 1998: 15). Rents were still too high for many unskilled workers and qualification criteria often excluded those in casual employment. Despite its philanthropic ambitions, Peabody still needed to ensure revenue through-flow: the investors had to be paid their five per cent dividend. This meant that rent revenue needed to be certain and tenants were asked to provide letters of reference from employers and to pay rent in advance. In order to maintain higher sanitary conditions, the general rule was one person per room, and no noxious 'industrial' activities to be carried out within Peabody tenements. Such rules – although not unreasonable – increased the cost burden on tenants. The decision to house only the 'self-supporting' and regularly employed was justified by Robert Vigers, a representative of the Trust, before the 1881 Committee on Artisans' Dwellings:

> we house the deserving class that wants accommodation [. . .] there are people that are so low, that they could not live with our people (quoted in Jones, 1976: 185).

The 'dangerous classes' or the 'undeserving poor' – as they had now become known – would not find any help from the philanthropic trusts, whose mission was to assist those of 'good moral character'. The link between destitution, desperation and immorality was not accepted: strong moral fibre was incorruptible. Hence, some people deserved charitable assistance while others would be left to fester in their own sin. This distinction between the 'deserving' and the 'undeserving' poor, although no longer couched in the same moral terms, still has a place in UK housing policy. Local authorities have a duty to house those deemed to be homeless by no fault of their own, but not those who have created their own predicament (perhaps being ejected from a private tenancy for 'anti-social' behaviour). The moral debates of the nineteenth century continue to shape today's policy objectives.

Another issue faced by the trusts in the middle of the nineteenth century – and which is often faced by Registered Social Landlords (see Chapter 3) today – was that of rising land costs and their consequent inability to compete in the land market. In London, land values in the central areas almost doubled in real terms in the 30 years after 1840. In the most popular areas, values rose by up to five times during the same period forcing the trusts to constantly increase rents in order to fund further development and maintain dividends to share holders (Cherry, 1972: 51). Many of the model dwellings developed by Peabody and other trusts became home to the Victorian period's 'key workers': by the 1880s, more curates and policemen were being housed than unskilled casual labourers (Jones, 1976: 187) confirming that the poorest strata of society was, by and large, unable to access the decent homes provided through charitable, voluntary action. Apart from economic reality, another reason for the systemic social exclusion of particular groups related to the religious rationale of the philanthropists, many of whom were active members of non-conformist churches: a factor that led many to distinguish between the deserving and the undeserving poor. The religious fervour of some philanthropists drove them to intervene in the way people lived their lives, trying to condition them and impart a particular set of moral standards. In some instances, this did result in efforts to house and engage with those considered to be in the lowest echelons of society. For example, having clubbed together with a group of female co-workers and supported by rich and influential friends, Octavia Hill purchased leases on a number of run-down properties in London. Her particular claim to fame was her subsequent 'maternalistic' approach to housing management, driven by a belief that she could re-condition members of the 'underclass', turning them into model tenants (Whelan, 1998: 15–16). The only thing she required of prospective tenants was a keen desire to improve their condition. Those who were subsequently unable to rise above immorality were quickly ejected (Holmes, 2006: 3). In December 1874, her achievements and approach were set out in a letter to co-workers:

> We have now 15 blocks of buildings under our care; they contain between two and three thousands tenants. Each block belongs to a different person or company, [. . .] Each block is placed by me under a separate volunteer worker, who has the duty of collecting rents, superintending cleaning, keeping account, advising as to repairs and improvements, and choice of tenants and who renders all personal help that can be given to the tenants without destroying their independence, such as helping them to find work, telling them of good trade to which to bring up their children, collecting their savings, supplying them with flowers, teaching them to grow plants, telling them of provident dispensaries, of good schools, arranging happy amusements for them, and in everyway helping them to help themselves.
>
> (Hill, 2005: 32)

Like a great many of her contemporaries, Hill was opposed to publicly subsidised housing, to state pensions and to free health care. It was individuals not the state who were responsible for the housing and social problems of the Victorian era: the rich – who should be offering moral guidance and financial support to the poor – had dispersed to the suburbs: they had, essentially, 'deserted their posts' (Jones, 1976: 229). State intervention in issues of social welfare was thought to be pernicious, providing the necessities of life but in doing so demotivating the poor and eradicating any sense of social responsibility. These same debates echo in current political discourse, where 'responsibility', choice and self-help are viewed as positive alternatives to the 'nanny' state. But in an era of non-progressive taxation, and no official redistribution of wealth, it was believed that state intervention would cause the rich to abdicate their natural responsibilities towards the poor, thus becoming less active citizens.

Like many philanthropists of the time, Hill believed that were her ideas to be applied more universally, the housing and social crisis of the time could be overcome. But such maternalism was generally rejected in the twentieth century when an emergent planning system, built on strong state intervention, came to focus far less on people as individuals, and became far more concerned with land-use and bricks and mortar. And yet, the very latest debates concerned with 'community' (see Chapter 8) are, unwittingly, grounded in a revival of Hill's ideas. Indeed, her desire to 'build communities' is reflected in many contemporary regeneration programmes and community-led projects: the 'sustainable communities' plan is concerned not only with housing and physical development, but also with the way that places provide a context for living and all this entails. Hill, like the modern exponents of sustainable communities, was well aware that the housing crisis could not be reduced to the simple provision of shelter. Hers was a 'housing plus' agenda (again, see Chapter 8) embracing social, health and educational dimensions, and addressing issues of social exclusion.

The economic motivation behind some philanthropy – ensuring healthy and therefore more productive workers – was noted at the beginning of this section. Some mill and factory owners also wanted their workers to live nearby, enabling them to work longer hours. While questions of sustainability were never raised, industrial philanthropy did reflect a desire to ensure proximity between home and work. In 1846, John Grubb Richardson conceived the idea of a model village adjacent to a mill that his family had purchased at Bessbrook near Newry in the previous year. Bessbrook 'was not on a main road and Richardson believed that, with this isolation from the major towns and their distractions, he would have a temperate and controllable colony' (http://cloghmore.bravepages.com/bessbrook/bessbrook_history.html: accessed 25 May 2006) and therefore a ready supply of good workers for the family business. At around the same time, similar model villages were built up and down the country. In 1850, Titus Salt announced plans to construct a 'new industrial community' next to the River Aire, 3 miles from Bradford. The centrepiece of 'Saltaire' was a textile mill, eventually surrounded by 850 terraced cottages, housing workers who had previously walked to work from Bradford. Later in the century, housing schemes were developed at Bournville (developed by George and Richard Cadbury) in 1880 and at Port Sunlight (developed by William Hesketh Lever) in 1888. Both schemes, intended to house chocolate and soap workers respectively, were innovative in terms of layout and housing design and exemplified cottage-style working-class housing in relatively green settings that afforded occupants with ample open space. The Cadbury brothers purchased land 4 miles from Birmingham city centre in 1878: 'driven by a passion for social reform linked with his Quaker beliefs, George Cadbury's objective was to provide decent quality homes in a healthy environment which could be afforded by industrial workers' (www.bvt.org.uk: accessed 11 May 2006). A Trust was founded in 1900 to manage the village created by the Cadburys, and this exists today, currently providing homes for 25,000 on a 1,000 acre site. Eight years later, Port Sunlight was founded as a 'garden village', designed by a team of more than 30 architects, reflecting Lever's desire to create an interesting picturesque environment. He possessed what today might be labelled a 'place-making agenda' (Chapter 8).

What all these philanthropic projects did was to demonstrate what was possible with sufficient motivation and finance. The plight of the working classes could be eased and an antidote to the squalor and disease of the slums was within reach. Not surprisingly, the extent of Victorian philanthropy was insufficient in the face of the huge housing and social problems that plagued towns and cities in the nineteenth century, in much the same way as the efforts of Registered Social Landlords today are dwarfed against the scale of demand for affordable homes (see Chapters 3, 4 and 5). However, like the exemplars of sustainable housing that are commonplace in the UK today, the model villages of the nineteenth century pointed to at least the possibility of a brighter future.

State intervention

It was perhaps inevitable that given the scale of the mounting crisis, the case for direct state intervention would become irresistible. Early concern had at least resulted in a monitoring of urban problems: the Poor Law Commission (set up in 1834 to make inspections of poor relief and draw up tables of poor rates) together with the General Register Office (1837) began to provide a statistical record of declining health and housing standards within the cities. In the following decade, four government-sponsored investigations were undertaken into working-class conditions: the Royal Commission chaired by Edwin Chadwick and subsequent report into the *Sanitary Conditions of the Labouring Population of Great Britain* (1842) is perhaps the most famous and the most widely cited. More than 7,000 copies of the report were published and distributed, many being sent to parliamentary members and other people of influence considered sympathetic to the social welfare agenda. Drawing on information collected from visits to some of the country's worst slums, Chadwick was able to reveal a direct linkage between a lack of sanitation, overcrowding and disease, concluding that concerted action was needed in relation to foul-water drainage, refuse collection and the supply of clean, safe drinking water. According to the report, both local and central intervention was crucial: ad hoc philanthropic endeavour was simply insufficient.

> on considering the evidence before given with relation to the effects of different classes of buildings, the suggestion immediately arises as to the extent to which it is practicable to protect the health of the labouring classes by measures for the amendment of the existing buildings, and for the regulation of new buildings [. . .] where neither private benevolence nor enlighten views can be expected to prevail.
>
> (Chadwick, 1965 (reprint): 339)

Neither philanthropy nor inaction was viewed a viable option in the long term. Although the liberal attitude to self-help and limited state intervention in private affairs remained dominant, the belief that government could sit back and do nothing was rapidly losing support. Appealing to common decency, John Stuart Mill – a champion of individual freedoms – argued, in 'On Liberty' (1859: see also Book 5, Chapter 11 of 'Principle of Political Economy', Mill, 1848) that a person may well cause harm to others not only by his actions, but also by his inaction:

> in all things which regard the external relations of the individual, he is *de jure* amenable to those whose interests are concerned, and if need be, to society as their protector.
>
> (Mill, 1859: annotated text edited by Gray and Smith, 1991: 31–32)

A real step-change in government thinking occurred in the late 1840s, prompted by recognition of a 'working-class problem', which was seen to encompass an economic, a social and a politic threat to the country as a whole. A philosophy built on the principles of self-help and individualism began to slowly shift, embracing the need to protect (wider political and economic) interests through steady and incremental state intervention. Once the floodgates opened, there was no going back. In the four decades after 1850, more than 40 major pieces of legislation concerned with housing and the working classes passed before Parliament. At first, much of this legislation lacked real bite. Politicians wanted to be seen to be reacting to the issues, but in reality, very little actually happened on the ground. Legislation embraced the issues of slum clearance and urban renewal and there was, at the very least, some thought given to what might eventually be done. Lord Shaftesbury, although suspicious of direct state intervention (see above) was an ardent supporter of social reform and some early legislation carried his name. In 1851, two Acts of Parliaments were passed and these became known at the Shaftesbury Acts: the first of the 'Labouring Classes Lodging Houses Acts' was simply about ensuring gender segregation in lodging houses, while the second sought to increase the number of lodging houses being built.

These were rather piecemeal efforts and most local authorities (which were, at this time municipal councils created in 1835) remained reluctant to become embroiled in the affairs of lodging houses, and only a few engaged in the direct provision of municipal lodgings (Ward, 2004). Shaftesbury, with the support of the metropolitan police (who saw municipal control of housing as a means of controlling people), was keen to extend his legislation. A Crowded Dwellings Prevention Bill passed unhindered through the House of Lords but was rejected in the Commons where it was argued that the bill was 'contrary to the spirit of liberty and violated the sanctity of the Englishman's Castle'. Intervention of this kind was still viewed as unwarranted, despite overwhelming evidence of a crisis in private housing. However, a string of subsequent bills did reach the statute book. In 1866 the Labouring Classes Dwelling Houses Act permitted local officials to borrow money from the Public Works Loans Board to erect and improve dwellings. An Artisans and Labourers Dwellings Act two years later (1868) handed the same local officials the power to demolish unfit dwellings. Shortly afterwards, in 1875, a further Act – championed by Sir Richard Assheton Cross – with the same name extended this power beyond individual dwellings to the demolition of entire neighbourhoods. In theory, at least, the power to engage in 'slum clearance' had been established, but in reality a compensation clause in the legislation again created a reluctance to use the new law (Cherry, 1996: 12). Direct action still stood in opposition to the view that housing conditions and the plight of the poor could be improved through 'patience, perseverance, determination, charity and private enterprise' (Cross, 1885; cited in Jones, 1976: 228).

But while reluctance to intervene in private housing matters remained, there was less reticence about the need to deal more generally with the issue of public health. This concern for health was perhaps more important in the early development of 'planning' than the housing Acts of the same period. It resulted in the introduction of an embryonic planning regime. In 1848, the Public Health Act stipulated that plans for buildings, streets and drainage would need to be submitted to local officials before construction began. A decade later, in 1858, a Local Government Act tightened state control over building regulations and all major towns issued 'by-laws' under the 1848 and 1858 Acts. But as with some modern legislation, legal uncertainties and weak enforcement powers made these building regulations difficult to uphold. The same was true of the Sanitary Act of 1866: this insisted that houses should be connected to a mains sewer and set limits to occupancy in the hope of securing public health improvements. But the act was complex and interpretation varied from one area to the next. For this reason, the Public Health Act of 1875 handed local bodies new powers of enforcement relating back to the 1866 legislation (Cherry, 1996: 11) and by the 1880s the term 'by-law' housing had become synonymous with the 'planning' and development of the Victorian city.

It was also in the 1880s that the 'fear of the mob' again became apparent. Urban development, and particularly clearance to make way for civic buildings and railways, had caused significant displacement in many inner cities, and those displaced were rarely rehoused (Hall, 1996), which resulted in a growing resentment towards local powers. But perhaps more significantly, an economic recession in the same decade resulted in new hardship, with many members of the 'decent' working classes suddenly finding themselves thrown into poverty and mixed up once more with Marx's 'dangerous class' (Sims, 1889: 11). This issue – of undesirable 'social mixing' – rather than overcrowding and poor public health aroused new anxieties, which now found expression among the working classes through trade unions and other political movements. Whereas the Reform Act of 1832 (extending voting rights to homeowners with an annual income of at least £10) was considered a major disappointment, the Second Reform Act of 1867 had tripled the size of the male electorate, and a further Act in 1884 extended voting eligibility to agricultural workers (Stoker, 1991: 2): a move which was followed in 1888 by the creation of County Councils. The working classes now had a political voice and this was uniting around the unions. In the same year, the Social Democratic Federation and the Fabian Society were formed, followed by the independent Labour Party in 1893, which had the stated intention of putting working-class members in Parliament. But during the 1880s, formalised political empowerment seemed to go hand-in-hand with insurrection: for many, the changes afoot at this time were simply not progressing at sufficient pace. Hall (1996: 24) has observed that 'during the mid-1880s, throughout the cities and above all throughout London, there was a spirit of cataclysmic, even violent, change in the air'. On 8 February 1886, a meeting organised by the Fair Trade

League and attended by 20,000 unemployed dock and building workers suddenly turned violent. The workers – who were demanding job protection – were joined by members of the Social Democratic Federation calling for socialist revolution. Rioting ensued, windows were smashed and in Hyde Park carriages were over-turned and their wealthy occupants were robbed (Jones, 1976: 291).

These and more serious rioting in Liverpool (1886 and 1887) provided the backdrop for a survey of living conditions among the London poor under-taken in 1887. *Life and Labour of the People of London* (1889, and published in full in 1902) was a cross-sectional study of London's population led by Charles Booth. It divided the city's population into four major groups: the criminals and loafers who led a savage life of extreme hardship; the perennially poor engaged in casual and irregular labour; a 'pitiable' class who struggled against hardship and economic depression; and a fourth class of people with more regular incomes, who were patient and hoped for new opportunities and a better future for their children. Again, Booth seemed to confirm the distinction between a true 'working class' and a 'residuum', but for the first time, was able to convince many of his peers of the need to create opportunities for the true working class. This was seen as the decent thing to do, but also a means to win political support and quell revolutionary sentiment.

It seemed that by the 1880s, Parliament was ready to listen to calls for change. During the previous 60 years, 'by-laws' – usually relating to public health – had been used in a number of towns and cities by municipal councils concerned about sanitation and slum conditions. In some instances, private bills had been passed allowing wholesale slum clearance. But by the 1880s, the municipal coun-cils themselves had become convinced of the need for more general powers, perhaps more wide-ranging (Ashworth, 1954: 180). This was also a time of reflection. We have already noted the reluctance – between the Shaftesbury Acts of 1851 and the 1880s – of many local authorities to engage in positive action, partly because of legal complexity and partly because of compensation require-ments. A Royal Commission of the Housing of the Working Classes – under the chairmanship of Sir Charles Dilke – highlighted this reality in 1885, revealing that only two London boroughs had enacted by-law measures. It was concluded, therefore, that further powers were unwarranted but that the raft of legislation introduced in the previous 30 years should be consolidated and simplified and that municipal councils should be empowered to deliver what should henceforth be considered a national health and, by implication, a housing agenda. It was recommended that local authorities be given greater resources, that staff should be better trained, that new powers of inspection should be rolled out and that authorities should be allowed to borrow money from the Treasury at a low interest rate (Dilke, 1885).

Plate 3 Victoria Square, Manchester – one of the country's first public housing developments, undergoing remedial works in 2002

These recommendations were implemented in an immediate Housing of the Working Classes Act (1885) and, five years later, another Act of the same name (1890) consolidated all previous legislation and marked the beginning of an era of municipal clearance and housing provision, specifically for the 'working classes'. Local authorities were, for the first time, able to build and manage public housing on a significant scale using money that could be borrowed from the Treasury. Slowly, some urban authorities (County Borough Councils after 1888) began to develop small stocks of working-class housing. In London, the first suburban estates were developed by the newly instituted London County Council. In 1890, it identified land at 'Totterdown Fields' in Tooting as a potential site for housing development. This was developed, with a view to relieving overcrowding in the inner city, in 1899. Further schemes were developed across the city in the early years of the twentieth century (Holmes, 2006: 7). Reflecting the findings of the Booth Report (1889), these early housing schemes were targeted at the 'patient' working classes: rents were set at a level that would only afford access to those with regular employment. The era of working-class housing had begun.

Early planning

But during this same period, a concern for building regulations and sanitation, and for concerted action led by the public sector, had also resulted in the de facto creation of a planning system. It was important, during these early years that housing for the working classes was to become the responsibility of local authorities. This responsibility handed authorities the simultaneous task of land acquisition and assembly and subsequently charged them with development planning. The move to state intervention in housing matters was central to creating a system of public-sector planning, which was reinforced by decentralisation marked by the creation of multi-purpose county councils in 1888 and elected authorities below the counties in 1894 and 1899 (Stoker, 1991: 2). This provided a framework in which to plan. The earlier Booth Report had also recognised that wider 'planning' (of transport linkages) was crucial if the problem of overcrowding in the inner cities was to be resolved (Hall, 1996: 49). Booth had been concerned with broader considerations and pointed to the need for private enterprise to become more generally involved in infrastructure provision, looking beyond issues of simple sanitation. This view was subsequently reflected in legislation at the turn of the century, with early supporters of integrated planning emphasising the continuation of Victorian housing problems into the new century (Sutcliffe, 1981: 60; see also Ward, 2004: 17). Charles Booth, like others, had viewed radial transport and suburban housing development as a solution to the urban problem. Suburbanisation would result in a thinning of the inner urban population, creating opportunities for slum clearance and improvement. At the same time, a more planned and manageable environment could be created on London's edges. But echoing the Victorian philosophy of free, private enterprise, 'planning' need not only be a framework for public intervention. The private sector might also benefit from operating within the parameters of such a system (Hall, 1996: 53). At first, planning was viewed with suspicion: as a socialist tool threatening the freedom of the market. But some clever arguments from the supporters of municipal planning seemed to quell these fears: John Nettlefold, Chairman of Birmingham's Housing Committee, suggested that public housing (still disliked by many) had only become necessary because of disorderly, poor quality private development based on unfettered speculative building, especially around the urban fringe: 'town planning' he argued, 'will show municipal house building to be unnecessary' (Nettlefold, 1908; cited in Ward, 2004: 25), providing the framework 'within which the private developer could operate' (Hall, 1996: 53).

This argument, aired with some regularity, was instrumental in winning support for the Housing, Town Planning, etc. Bill (1909):

The object of the bill is to provide a domestic condition for the people in which their physical health, their morals, their character and their whole social condition can be improved by what we hope to secure in this bill. The bill aims in broad outline at, and hopes to secure, the home healthy, the house beautiful, the town pleasant, the city dignified and the suburb salubrious.

(quoted in Cullingworth and Nadin 1997: 15)

The Act, when it was passed, gave authorities the power – if they so wished – to prepare a town planning scheme for land within their area of jurisdiction that was likely to be used for building purposes. This early planning looked to what might happen in the future (an important point in relation to Chapter 9), but was not concerned with the planning or re-planning of what already existed. The legislation was a disappointment to many activists who had been motivated by an awareness of the powers enjoyed by early planners in Germany (Horsfall, 1904). Planning was not viewed as sufficiently pro-active particularly with respect to land acquisition: the system did not challenge existing private property rights. On the face of it, 'statutory town planning immediately after 1909 was *a mild, uncertain affair.* Town planning for all was a novelty which might be gingerly tried, but there was every deterrent to prevent anybody from indulging in it to excess' (Ashworth, 1954: 188, emphasis added).

But, the new legislation made planning a local government function and this has since been viewed as a significant step. It also suggested, for the first time, that housing issues should not be addressed in isolation as they had been for much of the Victorian era. And this sentiment is echoed in the modern 'communities plan' (see Chapter 8). However, planning remained largely unspecified in its central purpose: it seemed to be a bundling together of existing powers with no underlying philosophy. Local authorities were called upon to 'do things' but how they should integrate their actions was left for them to find out for themselves. Following the 1909 Act, regulations were issued by government (from 1910 onwards) setting out the practical scope of planning (Ashworth, 1954: 189).

But the overarching feeling in 1909 was that this 'consolidating legislation' was a disappointment, dealing in broad aspiration (see the much-cited quotation above) but lacking substance. Clearly, the 'problems posed by the big city – moral, social and technological – commanded the intellectual energies of the Victorians, and town planning, which embraced solutions for urban growth, owes much to this setting' (Cherry, 1974: 8) but a desire for a more pervasive and powerful planning system had developed not only on the back of the urban crisis, but on other emergent factors. These included a desire to bring about land reform; an international perspective which seemed to suggest that stronger planned intervention in the shaping of cities was desirable; a concern for public amenity and conservation; and the Garden City movement, which saw planning as a key tool in delivering what might be thought of today as sustainable communities. Indeed, 'town planning began from a different set of influences, but found itself accommodating a similar set of objectives' (Cherry, 1978: 315).

Land reform

Land reform was of concern to both the social reformers of the nineteenth century and the early planners of the twentieth century. It was about allowing the state to intervene in private land matters where there was an economic justification. In the countryside, it was felt that absent landowners were unable to respond to changing market conditions and foreign competition, affecting the viability of British farming. In the towns, land speculation made it impossible to provide cheaper housing even with the arrival of low-interest Treasury loans to municipal councils (see above). Here, the case was made for some form of intervention that might regulate speculation and bring down the expectation of huge profits from development. In *Progress and Poverty* (1880) Henry George suggested that some of the profit from land development should be creamed off by the state, pre-empting calls for a 'betterment tax' in the twentieth century and a Planning Gain Supplement (see Chapter 7) in the twenty-first century. The idea that planning could somehow control land values, and dampen speculation thereby delivering a wider social agenda was an idea with some support, but no effective mechanism at this stage. Land reform held out the promise of a more responsive, planned economy (especially in relation to agriculture) and was also viewed as key to achieving a fairer society. But with no effective way of controlling development or assessing land value uplifts, it remained little more than a pipe dream. Land reform was a driving force behind the creation of a planning system, but until that system was in place no progress could be made on actually implementing reform, and until the rights of private landowners was subjected to fundamental challenge, no real headway could be made towards a more pervasive and powerful form of planning.

International experiences

While Britain's housing, health and public planning debate followed its own distinctive path, an awareness of international experiences and practices also exerted some influences over domestic development. In France, for example, major schemes for the improvement of Paris between 1858 and 1870 – under the steerage of Napoleon III and Georges Haussmann – impressed the British for their monumental scale. Following an initial programme of public works completed in 1858, Haussmann – in his capacity as Prefect of the Seine – negotiated a treaty between Paris and the French state that handed central funds to Paris for major public works. Haussmann was known for his extravagance, but despite the state keeping a tight rein on Haussmann's work, he was able to impose an entirely new primary pattern of main thoroughfares and principal civic buildings. Although Paris's transformation did not extend to the reconstruction of older districts, to slum clearance or to rehousing (Sutcliffe, 1981: 133), it demonstrated the power of planning in bringing about fundamental urban change. And although the transformation was not universally endorsed in France itself – an article in 'Temps' (1867) argued that 'one must suppose that Paris planning has for fifteen years been given over to geometricians, who have amused themselves drawing lines indiscriminately from one point to another' (http://gallery.sjsu.edu/paris/architecture/Haussman.html; accessed 18 May 2006) – in Britain and elsewhere, the achievements in Paris were a cause of considerable envy.

Paris's transformation was certainly influential in shaping America's 'City Beautiful' movement, which was initiated by the World's Columbian Exhibition held in Chicago in 1893. The exhibition – held in celebration of the four-hundredth anniversary of the discovery of the continent in the previous year – involved the transformation of swampland into a 'white city' of classic buildings and public space. It was conceived and planned by Frederick Law Olmsted and designed by the architectural practice of Daniel Burnham and John Root. The site was developed in the French Beaux-Arts style and comprised a series of white surfaces, long rows of free-standing statues and public spaces. Again, many British visitors were impressed with what could apparently be achieved on a blank canvas (Sutcliffe, 1981: 98). The City of Chicago itself was clearly impressed by Burnham's creation, handing him the task of comprehensively re-planning the city in 1909.

But it was perhaps developments in Germany, more than anywhere else, that most influenced British thinking. In 1904, just 5 years before Britain's first planning act, Thomas Horsfall published his influential text 'The Improvement of the Dwellings and Surroundings of the People: The Example of Germany'. Horsfall introduced a British audience to the detail of Germany's housing and town planning legislation. He drew attention to practical powers: the way in which German cities were able to purchase and assemble land in anticipation of urban growth, give low-interest loans to the builders of municipal housing, and – most importantly – draw up comprehensive building plans well in advance of development (Ashworth, 1954: 177). Much was admired in the framework of German planning although the outcomes were not always applauded. Barrack-style five-storey tenements contrasted markedly with the low-density suburban cottages that had become popular in the UK in the years after the developments at Bournville and Port Sunlight (see p. 38) and which were now being rolled out at Letchworth (see p. 49) (Ward, 2004: 26). But again, it was the procedures of German planning, and its comprehensiveness, that proved attractive and not its products. The model also proved popular in the United States where Sylvester Baxter praised German achievements:

> In no other country has the art of city planning been carried to so high a degree as in Germany today. This is due to several important factors. Among them are the extraordinary industrial progress in the past quarter century, the highly organized character of German institutions, the thoroughness with which the Germans attack their problems, and the strongly idealistic quality of the national temperament.
>
> (Baxter, 1909: 72)

The pervasiveness of German planning and its capacity to 'attack problems' was attractive to the early advocates of UK planning, but it created an aspiration that could not yet be realised in Britain. The first act fell well short of this aspiration, adding to the sense of disappointment felt in 1909.

Public amenity and conservation

In the early years of the twentieth century, support for planning was also built on early concerns over public amenity and conservation. Half a million acres of agricultural land was built upon in the 15 years before 1908: urbanisation had meant the loss of farmland and of open spaces (Ashworth, 1954: 182) and a new concern for these spaces found expression in the Garden City Movement (see p. 49). There had been little interest in the 'green space' agenda during the Victorian era (except when exemplar projects had promoted the picturesque in new cottage developments) and by-laws were, by the beginning of the twentieth century, held responsible for creating a sterile urban environment devoid of greenery. Horsfall – again reflecting on German experience – argued that the plight of the urban working classes was not only attributable to bad housing and unsanitary conditions, but also to the absence of anything positive to counterbalance these negatives (see Ashworth, 1954: 172). Open space and public amenity could provide this counterbalance, and Horsfall argued that these are essential components of any urban fabric. The German approach to planning had already embraced this idea, with 'organic' civic design embodying many of the principles set out by Camillo Sitte in *City Planning According to Artistic*

Principles (1889). Sitte had studied Italy's Medieval, Renaissance and Baroque spaces – especially Florence's Piazza della Signora and Venice's Piazza San Marco – and looked for ways to create similar public amenities in modern cities. Again, the German model – with its encapsulation of artistic principles and concern for public amenity – was influential in Britain. Raymond Unwin, already heavily taken with William Morris's call to build a modern art on medieval foundations, saw a clear need to incorporate art and amenity into planning. In a pamphlet titled *Nothing Gained from Overcrowding!* (1912) Unwin again argued that Victorian by-laws had needlessly created tightly packed narrow-fronted housing, erasing amenity, public space, and interest from Britain's towns and cities. Unwin called for a move from the formal to the informal and from the inorganic to the organic. Such principles resonate in current planning practice and in the urban design debate examined in Chapter 5. More generally, the public amenity, 'live-ability' and green space agenda have, despite early setbacks at the beginning of the twentieth century, now become integral to modern planning and housing debate (see Chapter 8).

The Garden City Movement

These same debates were taken forward by Ebenezer Howard's Garden City Movement. In *To-morrow: A Peaceful Path to Reform* (1898) Howard proposed a highly planned strategy for addressing the pressures of urban growth through the creation of self-contained communities beyond existing built-up areas. Through comprehensive planning, Howard argued that it would be possible to achieve a new balance between economic life, residential development and the demands for public amenity. The approach set out by Howard was highly prescriptive: create settlements of around 30,000 persons and try to achieve a reasonable social mix; move away from central locations to find cheaper land; give ownership of the land to the community itself, enabling them to profit from its development and use that profit to invest in public amenities. This vision of comprehensive urban planning (of 'master-planning'), bringing together aspects of the 'City Beautiful' and German procedural order (see p. 47) has shaped thinking on the purpose of planning for the past century.

Indeed, the early Garden Cities seemed to point to what a comprehensive system of national planning might achieve. Letchworth in Hertfordshire was started in 1904 and had 2,000 inhabitants within two years. The Garden City Company established to oversee the project ran into financial difficulties (it took until 1945 to pay off its accumulated debts – see Miller, 1989: 144) but this only seemed to confirm the need for central support in such comprehensive develop-ment. Financially, the Garden Suburb scheme in Hampstead (London) was more successful. It secured the patronage of Dame Henrietta Barnett in 1904 and was planned by Raymond Unwin and Barry Parker. A Hampstead Garden Suburb Act passed before Parliament in 1906, permitting a comprehensive 'cul-de-sac' style development. The Act was perhaps important insomuch as it signalled government's general support for low-density planning and urban extension (Ward, 2004: 26). Yet, the powers to promote this model more widely were not forthcoming in the 1909 Act.

The development of early planning in the twentieth century was judged against these four goals: more direct control over land through fundamental reform; a comprehensive style of planning that could achieve fundamental transformations; a move away from the narrow by-law agenda to a brand of planning that displayed a broader concern for place and amenity; and a master-planning approach that could deliver positive results across several fronts. These goals, or aspirations for planning, remain largely unchanged today. The issue of providing enough housing in the right places and of the right quality remains a primary consideration, but this is accompanied by wider concerns relating to place making, liveability and the power of planning to deliver positive outcomes. The debates that we examine in the remainder of this book are firmly rooted in Victorian reform and in the disappointments and debates of the early twentieth century.

Planning's evolution

The purpose of this chapter has been to demonstrate how contemporary housing and planning debate finds its origins in a number of historical antecedents. Current debate is also a product of the failure – during much of the twentieth century – to satisfactorily resolve many of the problems identified more than 150 years ago. Despite the powers handed to local authorities to build 'council housing' after 1890, only 24,000 dwellings were built in the period up to 1914, and this represented only a small fraction of what was actually needed (Malpass and Murie, 1994: 51). The undersupply of affordable homes is one clear issue that remains unresolved today, with Registered Social Landlords finding it difficult to stretch grants and set rent levels low enough for the poorest households. In the 1910s, this resulted in social exclusion: today, it means that many households rely on state benefit to meet rent costs and find themselves in a subsequent poverty trap. In much the same way as Labour promised 'Decent Homes for All' after its election victory in 1997, Lloyd George came to power in 1919 on the back of a promise to rectify a broadly similar problem; namely, securing 'homes fit for heroes'.

Like the late Victorians before him, Lloyd George spoke of the need to address the scale of the contemporary housing crisis through comprehensive action. In this respect at least, the Housing and Town Planning Act, etc. 1919 was yet another disappointment. It did little more than encourage local author-ities to pick up the responsibilities – for planning scheme preparation – that they were handed in 1909 while empowering them to draw up plans for existing built-up areas 'if they so wished' (Hall, 1996: 104). Yet the Act itself did reinforce the message that housing is a primary consideration in the planning process, extending the powers and responsibilities of local authorities in the provision of council homes, and charging them with the assessment of local housing needs. It represented a final break from the reliance on philanthropic effort that had characterised the Victorian era and resulted in the further promotion of public house building (Cherry, 1996: 74). A period of municipal house building began, which was only ended with the arrival of the first of Margaret Thatcher's govern-ments in 1979 (see Chapter 3).

There were political reasons for promoting Council Housing after 1919. The shock of the Bolshevik revolution in Russia in 1917 resulted in strong Parliamentary support for the 1919 Act, though this support faded as the threat of a similar uprising in Britain seemed to melt away. The period between 1919 and 1939 was then characterised by a political tug of war between liberal supporters of planned municipal housing development and conservative ele-ments, opposed to state provision (see Malpass and Murie, 1994). However, planning seemed to become increasingly important during this period. The Conservative Housing Act of 1923 offered subsidies to private house builders while the Labour Housing (Financial Provisions) Act of the following year led to a return to the exchequer subsidies for council housing introduced in 1919. This toing and froing continued throughout this 20-year period, creating golden periods for private and public housing successively. Planning flourished when public housing was in the ascendancy, but it also played a major role in the setting out of middle-class suburbs that sprang up as a result of low building costs, low interest rates, and the subsidies introduced by the Conservatives. Four million new homes were built at this time: just over one million by local authorities and three million by private developers. And of these private homes, 400,000 were built on the back of government subsidy (Holmes, 2006: 14).

The pattern of housing tenure – public/private – established in the inter-war period remains more or less intact today although the level of direct public provision has been reduced by the Right to Buy and other forms of privatiza-tion (see Chapter 3). During this period, the pattern of inner-urban terraces and suburban semi-detached homes that remains familiar across many British cities was established, largely by the planning of public housing in the inner cities and less dense and greener private housing beyond the centre. And yet, the weak-nesses of planning identified in 1909 remained. The 1919 Act and a further Act in 1925 were superseded in 1932 by a new Town and Country Planning Act which, among other things, tried again to coordinate local authorities in the effort of producing local planning schemes and gave greater priority to conservation objectives (hence the insertion of the word 'country' into the Act's title). Pre-empting contemporary debate over the future of 'sub-regional' planning (see Chapters 7 and 9), the 1932 Act also encouraged the creation of inter-local authority committees dealing with cross-boundary issues. By 1938, there were 138 of these joint committees and 60 embryonic sub-regional plans (Cherry, 1996: 70). Planning was starting to think at a more strategic level, but its range and influence was still limited by the barriers identified in 1909: it was constrained by private interests, was built on incremental legislative change and lacked a deeper philosophy, often failed to be comprehensive or integrative, and was not grounded in any clear consensus over where planning should go in the future.

In essence, it needed a new impetus. This impetus came from two sources. First, a modernist architectural movement that demanded not the carte blanche planning of suburban sites (as in the case of the Garden Cities model), but the comprehensive re-planning and redevelopment of existing urban areas: a modernist solution to the hardships of the Victorian era. Second, one of the most destructive wars in modern history, which would see planning called upon to lead the wholesale physical and economic restructuring of the nation.

The Modernist movement emerged in the 1930s, infiltrating into Britain from mainland Europe. Modernists experimented with new building forms, layouts, densities and materials, grounded in a socialist tradition of state action and intervention. But in the context of pre-war Britain, it was difficult for the movement to gain any foothold. However, by the mid-1930s, modernist ideas were being aired in planning and architecture schools, and a future generation was being influenced by the view that mass housing might, in the future, be delivered along the lines set out by such influential modernists as Walter Gropius, Adolf Mayer and Le Corbusier, all of whom were advocates of prefabricated and standardized housing (Gold, 1997: 50). Modernist thinking held out the promise of ordered, cheap and fast development which was seductive at a time of continuing housing shortages. It also offered a possible solution to the inner-urban problems that tended to be neglected by the Garden City-type solutions of the turn of the century (ibid., 172). Indeed, while low density family housing might be suited to the suburbs, cities would be better off with denser, perhaps high-rise solutions (Mumford, 2000: 50). By building at higher densities, land would be used more efficiently, but at the same time, spaces could be created between buildings as an antidote to the dark, densely packed slums of the nineteenth century (ibid., 38). Modernism promised, quite literally, a brighter future for the inner cities, and some early experiments occurred in Leeds, Liverpool and Manchester in the years immediately before the war (Cherry, 1996: 79).

Modernism offered a radical rethink of the way in which urban space might be used in the future, but its direct influence on British architecture and planning was cut short by the onset of war. All other political and social considerations were then eclipsed, during the next six years, by the fight against fascism. But on the cusp of victory in 1944, attention once again turned to the future of planning. After 5 years of war, many British cities – and the national economy – lay in ruins. Suddenly, the opportunity presented itself to give planning the bite that its supporters had long argued for. Wartime production and the need to offer the prospect of a post-war economic revival resulted in 'acceptance of the need for economic planning' (Simmie, 1994: 2). And this was combined with the need for reconstruction, both real reconstruction of bombed-out inner cities, and 'a morale-boosting vision of post-war society' (ibid., 2). The Planning White Paper of 1944 – 'The Control of Land Use' – emerged in this context. The White Paper offered a comprehensive view of the future role of planning: after the war, planning would play a pivotal role in coordinating different policy streams – housing, agriculture, schools, the distribution of industry, and conservation and recreation through the proposed 'national parks'. But the Act that followed in 1947, despite backing away from control over agriculture, was at least as radical in its outlook as the White Paper, bringing about land reform

Plate 4 The Barbican – one of the most successful British modernist housing schemes (London, 2005)

(nationalizing development rights) and vesting the power of planning control over all future development in local government. It handed these powers to a smaller number of stronger, larger local authorities, suggesting that future planning would be more strategic and more comprehensive. Development planning would become a statutory duty and local authorities would have a power over private interest that was inconceivable in the Victorian era.

The first challenge for the new system was that of reconstruction and it was in relation to this challenge that the system now re-engaged with the modernist agenda. The 1947 system sought: to prioritise the redevelopment of city centres; to separate residential from industrial land-uses; to create comprehensively planned neighbourhood units (which could be provided in the form of single apartment blocks); and to segregate motorised transport from day-to-day residential activities. How this might be achieved was demonstrated in the 1951 Festival of Britain: the Lansbury development in Stepney/Poplar comprised medium-rise prefabricated slab blocks of no more than six storeys interwoven with more traditional housing (Gold, 1997: 214). Yet early, 'soft-modernism' – favoured by the post-war Labour government – eventually gave way to bolder schemes designed to eradicate and replace the Victorian slums. Experiments in 'brutalism' and in system-built social housing have often, in hindsight, been viewed as flawed (see the discussion of Hulme's redevelopment in Chapter 5) and planning's support for such schemes in the 1950s and 1960s is often presented as evidence of the system's failure to deliver organic solutions or understand that housing is more than simply bricks and mortar or, in the case of brutalism, concrete and steel.

Despite the promise of the 1947 Act, planning's role in housing provision over the last 50 years has not always been viewed as positive. Despite promising the first integrated and comprehensive form of planning that the country had seen, the 1947 system fell short of this goal, prompting the debates and reforms that are examined in the remainder of this book.

Conclusions

Today's housing and planning debate is a continuation of themes and unresolved dilemmas that have been inherited from the Victorian period and the early years of the twentieth century. The privatization of public housing (Chapter 3) – which has exposed planning to a greater weight of responsibility for the supply of affordable homes – is another phase in the debate over state versus private (or voluntary) action. Broader house-building debates (Chapter 4) reflect the same key themes – including that of residential density and how much housing should be built – that were of concern to the late Victorians and especially Howard.

Plate 5 Social housing – Trellick Tower by the architect Erno Goldfinger was awarded a Grade 2* listing in 1998. Flats in this iconic building are sold privately for upwards of £200,000 (London, 2005)

Questions relating to the affordability of homes and to design (Chapter 5) are the same questions raised more than a hundred years ago: how can housing be accessed by the poorest sections of society and, again, will this goal only be achieved through state intervention? And how can we create organic spaces that work with rather than against people, echoing the questions raised by Raymond Unwin at the beginning of the twentieth century.

In relation to the new planning system introduced in 2004, the questions that we have returned to seem perhaps even closer to those raised in the nineteenth century. Modern housing-supply debate (Chapter 7) takes us right back to fundamental questions surrounding the public sector and the market, and the need for state intervention if the market is allowed to perform at its optimum. Nettlefold (1908) favoured a brand of planning that could do away with the necessity for state housing provision, and this seems to be the goal again today. But it is the Communities Plan (Chapter 8), more than anything else that brings planning and housing debate full circle. There has been too much emphasis, we are told, on a simplistic housing supply agenda and planning has forgotten its role in place-making and in helping to create communities. As we noted earlier in this chapter, the plan echoes those sentiments expressed by Octavia Hill (housing is more than housing), by Ebenezer Howard (jobs, homes and amenities need to be brought together) and Raymond Unwin (planning should concern itself, centrally, with the spaces in between what is built) and sets a wider agenda and role for the planning system, but the system may not be equal to this task. In 1909, it was felt that the planning framework was insufficiently comprehensive: this was also true in 1919 and 1932. In 1947, it was generally believed that planning would henceforth be able to shape places and have a positive influence over built form. This belief, however, diminished during the next half-century as the system sank into a regulatory mindset, defending a status quo, rather than offering any positive vision of change and, generally, leaving communities feeling disenfranchised by a bureaucratic process. Planning's rejuvenation (Chapters 9 and 10) is the last theme we consider in this book. But it is also a familiar theme: there have been false dawns throughout the twentieth century: it is perhaps not always the legislation that has been at fault, but the culture of planning.

Chapter 3

The (re)birth of private housing provision

Introduction

Recent housing debate in the UK has focused, largely, on undersupply. We noted in Chapter 1 that the rate of housing completions in Great Britain fell to a 54-year low in 2001. The recent Barker Review (2004) blames undersupply – and the volatility of housing supply in the UK – for a crisis in housing affordability that prevents many households from getting on the 'housing ladder' in the first place, and stops others from moving within the market (perhaps from less suitable to more suitable accommodation). Clearly, patterns of housing completions in the private sector are critically important in determining housing affordability and access. However, another issue – the changing fortunes of public sector housing provision – has played an important part in shaping the UK's current affordability crisis. Half a century ago, the public sector was the principal provider of housing in the UK, but its role has diminished over this period, giving the private sector far more importance. Government subsidies for housing provision in post-war Britain shielded many households from market pressures. But a belief in the benefits of homeownership and, latterly, personal responsibility as a 'stakeholder' has resulted in a withdrawal from direct public sector provision. In more recent times, government has preferred to rely on market mechanisms (and indirect interventions via planning gain) that might, with some luck, satisfy demand and meet different needs.

Market mechanisms, however, are often unable to meet the full range of housing needs. Arguably there are two key issues in relation to housing supply and housing access: first, the general 'affordability' of housing and second, access to 'affordable homes'. General affordability is about the balance between supply and demand, and about ensuring that housing of the right type and price is built in the right locations. This is a central concern of the planning system and one that we focus on in Chapter 7. But 'affordable homes' or housing is a more specific term – and need – for housing built with some form of direct or indirect subsidy. In the era of public housing as mass provision (the early to mid-twentieth century), this subsidy was direct, with government funding land and construction costs. Today, the planning system takes much of the strain (see Chapter 5) creating an indirect subsidy from planning agreements. But in both the past and in the present, the concept of subsidy-derived affordable housing exists. There are two reasons why the provision of affordable housing remains necessary today. First, general undersupply (which is partially the result of planning restraint – but see our comment on this issue in Chapter 1) keeps house prices high in many areas, preventing many people from buying or renting homes, and leaving them in need of some form of assistance. Second, successive governments have sold 'affordable housing' (mostly council housing) to sitting tenants removing it from the public (and sometimes the voluntary) sector. Policies aimed at providing affordable housing today (including planning gain policies – see Chapter 5) must be viewed in the context of privatisation policies in place since the 1980s. The number of affordable homes being built now is minuscule compared with the number of affordable homes 'lost' over the last 20 years. In 1981, more than 6 million households rented homes from the public sector at 'fair' (controlled) rents; in 2004, this figure had fallen to 2.9 million. The shift from public to private housing provision has undoubtedly created difficulties for those households who, 20 years ago, might have accessed council homes but who, today, struggle to pay market rents or keep up mortgage repayments.

In this chapter, we are concerned with the supply of affordable housing, and more particularly with the loss of council housing through the Right to Buy (RTB). It should be read as further context for current housing problems. In a nation without significant public provision, resolving private housing supply problems becomes critical: the 'safety net' has become increasingly patchy and there is little room for error in the private sector. This chapter looks at what has happened to Britain's stock of council homes over the last quarter of a century; the efforts made to deliver affordable homes in other ways (especially via the voluntary sector); and, the way in which the public sector has taken on an enabling role – a role that has been extended by more recent 'planning and affordable housing' initiatives (see Chapter 5). Although this chapter touches on the role and input of the private sector in the provision of affordable housing, this is a topic that is dealt with more fully in later chapters, and particularly in Chapter 7 which deals with more general 'market affordability' and planning.

The sale of public housing: background

The sale of public housing under discretionary policies (local authorities able to sell but not obliged to do so) was already significant when the Conservative government gained power in May 1979, and had been growing steadily since the Housing Subsidies Act 1967 and the subsequent Housing Rent and Subsidies

Act 1975, which allowed sitting tenants of local authorities to purchase equity shares in their council homes (10 years later, the Housing Act 1985 was to establish a similar scheme under the auspices of the RTB legislation, which permitted tenants to secure a 'shared ownership' lease (Cooper, 1985: 97–99)). Data concerning pre-1980 sales are shown in Table 3.1. Despite the gradual increase in sales throughout the 1960s and 1970s, the obligatory demunicipalisation introduced by the Housing Act 1980 – in the form of an individual Right to Buy – was to produce an unprecedented decline in public sector housing provision (Malpass and Murie, 1987: 98; see also Jones and Murie, 2006). In the immediate aftermath of the Conservative election victory of 1979, the introduction of an obligatory sales policy was seen as the 'most effective way of expanding homeownership' (Malpass and Murie, 1987: 99). It also shifted the the emphasis of housing policy onto private rather than public sector solutions.

Condemnation of the 1980 legislation on the part of the Government's political opponents was swift; the housing organisation Shelter, claimed that 60 per cent of all local authorities in England and Wales were opposed to the obligatory sale of public housing (including 30 per cent of Conservative-controlled councils). Similarly, 'the Labour Party Conference of 1979 endorsed the National Executive Committee's statement condemning the Conservative policy of selling council houses, and carried a motion that the next Labour Government would repeal the 1980 Act' (Balchin, 1981: 137). But despite considerable opposition to the legislation, the new Housing Act was passed through Parliament on 8 August 1980. Eight weeks later, on 3 October, Chapter I of Part I of the Act relating to secure tenants' RTB came into force (Aldridge, 1980: 4). Our intention now is to consider the background to the 1980 Housing

Table 3.1 Council homes sold (1970–1978): England and Wales

Date	Units
1970	6,231
1971	16,851
1972	45,058
1973	33,720
1974	4,153
1975	2,089
1976	4,582
1977	12,019
1978	28,540

Source: Balchin and Rhoden, 2002: 187; from Department of Environment (DoE), Housing and Construction Statistics

Act and those developments in housing policy that made it possible for the state to essentially drop the well-established idea of public provision of affordable housing. Investment in housing associations created a context in which housing policy was able to move in a different direction (away from public sector intervention), but this does not explain the apparently seismic ideological shift that appeared to occur in 1980. But the Housing Act of that year was not a departure from past thinking (on the part of the Conservatives) but simply the fulfilment of an ideological vision that had been present for a hundred years. Successive Conservative governments had sought to rein-back support for public housing but none had had a mandate for a full withdrawal (or the right plan for such a withdrawal) until 1979. The arrival of the first Thatcher government began a chain of events – a golden age for housing associations followed by their decline and a new reliance on private provision – that set the stage for the current policy context: where public provision is minimum, housing associations (now RSLs) struggle to make any impact in the housing market, and the private sector is called upon to 'trailblaze', embracing all manner of new initiatives – sustainable communities, planning gain, planning tariffs, £60,000 homes, affordability targets – aimed at recreating the pool of affordable homes that the country appears to so desperately need, but which has been depleted over the last quarter of a century.

What we offer in this chapter is a continuing narrative: a story of state withdrawal from public housing provision; the emergence of a public sector enabling rhetoric (running parallel with the decline of council housing); and a shifting balance of responsibility which, today, means that government must 'facilitate' housing provision by forming a stronger relationship with the private house building industry. This relationship centres on the planning system that has become central to the delivery of decent homes, which, more than ever before, tend to be private homes.

There are many books dealing with the tos and fros of UK housing policy in the twentieth century and there are many points at which a retelling of the story might commence. But because our central concern is with the withdrawal from direct public housing 'solutions' and the shift through voluntary to largely private responses to housing supply needs, a logical starting point is the creation of the Housing Corporation in 1964. The purpose of this new body – established through an Act of Parliament – was essentially to provide a more centralised framework for the development of a voluntary housing sector. The Housing Corporation took over the former role of the National Federation of Housing Societies, acting as an umbrella organisation for housing associations. But the government's intention was that this new body should help develop a more strategic housing role for local associations, encouraging them to work more closely with local government by controlling and rationing grants. It was the beginning of a new era in 1964, when housing associations would no longer simply 'do their own thing' but would, increasingly, be at the beck and call of government. A context was being created in which the 'voluntary sector' – comprising a network of independent housing associations run by local volunteers – might play a bigger role in affordable housing provision, lifting some of the burden from local authorities. Harrison (1992: 12) suggests that the arrival of the Corporation might be considered a milestone, greatly empowering housing associations; though the question of what was behind this empowerment is not addressed. In reality, 'associations were [still] eclipsed by the growth of council housing until the 1970s' (Langstaff, 1992: 30) and it was not until the Housing Act of 1974 that really significant gains on the public sector were made, or that the state was ready to shift responsibility further from local government.

The Housing Act of 1974 brought about two key developments that further changed the context for public housing provision, and slid responsibility further towards associations. First, local authorities' ability to adequately fund new-build projects was restricted by Housing Investment Programme (HIP) cuts. Second, although total housing spending was curtailed, the Housing Corporation was assigned a greater role in directing grant subsidy to housing associations: in the form of Housing Association Grant (HAG), or Social Housing Grant as it is now known. All housing associations registered with the Corporation qualified for receipt of HAG, which averaged between 95 per cent and 99 per cent of development costs in London, and marginally less elsewhere. Nationally, HAG averaged 85 per cent of scheme costs (it could cover 100 per cent of development costs in some special needs schemes). Furthermore, this basic capital grant receipt was often 'buttressed by discretionary revenue grants (Revenue Deficit Grant [RDG] and Hostel Deficit Grant [HDG]) covering annual deficits which arose because of stock development under pre-1974 régimes, the effect of rent restrictions after the calculation of HAG and the high cost of managing hostels' (Langstaff, 1992: 31). This fairly generous system of subsidy in the years following 1974, along with the involvement of urban housing associations in Housing Action Area [HAA] and General Improvement Area [GIA] rehabilitation schemes, was to lead to a period of rapid expansion for many housing associations (Harrison, 1992: 13), and to a quickening convergence of (and a new balance between) the roles of both the public and voluntary sectors in direct affordable housing provision.

Indeed, by 1979 the new financial regime created by the Labour government in 1974, had provided a platform on which further change could be built. The narrowing of public sector provision was already apparent, and so too was a broadening of support, on the part of local government (through its enabling role – see p. 66), for the private and voluntary sectors. These changes were a clear product of political and fiscal pressures applied by central government (Malpass and Murie, 1987: 95; see also Cope, 1999). And yet, the new funding system of 1974, preceded by the establishment of the Housing Corporation in 1964, brought with it greater state interference in housing association activity, and loss in local autonomy. This was the price that associations would pay as they moved towards centre stage in the provision of affordable housing. Government wished to have less direct involvement in housebuilding, but it did not wish to relinquish control over social housing programmes: this control could still be exercised through grant setting, and through the planning system.

The Housing Act 1980

As we noted above, the introduction of a more radical privatisation programme in 1980 did not mark any sudden ideological shift: the Conservatives had never been the friends of state housing provision (see Chapter 2), and given the right mandate and a workable withdrawal strategy, it seemed inevitable they would eventually seek to break down the state's housing 'monopoly'. The right mandate was handed to Margaret Thatcher in 1979: the workable strategy came in the form of the RTB, a privatisation scheme that convinced UK tax payers of the wisdom of breaking up a national asset that had taken a hundred years to build, and which would eventually be replaced by piecemeal efforts to provide replacement affordable housing, and regular references to the UK's affordable housing crisis. But in 1979/80, these were issues for the future. The Conservatives had pledged to give council housing tenants the right to buy their homes with a discount, and this appealed to many voters in the 1979 general election. The RTB policy was counter-balanced by a tightening of restrictions on the internal affairs of housing associations, which could be hitherto influenced by local authorities as the gatekeepers of housing association grant (Aldridge, 1980: vii). The intention – as it eventually became apparent – was to edge local authorities towards a 'strategic enabling role' by giving them greater leverage over the housing associations.

The impact of the Housing Act 1980 on the stock of public housing is well documented, and we provide figures relating to sales when we look at 'shifting responsibilities' later in this chapter, but perhaps less attention is given to the Act's impact on the voluntary sector. Essentially, the controls that were introduced in 1980 (and other controls that have since been implemented) were designed to create a housing sector that could be manipulated by government to meet what are viewed as state responsibilities – to ensure that the majority of voters have decent homes and are reasonably content. Three key changes affected housing associations at this time. The first of these involved extending the activity of associations; no longer would they simply be assigned the task of providing rented accommodation, but would be expected to buy, improve and – where applicable – dispose of homes (Aldridge, 1980: 132) through the same RTB mechanism affecting public sector stock. This final role affected 3 per cent of association (secure) stock between 1980 and 1992: more recently, some assured tenants have been able to take advantage of a softer Voluntary Purchase Grant (VPG) scheme introduced in the Housing Act 1996 (HM Government, 1996), and latterly, the Right to Acquire (Balchin and Rhoden, 2002: 245) and Home Buy (ODPM, 2005j). The second change facing associations at this time was the tightening of the Housing Corporation's grip on internal affairs. The finances of those housing associations registered under Section 13 of the Housing Act 1974 would henceforth be under constant scrutiny. New accounting and auditing requirements meant than an association was obliged to furnish the Corporation with 'a copy of its accounts and auditor's report within six months of the end of each accounting period (s124 (3))' (Aldridge, 1980: 136). And third, this tightening of central control was also manifest in the establishment of the Grant Redemption Fund (GRF) (Aldridge, 1980: 140). The setting up of the GRF meant that associations would now have to repay any HAG received if surplus rental income was accumulated from the projects undertaken using the grant. The exact calculation of 'surpluses' was defined by the Secretary of State and from 1980, the accounts of individual associations had to show a GRF to which surplus income was credited.

What these mechanisms did not do, despite the rhetoric of a broader role for housing associations, was to create a housing sector able to replace public provision. But this was never the intention. Rather, the long-term plan was (a) to provide an arms-length housing safety net and (b) move to a market system in which homeownership would be by far the dominant form of housing tenure. Again, this pattern of shifting responsibility is returned to later on. The first stage in this ideological project was to bring housing associations to heel. Hence tighter controls in 1980 also included the introduction of an Approved Development Programme (ADP), administered by the Housing Corporation (which had been waiting in the wings) and delivered via local authorities. The ADP brought with it an annual bidding process in which associations require the assistance and support of local authorities when forwarding a bid. It removed the need for the Secretary of State's approval of grant funding for an association project where that project fell within the conditional parameters and the cash limits of ADP. So in a sense, it simplified what had been a fairly complex set of past procedures.

These cash limits were clearly defined within each Housing Corporation region by an 'objective' measure of regional needs using a Housing Needs Index (HNI). The adoption of the ADP meant that for the first time, housing association funding could be administered wholly or jointly (with the Housing Corporation) by the local authority, which could therefore influence the nature of association schemes as a means of fulfilling its own development objectives, and what it saw as its own obligations or political priorities. For local authorities, the 1980 Act seemed to represent a major step towards a more strategic (enabling) housing role. In the 1980s, the key task was to enable voluntary action; in the 1990s, a new emphasis was placed in influencing private action – and the delivery of affordable housing – through planning.

Developments in the voluntary sector during the 1980s can, and have, been interpreted in a variety of ways. On the one hand, the creation of a more strategic voluntary sector might be viewed as a means of maximising the amount of affordable housing delivered by associations. On the other, these developments might be viewed as a smokescreen, giving government the opportunity it needed to set in motion an ideological agenda in which there was no role for state housing provision. The rationale behind the right to buy seems to centre on Thatcher's hard-line brand of conservatism. There was no simple economic case for the policy: it has since proven more expensive to place families in housing need in expensive and temporary private accommodation. The capital receipts from private sales total in the billions of pounds but are minuscule compared with the market value of the properties sold (and therefore with the value of the asset that the state has lost). The social case is also unclear: public housing was often of very high quality, whereas private housing may provide poor space standards for those unable to afford better accommodation. The RTB seems to be underpinned by wholly political and ideological objectives. Conservatives often defend the policy by pointing to the number of homeowners created, never conceding the economic cost to local authorities or the social cost expressed in terms of a recent surge in homelessness since 1997, or the emergence of a housing underclass who, after the demise of council housing, found their housing access opportunities severely restricted. A more reasonable claim is that the policy created a lot of Conservatives, who returned the party to power in 1983, 1987 and 1992. It was only an economy out of control in the early 1990s that eventually saw the 'right to buy Conservatives' withdraw their support for the parliamentary party.

But the political wisdom of the RTB rested, more fundamentally, on an ideological dogma that led the Conservatives to run a sustained campaign of denigration of local authorities as inefficient housing managers (Birchall, 1992: 15). Thatcher's view was unequivocal:

The state, in the form of local authorities, has frequently proved an insensitive, incompetent and corrupt landlord [therefore ...] as regards the traditional post-war role of government in housing – that is, building, ownership, management and regulation – the state should be withdrawn from these areas just as far as possible.

(Thatcher, 1993)

Again, the result is well documented: 1980 marked the beginning of the end of more than half-a-century of growth in public housing provision. Inevitably, the relationship between local and central state was strained by this sudden change, making it difficult to convince authorities to reappraise their housing role. On the one hand, government attacked the credibility of continued local authority involvement in provision *because* of administrative inefficiency, while, on the other, attempted to define a new administrative and strategic role for local government arguing that this was where local government's strength lay. The year 1980 can also be seen as a cross-roads in the narrative of UK housing policy: a juncture at which association and authority roles at first appeared to converge, but then departed in opposite directions. Authorities had been the main provider of social 'affordable' housing since the notion of liberal intervention in the housing market first appeared in the early years of the twentieth century. And associations had always played second fiddle, providing new homes of specific types but never making significant inroads into direct provision. This did not suddenly change in 1980, but what happened subsequently – and the way the RTB affected local authority stock – meant that authorities would no longer be seen as the providers of new affordable housing in Britain. It marked the beginning of a period of transition when, increasingly, the public sector lost ground to (and control over) the private sector. Eventually, it led to a situation where the state's influence in housing provision became indirect, not concerned with spending money, giving grants or providing building land, but simply trying to exert influence through the land-use planning system.

After 1980, it was recognised, of course, that the sale of council homes might have some undesirable knock-on effects. The discounts granted on property sales could of course generate big profits for some former council tenants, and this might result in adverse publicity. This has since proven to be the case, especially in London (Murray and Evans, 2002: 18). Government initially attempted to avoid this situation by stipulating that discounts granted (at 33 per cent of market value, rising to a maximum of 50 per cent depending on a purchasers period of occupancy) would be repayable to the local authority, or other public body, if the purchaser sold-on before a specified period of time had elapsed (HM Government, 1980: Section 8 (2)). There was also some concern that a loss of rent revenue would prevent local authorities from servicing the outstanding debts against council homes (they were being sold before their construction had been paid for) (Balchin and Rhoden, 2002: 191); a concern that heightened after 1988, when government removed the so-called 'cost floor' rule which had hitherto prevented the discount granted on a local authority property from exceeding the amount of money still owed on the property by the local authority (Shucksmith, 1990: 154). There were also more particular concerns over the reduction of affordable housing in more attractive rural areas, some of which might be sold on as second homes. Under Section 19 (1) of the Housing Act 1980, special restrictions on the resale of former council properties applied in designated rural areas, including National Parks, Areas of Outstanding Natural Beauty (AONB) and other areas designated by the Secretary of State. In such areas it was possible to apply covenants limiting 'the freedom of the tenant and his successors in title to deal with the dwelling house' (Aldridge, 1980: 55); these limits were designed to ensure that homes continued to be occupied by local people. But the Section 19 provisions were weak: few authorities outside the National Parks and AONBs were granted the power to apply covenants, therefore early predictions that 'sales [would] lead to a reduction in the ability of councils to carry out social and planning objectives' (Phillips and Williams, 1983: 91) proved well-founded. This is an issue we return to in Chapter 6.

But generally, the potential disbenefits of privatisation were thought to be outweighed by the benefits, which included the creation of personal wealth and responsibility. Many households did indeed benefit from the 1980 legislation; it provided them with capital releasable for home improvements; it handed them the means to compete for housing in the open market and leave the social sector if they so wished. It is only over time that the disbenefits have surfaced, as the private and voluntary sectors struggled to meet those housing needs that might previously have been met within the public sector. Indeed, the current crisis in housing supply and affordability is, arguably, only a 'crisis' because the public sector safety net has disappeared.

Strategic housing enablers

Privatisation of previously public housing has reshaped the role of local authorities in housing provision. A surge in private sales in 1981 (100,000 units sold) and 1982 (200,000 sold) together with the new administrative regime for housing associations meant that many 'policy statements began to refer to authorities playing an enabling role, facilitating provision by non-municipal agencies' (Birchall, 1992: 25). Implicit in these statements, was a drive to create new partnerships, and forge stronger links with the voluntary housing sector in the short term, and the private sector over the longer term. The partnership with associations was defined by three factors. First, by the decreased resourcing to local authorities; second by lower net housing spend, eventually affecting the entire housing sector including associations; and third by the introduction of an ever greater element of private funding for new social housing. The first factor was immediately apparent in 1980; the second became more gradually apparent as the decade wore on; and the third, was something that associations feared but did not have to face until much later in the 1980s.

These factors prompted a new voluntary–public relationship during this period, but perhaps even more fundamental to the longer-term development of housing (and planning) policy was the view that tenure was not of paramount concern in the provision of affordable housing. Indeed, government was keen to explore new ways of promoting 'low cost homeownership', and argued that local authorities should play a strategic enabling role in the pursuit of this objective. It was at this time that government began to 'encourage' local authorities to enter into partnerships with private builders, granting permission to provide 'starter homes' on publicly owned land (thereby generating a land-cost subsidy: Malpass and Murie, 1987: 287). The sale of public land to private and voluntary providers was a common activity after 1981 and much of the Housing Corporation's capital funding programme was diverted into schemes linked to this form of land release. Again, little thought was given to the tenure of the homes that should be built: the view that 'affordable housing' (of any tenure) and 'social housing' (long associated with renting) was one and the same was not challenged. Government had come to believe that the country's principal housing problem was one of supply rather than housing type or tenure. In 1980, the Minister for Housing and Construction argued for a 'striking similarity between the household incomes of a significant number of owner-occupiers and an equally significant number of council tenants'. In response, government's 'low-cost homeownership' experiment brought together 'voluntary and community groups, landlords, builders, and financial institutions for new house building' (Ball et al., 1988: 207) based on an assumption that the benefits of extra supply would naturally trickle down to those in greatest need. Critics argued then, and continue to argue today, that an overwhelming emphasis on market mechanisms fails to overcome the obstacles posed by access and affordability affecting a significant housing underclass. A market philosophy has created a comfortable, fairly well-housed majority, but left a very badly housed minority in its wake.

The enabling role of local authorities has had two dimensions since the early 1980s. The first dimension is the relationship between authorities and the private sector, addressing the needs of the majority by facilitating housebuilding. The second is the continuing link with housing associations, which has been shaped by the assumption that market mechanisms can cater for the needs of a majority of, but not all, households. This resulted in commitment to retaining a residual supply of social rented housing, funded through HAG channelled via the Housing Corporation's development programme. Within this second dimension, local authorities would – and continue to – act as strategic overseer, contributing land to new developments where possible, and encouraging the provision of some social rented housing as well as housing for low-cost homeownership or for shared equity. By providing land and acting as funding 'gatekeeper', local authorities won the right to nominate housing applicants waiting on their own housing registers to housing association tenancies. This enabled local authorities to meet their obligations to rehouse those in acute need, or accepted as statutorily homeless. In turn, many associations grew rapidly on the back of more generous funding, but were being encouraged to develop ownership rather than rental schemes, even where the apparent need was for rented accommodation. That said, many associations maintained their rental programmes, sometimes by implementing mixed tenure schemes and subsidising the rental element.

The rental sector

Many associations saw this strategy as one of desperation: government, on the other hand, viewed it as a model for future innovation, bringing together different tenures and generating a private subsidy from market housing. Such strategies were held up as exemplars in the 1987 Housing White Paper, in which government sought greater innovation in provision, and greater stability in the private rented housing market. Private renting, after 1987, was touted as the obvious antidote to the access barriers erected by a policy focused almost exclusively on homeownership. Government continued to attack council housing, but started to talk about the need to maintain a healthy rental sector. In 1986, the Audit Commission published a report into Managing the Crisis in Council Housing in which it criticised the excessive politicisation of management activities, and outlined the failure of local authorities to successfully fulfil the day-to-day obligations of repair and maintenance (Hallett, 1993: 81). Because they were such bad landlords, it was 'necessary to develop policies to encourage investment in private renting and housing associations' (ibid.), together labelled the 'independent rented sector'. A new Housing Act in 1988 (HM Government, 1988) sought to deregulate the private rental market, not to promote renting as a realistic tenure choice for a significant number of households, but to at least stabilise the sector.

Hence the narrative of decreased emphasis on public provision and increased private responsibility over the last 25 years has a twist in its tail. The programme of privatisation continued unabated (as we will see shortly), but government came to recognise the need to provide rental opportunities for those households at a life-stage when renting was the preferred tenure, or because homeownership was unachievable. A new housing Bill, introduced before Parliament in November 1987 reflected a belief among many Conservatives that the series of Rent Acts (following on from the Rent and Mortgage (Restrictions) Act 1920) consolidated by the last Labour government under the Rent Act 1977 has been 'responsible for a steady decline in the private rented sector of the housing market' (Rodgers, 1989: 1). The argument might, of course, be viewed as perverse. A Conservative government that had spent the previous eight years selling council homes to sitting tenants now argued that a scarcity of rental opportunities was the result of the 'fair rent system' introduced in Section 70 (2) of the Rent Act 1977. This system saw rents regulated by local authorities and, it was argued, meant that there was an 'insufficient return for landlords to invest in improvement, repair and enhancement of rented property' (ibid) because of the way 'fair' rents were calculated; that is, with an assumption that the number of tenants seeking accommodation in similar dwellings is not substantially greater than the number of such dwellings available. If, on the other hand, free-market principles were applied, rents would be permitted to rise, and reinvestment in the rented sector would follow. The first major change brought about by the Housing Act 1988, was the abolition of Rent Act protection and the creation of 'assured tenancies' after 15 January 1989. Assured tenancy agreements would be settled by negotiation between landlord and tenant for all new lettings after this date, while the 'rights of previous housing association [or private sector] tenants remain the same as before and their tenancies remain unaltered' (Harrison, 1992: 17). The new freedom of contract amounted to a reversal of successive Rent Act legislation, but the apparent removal of contractual tenant protection, it was argued, would not infringe upon personal rights, but simply align the status's afforded to tenant and landlord, and improve mutual cooperation. However, although landlords would benefit from a more competitive rate of return, tenants would no longer be immune to market forces, and as far as housing association tenants were concerned, would no longer have the RTB.

For housing associations, changes in tenancy agreements and a move away from 'fair rents' were combined with an overall reduction in HAG funding, and placed upward pressure on rent levels. Harrison (1992) argued that the move towards market rents had little to do with reviving the rental sector, and was more a result of government's belief that tenants in the public sector (now broadly defined) were paying too little for their housing. Rents increased and government responded by claiming that this would result in a better housing service. In reality, a growing number of association tenants found it impossible to keep up with these increases and, over time, many found themselves pushed into a poverty trap and realised that they would often be better off out-of-work and in receipt of Housing Benefit. This has been a recurring problem for housing associations since the late 1980s, with many tenancies becoming ever-more unaffordable. This affordability problem has been amplified by a reduction in available HAG from 1988 onwards – and more recently, continuing cuts in Social Housing Grant (SHG) rates since 1996. The shift to mixed public–private funding in 1988 (with associations having to rely on private finance to fund new-build schemes) was supposed to encourage greater cost efficiency. But it also created a riskier operational environment for associations: first, because of the need to borrow at commercial rates and consequently be in a position to service debt, and second, because grant levels were now to be agreed at the outset of a development. Any cost overrun would have to be met by the association. This led to far greater caution among associations, which has inevitably impacted on the supply of housing association properties.

Changes to tenancy arrangements were designed to free the rental market from regulatory constraint. Inertia in this market had become increasingly apparent, particularly as the public sector withdrew from rental provision, leaving little or nothing to fill the void. But this deregulation, as important as it might be over the longer term, was perhaps only a secondary component within the wider content of the 1988 Act. Government's real objective at this time was to consolidate the work it had begun in 1980: namely, to squeeze the local state from direct provision and define a new relationship between authorities and the other sectors.

Enabling and the independent sector

But these changes were a minor distraction from the bigger project. Government 'enabling' rhetoric was more explicit in the 1988 Act than it had been in 1980, and this time, greater emphasis was placed on the use of private finance in public or voluntary housing schemes: authorities were charged with 'encouraging innovative methods of provision by other bodies (such as housing associations), involving increased use of private sector sources of finance' (Rodgers, 1989: 7). Indeed, the 1988 Housing Act appeared only a year before the first PPG Notes. The finalised PPG dealing with planning and housing (1992) made the same references to local authorities as enabling housing provision – and especially affordable housing – through a variety of innovations (see Chapter 6). The mid- to late-1980s saw the emergence of new forms of public–private–voluntary collaboration across a number of policy areas (the importance of such collaboration was spelt out in Part II of the 1988 Act).

As well as changing the context for private and housing association renting, government contined to attack the public sector's management and ownership monopoly through voluntary stock transfers (VSTs) and through the creation of Housing Action Trusts (HATs). Essentially – and this is not a topic that we wish to examine in any great depth – HATs became the context for VSTs, the first being the vehicle for and the latter the process of, transferring large quantities of public sector housing to housing associations (often newly created 'transfer associations'). Associations became the new landlords for former council housing tenants, and borrowed money against their new assets to pay for essential repairs and maintenance. Private funding became the critical ingredient in housing provision and in the upkeep of remaining non-private (usually 'voluntary') housing stock. But private finance has dramatically altered the scale of voluntary housing provision: the post-1988 environment has suited larger associations, better able to deal with the new financial realities. The big associations – with more tenants and more rental income – have found it easier to attract private finance and use reserves to pay for development (Harrison, 1992: 21). Smaller associations have often been ineligible for some forms of Housing Corporation funding, have smaller rental income streams, and find it more difficult to secure loans against assets. These have responded by entering into development consortia, many have merged, and some have stopped developing new homes altogether, choosing simply to manage what they already have (Cope, 1999).

The voluntary sector has been transformed since 1988: grant rates have fallen year-on-year; some associations have disappeared, others have merged and grown; few associations rehabilitate older properties (because of the unpredictability of grant funding); most concentrate on new-build, behaving like private volume builders, and sometimes enter into development agreements with private developers.

Provision and regulation today

Thirty years ago, the context for housing provision in the UK was very different from the situation today (figures on who provides what, and how this has changed since 1981 are set out in Table 3.2). A belief prevailed that the needs of a large section of the UK population could only be met through public housing provision, and that the private sector met the needs of a distinctly different part of the 'market'. Similarly, housing associations were viewed as an ancillary mechanism for meeting special needs, particularly those of the elderly. This view was disputed and then completely abandoned in the 1980s. The belief that emerged during this period is the same belief that prevails today under the 'New Labour' administration: the private sector can provide for the vast majority

Table 3.2 Housing stock in Great Britain (1981–2001) (000s)

Date	Owner-occupied	Rented privately	Rented from RSL	Rented from local authority	All dwellings
1981	12,171	2,340	470	6,115	21,094
1982	12,345	2,322	484	6,110	21,261
1983	12,721	2,310	497	5,929	21,457
1984	13,038	2,300	512	5,812	21,662
1985	13,320	2,267	528	5,744	21,859
1986	13,660	2,205	550	5,655	22,070
1987	14,027	2,139	567	5,,558	22,292
1988	14,435	2,077	582	5,432	22,527
1989	14,848	2,069	586	5,239	22,742
1990	15,120	2,128	635	5,055	22,939
1991	15,162	2,150	701	4,966	22,979
1992	15,312	2,264	733	4,879	23,188
1993	15,464	2,332	811	4,759	23,366
1994	15,632	2,396	884	4,634	23,546
1995	15,828	2,441	976	4,496	23,741
1996	16,036	2,450	1,078	4,369	23,932
1997	16,253	2,455	1,132	4,273	24,113
1998	16,498	2,452	1,205	4,141	24,296
1999	16,737	2,433	1,319	3,983	24,472
2000	16,982	2,419	1,458	3,789	24,648
2001	17,212	2,419	1,616	3,558	24,805
2002	17,348	2,496	1,668	3,424	24,936
2003	17,547	2,581	1,824	3,149	25,101
2004	17,783	2,626	1,979	2,886	25,274

Source: ODPM (2006 – web source) Live Tables on Stock, ODPM: London (Table 102, Historical Series) (www.communities.gov.uk)

of the country's needs; an 'independent rental sector' (including housing associations) have an ancillary role to play in supporting homeownership (through
shared equity schemes) and offering rental opportunities; and the public sector
enables provision as grant gate-keeper, as strategic housing coordinator (leading
on local research and monitoring), and as planning authority. In this chapter, we
have traced this re-balancing of responsibility so as to set the scene for current
housing debates. The critical division today is the three-way split between the
sectors: the private sector as mass-producer, the public sector as facilitator and

gate-keeper, and the voluntary sector as ancillary delivery vehicle. A system of production and regulation has been created over the past 25 years – resulting, principally, from a withdrawal from public housing provision – that has moved the private sector to centre stage. Arguably, such a system is inherently less stable, or at least presents households with greater risk: those unable to compete for market housing, or pay market rents, may find that housing alternatives are few and far between. The partnership between the public and private sectors has become increasingly important over this period of transition: if great things are expected of the private sector, then the public sector must ensure that private developers are allowed to deliver. Any impediments must be removed, so that enough housing of the right quality and in the right locations can be provided. This leads to questions – concerned with the role of planning – that are not answered in this chapter, but that provide a focus for later chapters. The major impediment for private builders is land availability, and more specifically, land in the right locations. As responsibility for housing provision has left the public sector, this sector has taken on greater responsibility for ensuring that others are able to bridge the supply deficit. The 'enabling rhetoric' of the 1980s was flawed: the rhetoric saw authorities distributing grants and opening up land-banks. But grants have dwindled and public land-supply has dried up in many areas. The view of enabling in the 1980s is very different from today's view of authorities facilitating provision by controlling the land market. Planning (and influencing the use of private land) has becoming the principal enabling mechanism under New Labour.

However, 1980s debates over the 'disabling' of local government echo in current debate. Twenty years ago, it was felt that authorities had been left bereft of power or capacity by a Thatcher government that did little more that deride their management of public housing. Today, authorities have been called upon to facilitate general and affordable housing provision through a planning system that is complex and bureaucratic (according to its critics). Thus, most major critiques of housing supply issues in the UK today relate to the planning system and the operation of that system by planning bodies, either regional or local. Planning authorities are often seen as reactionary, and as failing to be forward-thinking in relation to housing provision; the planning system, more generally, is viewed as unresponsive to the needs of the housing market, and therefore as a barrier to meeting needs and satisfying demand (see Barker, 2004; and see Chapter 7).

But if the switch in emphasis from public to private provision is the dominant trend over the last few decades, a closely related trend is the transition from largely tenure-neutral policies, to a dominant emphasis on homeownership. Since Antony Eden's call for a 'property owning democracy' in 1955, housing debate has focused on the virtues of owning over renting. Owning one's home creates a sense of comfort, security and responsibility. However, Conservative promotion of 'low-cost homeownership' initiatives in the 1980s became diluted in the 1990s as new 'planning and affordable housing policies' tended to prioritise a need for low-cost rented housing (on the back of planning gain arrangements: see Chapter 5). The last Conservative government under the leadership of John Major sought to reverse this trend by redrafting planning policy guidance in favour of 'affordable housing' without any stipulated tenure. The incoming Labour government reiterated that affordable housing need be of no particular tenure type (in both 1998 and 2000: see Chapter 5). In reality, planning has been used to deliver an increasing proportion of lower cost homeownership opportunities, especially through shared equity schemes. This fits comfortably with the Blairite vision of a 'stakeholder' society, conferring individual responsibility through home-ownership. Of Britain's current housing stock of some 25 million units, nearly 69 per cent are in private owner-occupation, compared with 58 per cent in 1981. The non-private stock total is shrinking while provision by 'socal' landlords has levelled out. It is expected that a further 4.8 million households will form – in England alone– in the period up to 2026 (ODPM, 2006c). The swing away from public provision to private supply, and from renting to owning, will continue based on present policy trends. This is the most important message emerging from this chapter. Of course, the privatisation of public stock has caused significant inequities: some former tenants have accrued significant profits from onward sale, as we note below, while those in need of support may no longer be able to access social rented housing. The journey from where we were in 1980 to where we are today has produced a great many winners, and a similar if not greater number of losers. But the main impact has been to radically reshape the UK's housing system, from one characterised by sectorial and tenure mix, to one dominated by private interests and by a volume housebuilding sector. This is the context for the remaining chapters of this book.

Conclusion

At the beginning of this chapter, we set ourselves three questions: what effect did the RTB have on affordable housing supply, what other means were found to deliver affordable homes and how did the shift in policy emphasis shape the relationship between local authorities and other housing providers? This has been largely a historical examination of these issues, focused mainly on the 1980s and early 1990s. We have suggested that this was a critical period for authorities and housing associations: the former were eclipsed by the latter, though the latter – because of resource constraints – have failed to fill the housing supply deficit left in the wake of the public sector's withdrawal from direct housing provision. But it was never the intention of government that one form of social housing provision should replace another. The project begun by the Thatcher government of 1979 to 1983, and continued by successive Labour governments since 1997, was to create a substantively different housing system: one dominated by the private sector, but influenced and regulated by central state and local authorities, predominantly through the land-use planning system and, since 2004, by a broader emphasis on spatial planning (see Chapters 8 and 9).

In the Housing White Paper of 1987, the influence to be exerted by local authorities was painted in an 'enabling rhetoric'. Such enabling was only weakly resourced in the 1980s: in the 1990s it became conflated with planning policy; enabling general provision through the release of sufficient building land, and enabling affordable homes through planning gain or 'exceptional' permission mechanisms (both of which are examined in later chapters). But the problem in terms of delivering 'decent homes for all' is that despite the view that household incomes between a great many council tenants were comparable to a great many owner-occupiers, many households have been squeezed out of a more competitive, privatised, housing market. Bevan and colleagues have shown that a lack of social rented housing is a growing source of social exclusion in many areas (ibid., 2000). The market often provides housing of the right price, but in the wrong locations. In many rural and more affluent inner-urban areas, those on lower incomes frequently find that the average cost of a home close to where they work is at least ten times their household salary. They could afford a home elsewhere, out of London, but cannot move because of employment ties. Latterly, this has led policy makers to concentrate on the 'homes–jobs' balance in many areas, or to promote assistance policies aimed at supporting 'key workers'. The housing market has not worked well for everyone: despite talk of a country inhabited by a well-housed majority, the shift from mixed provision to dominantly private provision has created an inadequately housed underclass: people in rural areas, in inner cities, in affluent towns and suburbs who are locked out of the housing market, and who may have benefited greatly from access to council housing of the type that was commonplace before 1980.

There seems to be no going back to the era of mass public provision, but some mechanism needs to be found to ensure that those unable to compete for private owner-occupation have some alternative option. Past experience suggests that owner-occupation is not a sustainable housing choice for all households. Sudden fluctuations in interest rates and the cost of mortgage borrowing led to a market crisis in the early 1990s (Gentle *et al.*, 1994) showing that providing a safety net is essential. Alan Holmans continues to predict that a third of households forming in England during the next 20 years or so will require homes built with some form of subsidy assistance (Barlow *et al.*, 2002). This suggests that government should be looking to stabilise and increase the existing stock of affordable rented homes in England: however, RTB continues to threaten both the supply of affordable homes and the efforts of regeneration agencies attempting to rejuvenate many run-down inner-city housing estates. In London, for instance, many regeneration efforts run into difficulty with regeneration partnerships unable to buy back former council homes – because of escalating London prices – which become a barrier to comprehensive renewal programmes. Government has set limits on or restricted RTB sales in some London boroughs, and has also replaced RTB with a less attractive 'right to acquire' policy, which grants tenants a fixed sum discount rather than a percentage discount if they opt to purchase the home they have been hitherto renting.

And yet privatisation continues. Government remains committed to creating opportunities for people to purchase their council homes, and will not renege on the 'right' created by the Conservatives. In 2001, 18,000 new affordable homes were built in England: in the same year, 33,000 were sold through RTB, with many former tenants accumulating huge windfall profits (Table 3.3).

While the current government acknowledges that 'for every social home added to the stock in the last few years, at least two have been sold under the Right to Buy' (ODPM, 2003a: 28), it insists that it will continue to encourage 'homeownership, especially for social tenants who can sustain the commitments of homeownership, while modernising the right to buy' (ibid., 28). It remains unclear as to what exactly this 'modernisation' will entail, though it seems unlikely that there will be any significant retreat from privatisation. John Prescott recently stated that 'the Right to Buy scheme has brought tremendous benefits, and I've made it clear that it is here to stay' (ODPM, 2003b). This endorsement of Conservative housing policy seems all the more strange given that the Labour

Table 3.3 Resale prices for Right to Buy properties in London: 2002

Address	*Purchase date*	*Purchase price (£)*	*Discount (£)*	*Resale price (£)*	*Profit (£)*
Drury Lane, WC2	Sept 1988	60,000	35,000	400,000	340,000
Minton Mews, NW6	Feb 1990	38,640	45,360	219,950	181,310
Bartholemew Road, NW5	Oct 1993	45,600	49,400	290,000	244,000
Retcar Place, N19	Nov 1998	21,000	45,000	155,000	133,900
Parliament Hill, NW3	Apr 2000	230,000	50,000	525,000	295,000
Tonbridge House, WC1	Feb 2001	165,000	38,000	297,000	132,000

Source: Murray and Evans, 2002: 18

party was unequivocal about its intention to scrap the RTB in 1979. But the endorsement is not surprising given how much the context for housing policy in the UK has changed in the past quarter of a century. Government notes that homeownership remains an important personal aspiration (ODPM, 2003a: 7) and argues that 'owning a home gives people a bigger stake in their community, as well as promoting self-reliance' (ibid., 33). In this sense, the promotion of homeownership is presented as part of the means to deliver 'sustainable communities' (see Chapter 8), with some studies debating the policy's role in promoting social balance (Jones and Murie, 2006: 141).

But a policy of privatisation and self-reliance resulting in a single sector, single tenure housing system is clearly problematic. Evidence from elsewhere in Europe suggests that markets offering a wider range of tenure choice are less susceptible to housing shortages or to crises of affordability. Toynbee (2003: 10–11) argues that with the highest poverty and lowest social spending in the European Union, there are likely to be millions of people in Britain who will never be able to buy their own homes: therefore, does current housing policy – supporting and extending the status quo – really address long-term needs?

Plate 6 Tolmer's Square, London, a 1970s development of 36 split-level council dwellings (London, 2006)

In this chapter, we have outlined the importance of recent housing policy in creating a housing system – dominated by private provision – that will, inevitably, share a particular relationship (more arms-length and indirect) with the state. This dominance of private provision has meant an increasingly reliance on market mechanisms for general housing supply and, latterly, a reliance on planning intervention to deliver more 'affordable' homes where these are needed. Privatisation – of both the public housing stock and the means of future provision – has heightened the importance of planning in delivering 'decent homes for all'. A retreat from direct intervention has increased the role of indirect intervention. Public provision no longer shields households from market pressures, which are felt most acutely in areas of housing scarcity, but the public sector is able to exert influence over private house builders in the hope of ensuring the right types of homes in the right locations. In 2001 government embarked on reforms of the planning system aiming to improve efficiency and speed; in 2003, it launched a 'communities plan' setting out a vision of increased house building in the context of sustainable communities. But in 2004, a Treasury-sponsored review of housing supply in England concluded that not enough housing is being built in the right places, and that planning is a major impediment to adequate supply (Barker, 2004). The last three decades have borne witness to the emergence of a new housing system, dominated by the private sector. Government, at the present time, seems to find great difficulty in managing this system through planning. This is the historic context for current housing debate in the UK, and the narrative of public–private housing. In the next chapter, these recent debates are introduced in greater detail.

Chapter 4
The shifting policy landscape

Introduction

In the last chapter, we saw that Britain's housing system is one dominated by private sector provision and by homeownership. This system is regulated by central state and by local planning authorities. In recent years, the key issues in planning for housing relate to land and its supply. In this chapter, we aim to provide an introduction to recent house building and land for housing debates in England. Policy debate prior to 2004 provides the essential context to government's reform of the planning system (see DTLR, 2001c; ODPM, 2002b, ODPM, 2003a; HM Government 2004; see Chapter 9, this volume), and its desire to speed up the planning process; to ensure more efficient use of land through an emphasis on land recycling; to build more 'sustainable communities'; and to rethink the way planning deals with housing supply. Countless independent studies, commissioned reports and best practice guides have looked at the issue of – or issues relating to – new house building (Adams and Watkins, 2002; Carmona *et al.*, 2003; Barker, 2004). In this chapter, the intention is to provide a concise introduction to recent, pre-2004, debates and issues. We also deal with some of the key issues – relating to land recycling, density and design, affordable housing, and housing numbers in regional planning – that punctuate these debates. Current concerns, relating to sustainable communities and housing supply and the market, are considered in later chapters. Here, we consider:

- the broad parameters of the 'house building question';
- Labour's evolving policy agenda, as a lead-in to later chapters dealing with sustainable communities, planning reform and housing supply;
- the recent emphasis on more efficient use of land and the resultant 'greenfield good, brownfield bad' mentality permeating government thinking;
- A broad discussion of this land-use debate leads into further discussion of housing density and design issues, and the supply of 'affordable homes';

• housing numbers and how forecasts of future population growth have, in recent times, become housing allocations in local development planning (though in Chapter 7 we discuss how this process may be revised in the future).

This examination of the 'broad picture' leading up to the 2004 Planning Act focuses on the developing policy context, and the key issues emerging from this context. It provides a lead-in to later, more detailed, analyses of planning policy intervention relating to key housing issues in Chapter 5, and scales of intervention – strategic and local – in Chapter 6.

The house building question

There has been no singular house building question affecting the UK though particular groups have found it useful to present stark choices to the public: build on 'greenfield' land or recycle redundant urban areas; build more housing or face an affordability crisis; build at higher density or suffer the loss of the English countryside. By offering these types of simple alternatives, they (environmental lobbies, house builders, economists, etc.) have helped polarise the house building question and generated a new religious fervour, bent on either stopping

Plate 7 A new housing scheme on site (Stratford-upon-Avon, 2001)

Plate 8 Low-demand housing in East Manchester – built in the 1980s, demolished within 20 years (Manchester, 2002)

all development or on breaking down the constraints and pushing for ever higher house building rates.

But policy makers, planners, housing providers and local communities have faced different challenges in different parts of the country. In the south-east of England, there has been huge housing demand pressure and very few brownfield sites (with the exception perhaps of London's Thames Gateway: see Chapter 8) and this has led the Joseph Rowntree Foundation to argue that 'there will be cases where greenfield development will provide a more sustainable solution and other cases where it is essential for the UK's macro-economic agenda' (Barlow *et al.*, 2002: 10). In the north of England, demand pressures in many, but not all, areas can be far less pronounced and despite an abundance of brownfield (previously used) land in many areas, there is sometimes little interest in developing these sites. Part of the problem (particular in the north-west) has been the 'Manchester syndrome' (Rogers and Power, 2000: 149) with too much housing in the past being supplied on greenfield sites, leading to a situation of oversupply and the abandonment of some inner city areas – the so-called 'doughnut effect'. This leads to 'unused spaces in cities', which 'beget trouble: vandalism, fires and illicit activity' (ibid., 151). The problem of releasing too much land for housing is not only evident in the north-west, but also in the Midlands (east and west), Yorkshire and Humberside and Tyneside and Teeside. This situation contrasts significantly with the more affluent parts of southern England and London where it is far more common to build below the rate of household formation.

There are also different questions and challenges in urban and rural areas (see Chapter 6), though the processes underpinning these challenges stem from the relationship between town and country. In the countryside, Cloke *et al.* (2002) have recently pointed to the burgeoning problem of rural homelessness, some of which has been transported from cities and some of which stems from the displacement of households caused when rural markets become overheated as a result of urban–rural population movement. Second-home ownership in the countryside or the desire of many people to move to rural areas on retirement may also result in housing supply being outstripped by demand (Gallent *et al.*, 2003). The house building question in the countryside is driven largely by issues of land supply (and scarcity) and planning constraint (Hoggart, 2003) and debates over brownfield–greenfield are overshadowed by absolute supply problems, the sale of council housing (reducing the supply of affordable homes – see Chapter 3) and the problem of incoming and affluent households resisting future house building (the so-called NIMBY effect).

There are, therefore, many different house building questions: some relate simply to the quantity of new homes required (which varies significantly from place to place); some relate to the quality of housing provided by the private sector and this issue has gained prominence in recent years as government pushes for higher density developments. A final group of questions relate to location and recycling, and whether the 'right' option in different situations is to develop greenfields or previously used sites. But there are no simple answers: in the north, the need to prioritise regeneration efforts is clear, and elsewhere it is also important to make most efficient use of building land, but this may need to be balanced with the strategic release of greenfields in order to keep pace with demand. In urban areas, the emphasis will inevitably be on efficiency and on social balance; in the countryside, social balance is equally important though the overriding house building challenge is to release sufficient land for all new building. The different regional challenges have been summarised by Goss and Blackaby (1998), who also make a clear distinction between urban and rural parts of Britain (see Table 4.1). The challenges they pose extend beyond the issue of housing supply and embrace wider social concerns. They recognise that there is no singular housing or house building question, but a complex array of inter-linked issues that need to be addressed.

Table 4.1 Housing challenges: difference between regions and countries

Urban authorities in the Midlands and the north of England	Rural authorities in the Midlands and north of England
• Hard-to-let local authority and housing association housing association housing • Poor-quality stock across tenures • Public/private partnerships – levering in funds for regeneration • Community breakdown/social exclusion	• Complex housing market • Unemployment • Transport problems
Urban authorities in the south of England	Rural authorities in the south of England
• Shortage of land/resources to meet growing need/demand • Improving estate management performance • Poor-quality social housing stock • Tackling anti-social behaviour/crime	• Reducing resources and growing demand • Shortages of land and high prices of land • Greenbelt issues • Rural communities/social exclusion/ rural poverty • Problems of frail elderly • Transport problems
Urban authorities in Scotland	Rural authorities in Scotland
• Poor quality housing across all tenures • Need for regeneration • Surplus council housing in some areas • Community Care	• Depopulation of villages • Insufficient investment • Community care • Transport problems
Urban authorities in Wales	Rural authorities in Wales
• Poor quality housing across all private tenures • Social exclusion	• Need for regeneration • Depopulation of villages • Surplus housing in some areas • Poor quality housing across tenures • Transport problems

Source: CIH/LGA Survey of Local Authorities 1998 (Goss and Blackaby, 1998)

However, with all these caveats in mind, the issue of housing quantity – across England and Britain as a whole – can often dominate the housing agenda. In 2001, Holmans calculated that an additional 3.5 million households would form in England between 1996 and 2016, and more recent official projections (2006) put the figure, based on 2003 mid-year population estimates, at 4.8 million. Logic would suggest that this would generate a demand for the same number of new dwellings. But once demolitions (and the need for replacement), an increase in second homes (or an estimated 100,000 units taken from permanent use), and the increase in dwelling vacancy is taken into account, the absolute number of new dwellings needed and demanded in England during this 20-year period rises to 4.5 million (against Holman's figure of 3.5 million presented in Chapter 1). Based on the 2006 projection figures, the need and demand for dwellings could rise well beyond this figure.

These figures of course generate their own debates: relating, for example to the social inequity of owning second homes (Monbiot, 1999; Gallent *et al.*, 2003; Wallace *et al.*, 2005) and the 'injustice' of permitting increases in dwelling vacancy (Empty Homes Agency, 2002: 1). But given that government is unlikely to dictate the use of private property, increases in housing demand in the order of millions of units are unavoidable. This means that questions of how and where to provide new homes become vital: debates over recycling, density and design all piggy-back on the fundamental question of supply.

A spectre hung over the house building question in the early years of this decade: and this appeared to be one of inconceivable mathematics. Holman's calculations suggested a required building rate (if we were to provide for demand and meet need) of 225,000 units per annum (that would need to be sustained between 1996 and 2016). It was further estimated that two-thirds of this (63 per cent) would have to be provided by the private sector and the remaining third would have to be 'affordable' (see Chapter 3). But during the 1990s, total build across England averaged only 146,000 units per annum (private sector plus registered social landlords). If we assume little change in this rate between 2001 and 2004 (though the HBF has suggested that an all-time low in the building rate was reached in 2001), this means that a backlog of unmet need and demand was created between 1996 and 2004 totalling 711,000 units (that is 225,000 minus 146,000 for each year between 1996 and 2004). Therefore, for the period 2004 to 2016, the necessary building rate would have increased to more than 296,000 units, far beyond the house building rates that have been recently opposed on environmental ground. An added twist is that these figures – based on Holmans' calculations – reflect on the pre-Barker (2004) situation. Barker's analysis – as we will see in Chapter 7 – centres on the need to build at even higher rates to bring recent English house price trends in line with those experienced in mainland Europe. But, on the basis of recent building trends – in both market provision and the provision of affordable homes – it looked, in 2004, extremely unlikely that future house building would keep pace with demand unless there was a significant change in the way new housing was delivered. We consider the pressure for such a change in Chapter 7.

In the next part of this chapter, we look at how government has grappled with the fundamental planning processes underpinning housing delivery, and the housing problem outlined above, stretching from its early years in office to more recent attempts to speed up and increase development through embryonic planning reform before the Barker Review of Housing Supply, and Planning Act of 2004. This section is followed by brief introductions to the key themes – land recycling, density and design, affordability and regional debate – that are dealt with in later chapters.

Planning for housing: the modernising agenda

The Government's broader vision for the planning system during its first five years in office (1997 to 2002) was largely shaped by the household projections published by the previous administration (DoE, 1996b). Despite a range of criticisms levelled at the projections, particularly as a basis for regional decision-making (see for instance, Baker and Wong, 1997; see also, later discussion and Chapter 6), the 1996 projections were at the forefront of strategic thinking since their likely contents first emerged (DoE, 1995a). Indeed, the 1995 White Paper on Housing stated that 'half of all new housing should be on re-used sites' (DoE, 1995b: 11). The Labour government elected to power in May 1997 was keen to demonstrate its own environmental credentials and there was soon talk of 60 or even 75 per cent of all new development being guided onto recycled land (Planning 1245, 1997: 3). The consequent debate over land recycling – introduced above – is examined in the next part of this chapter.

By the late 1990s, it was already apparent in which direction the planning debate pertaining to housing supply was moving. Predictions of unprecedented household growth raised significant concern over the social and, moreover, environmental impacts of different development strategies (e.g. land recycling versus greenfield development). The main concerns were set out in Breheny and Hall's influential *The People: Where Will They Live?* (1996) though any debate at this point was overshadowed by the approach of the general election. In the latter half of 1997, however, the threads of the debate – which were to dominate the policy agenda in the following year – began to emerge. An implied acceptance that land recycling options were preferred over the development of greenfield land prompted a debate centring on the need to prevent town cramming while ensuring sustainable countryside quality. Already, the 'greenfield good, brownfield bad' axiom had taken hold and there were calls for the 'sequential phasing' of new housing development; that is, a presumption against building on greenfield sites if suitable brownfield options were available (a move eventually introduced in PPG 3 (DETR, 2000a). Similarly, there was some discussion of a possible 'greenfield tax', which might be used to discourage development of such sites and, in turn, make land recycling (relatively) more appealing. At this time,

Box 4.1 Planning for communities of the future – 1998

In February 1998, government published *Planning for Communities of the Future*, a document that dealt with broad strategy for future house building. Its concern was with the pressures generated by household growth, patterns of future development, issuing a response to the last government's Green Paper consultation (*Household Growth: Where Shall we Live?*) and with the relationship between new housing supply and future household growth (with the former being viewed as a part-driver of the latter). Talk of providing *decent homes* as a means to ensure greater quality of life first appeared in *Planning for Communities of the Future*, and this was to be achieved through a new approach to meeting demand for new homes and through a 'renaissance' of towns and cities, coupled with protection of the countryside (DETR 1998c: 5). The new approach to meeting demand would hinge on a revision of the way housing figures are calculated and cascaded down to local authorities: dubbed a move away from 'predict and provide' to a rationale of 'plan, monitor and manage' involving:

- greater involvement of local authorities and Regional Planning Conferences in the process of calculating household projections (a task undertaken by the Department of the Environment, Transport and Regions (DETR) at that time);
- draft figures to be set out in Regional Planning Guidance (RPG) and then subjected to a sustainability appraisal as well as an Examination in Public (EIP);
- the Secretary of State to accept or modify figures on the basis of the EIP Chair's recommendations and then to publish RPG;
- Regional Planning Conference (or its replacement) to 'accept more responsibility for measuring and dealing with any adverse consequences of their decisions on housing provision' (13). This would include monitoring house prices, standards and needs and to report on negative repercussions;
- problems to be taken up in the next set of household projections (hence there is a clearer feedback loop from the regional level to those charged with producing projections).

An urban renaissance and the protection of the countryside was to be achieved through:

- a new target (60%) for building homes on previously developed land, but with greater recognition of regional differences and therefore the problems of achieving this target (this recognition was to draw on a National Land-use Database, cataloguing information on site availability);

- the establishment of a Task Force charged to develop guidance on reusing previously developed sites and to promote 'development on key demonstration sites' throughout the country (17);
- a range of regional housing solutions (including development within urban areas, urban extensions, new settlements and infill and extensions) tying housing development more closely to public transport;
- a sequential approach to allocating housing land (emerging two years later in PPG3);
- reiteration of support for urban containment through the use of Green Belts;
- a combination of good urban design and increased densities (where feasible), with a commitment to revisiting this issue in a revised PPG3;
- a cautious acceptance of the role of new settlements, but also a clear commitment to the concept of 'urban villages', which bring together 'new housing with a mix of tenures, local shops and services [. . .] in a relatively compact, village development, with greater opportunities for walking or cycling' (23).

Planning for Communities of the Future set out Labour's broad vision of the role of planning in providing new homes. It linked some new thinking with a continuation of broader household growth debates, which the government had inherited from the previous administration.

---

the best ways of developing recycled (and particularly contaminated) land were being outlined (Syms, 1997) in the light of an acceptance that more housing would be needed and a greater proportion of it would have to be built at higher densities in already urbanised areas – for the sake of the nation's principal asset, namely its countryside (Countryside Commission, 1998). The house building debate during 1997 and 1998 was dominated by household growth and the need to accommodate that growth with minimum impact.

But at a more local level, it was also dominated by counties and unitary authorities ducking below the building rates (which partially explained the mounting crisis of mathematics noted above) and finding talk of huge household growth and house building completely unacceptable to a vociferous electorate, especially in southern England. Part of the problem was thought to stem from the philosophy of 'predict and provide' (i.e. government predicts housing growth and local planners facilitate provision through land release). This philosophy was considered too top-down and precluded any chance of adjustment (of building

Box 4.2 The Urban Task Force – 1999

The UTF was charged to 'identify causes of urban decline in England and recommend practical solutions' (Urban Task Force, 1999). The need for additional brownfield development, set out in *Planning for Communities of the Future,* was seen to go hand-in-hand with a need for broad regeneration, developing not just homes but also jobs and businesses on brownfields (Rogers and Power, 2000: 163): hence the UTF was to 'establish a new vision for urban regeneration founded on the principles of design excellence, social wellbeing and environmental responsibility' (ibid.). Its central purpose was to advise on the practical machinery needed by government to deliver on its 60 per cent recycling target.

The UTF reported in the same year that government issued revised household projections: the 1998-based figures reported that 3.8 million additional households would form between 1996 and 2021 (DETR, 1999b). On the basis of policy assumptions at the time, the Task Force advised that government was unlikely – given the need to provide significant numbers of new homes – to meet its land recycling target. It went on to paint a bleak picture of urban fragmentation, erosion of the countryside, depleted natural resources and social deprivation were the target to be missed, and so started with the premise that immediate action was required. The UTF made more than 100 recommendations, but of particular relevance (feeding into PPG3 and reform of the planning system) are its views on:

* how to increase the recycling of land and buildings;
* how to improve design standards and increase building densities;
* the improvements required in terms of 'leadership' and planning reform in order to realise (and surpass) government's objectives.

With regards to recycling, the UTF informed government that its objectives were broadly correct: having a stated target for land recycling was crucial to achieving an urban renaissance and this should mean limiting building on greenfield land. The UTF also argued that public bodies should lead the way by releasing redundant urban land and buildings for regeneration, a move that had already proven a successful catalyst for regeneration in the north of England (see Mills, 2000). Government was also to lead a national campaign for bringing contaminated land back into use by 2030, ensure an empty property strategy in every borough (hence satisfying some of the backlog housing demand) and, most controversially, harmonise Value Added Tax (VAT) on new build and residential conversions.

There was a clear recognition in the UTF Report that the image of urban areas needed to be fundamentally changed if people were to be attracted away from greenfield developments, and instead choose to live in cities. The need to improve urban design standards therefore emerged as a key message, driven by a national campaign to increase design quality through training, exemplar projects and the establishment of Local Architecture Centres. Better design would, it was hoped, create a platform for more 'suitable densities', which in turn would resurrect the fortunes of public and green transport modes.

Finally, all this would only be possible with 'excellence in leadership, participation and management', with local authorities given the means to lead the urban renaissance. The UTF spoke of the need to 'change the ethos' of the planning system: this message resonates in the PPS (see Box 4.4), following on from the Green Paper (2001), which called for a 'step change' in the culture of planning. It also sets out the importance of getting people involved in decision making: the Policy Statement introduces the concept of Community Statements as part of Local Development Frameworks (LDFs), which set out how communities will be engaged in the planning process. A more strategic focus for Local Planning Authorities (LPAs) (another of the UTF recommendations) has now materialised with the abolition of Structure Plans, causing (at least in theory) a drift of power upward to the Regions and down to local authorities.

Recycling, design, density and implementation emerged as key areas of concern in *Towards an Urban Renaissance*. There has been some disappointment that government has been slow to react to some key recommendations (for example, on VAT harmonisation), but many of the central messages have now been taken forward, both in PPG3 (with regards to recycling, density and design) and through subsequent planning reform culminating in the Planning Act 2004.

rates) in response to changes in demand, perhaps resulting from sudden economic shifts (for instance, the arrival or departure of a major employer in the local area). Government indicated its intention to move to a different philosophy of 'plan, monitor and manage' (DETR, 1998c: see Box 4.1) thereby, in theory at least, giving local authorities greater flexibility to interpret strategic housing figures. Government's intention was to allow authorities some leeway in working with official figures, using different strategies to manage housing demand. Some authorities viewed this as license to allocate fewer housing sites or withdraw from strategic developments arguing that more innovative solutions to meeting housing demand could be found elsewhere, often outside the local area. The

Box 4.3 Planning Policy Guidance Note 3 – 2000

PPG3 (DETR, 2000a) reflected many of the concerns set out in both the report of
the UTF and *Planning for Communities of the Future*, particularly:

- the implementation of planning policy in relation to new housing development;
- an emphasis on land recycling, but wedded to an acceptance of urban
  extensions;
- support for higher density housing development designed to a high
  standard;
- continued emphasis on securing affordable housing through the planning
  system based on delivery targets.

PPG 3 formally adopted the idea of 'plan, monitor and manage'. At the
regional level, housing figures were to reflect not only the latest household projections, but also an appreciation of the needs of the regional economy, the capacity
of urban areas to accommodate more housing, the environmental implications of
growth and the capacity of existing or planned infrastructure to cope with more
homes and people. However, the allocation to counties (or unitary authorities)
would still need to 'add up' to the regional total. The shift in PPG3 did little more
than ask regions to ensure that figures were not simply divided equally but were
allocated on the basis of economic and environmental capacity. The decisions
reached – based on regional judgements – were likely to raise political tensions
(see Chapter 6).

Locally, 'plan, monitor and manage' resulted in a new emphasis on 'urban
capacity' (studies) rather than the more general 'land availability' (studies) of
previous guidance notes. Authorities were to formally set a target (which was also
a national target) to develop 60 per cent of housing on previously developed land
by 2008, and would achieve this by adopting a 'sequential approach' to land allocations, placing a presumption of developing brownfield land before greenfields.
The sequential approach was to draw on the local intelligence derived from the
urban capacity studies, which would examine:

- the location of sites and accessibility to jobs, shops and services by transport means other than private car;
- the capacity of existing and potential infrastructure to service new housing
  developments;

- the ability to 'build communities' in particular areas – perhaps along the lines of the 'urban villages';
- the physical and environmental constraints on development.

PPG3 also emphasised the link between recycling, higher densities and better design. Its message to planning authorities and developers was that they should 'think imaginatively about designs and layouts which make more efficient use of land without compromising the quality of the environment' (ibid., para. 54). From a local authority point of view, this meant dealing specifically with design by issuing Supplementary Planning Guidance (SPG – or Action Plans), perhaps in the form of Village Design Statements (VDS) in rural areas or more general design guides elsewhere. Poor design would henceforth become a critical factor in refusing planning permissions: 'local planning authorities should reject poor design particularly where their decisions are supported by clear plan policies and supplementary planning guidance' (ibid., para. 63). One dilemma facing planning authorities in 2000, and which remains unchanged at the present time, concerns their lack of design-articulate staff: so while the majority of authorities recognise the need to embrace design issues (and have done for decades), they simply have not the skill-base to act on government advice.

Coupled closely with higher design standards is the view – set out in PPG3 – that the efficient use of land goes hand-in-hand with increased development density. The guidance stated that 'local planning authorities should avoid the inefficient use of land. New housing development in England is currently built at 25 dwellings per hectare [dph] but more than half of new housing is built at less than 20 dph. This represents a level of land take which is historically very high and which can no longer be sustained' (ibid., para. 57).

A large part of the density problem was blamed on car dependency and therefore local authorities were called upon to review all existing standards for car parking and road layouts, thereby addressing not just the size of dwellings but the use of space between dwellings. Authorities were also told to avoid permitting developments of less that 30 dph, with a new target set at increasing densities over the long run to between 30 and 50 dph. Rogers and Power (2000) praised the new target, arguing that if an 'average density of fifty dwellings per hectare were applied to all built up areas, including villages, and to all new developments, our requirement for green land would already be virtually satisfied by what is in the pipeline for the next 20 years' (188). However, there was not a total consensus on the wisdom of higher densities. Large segments of the public have been conditioned to equate higher density with town cramming or troublesome tower blocks and therefore house builders continue to build at lower densities on green sites, arguing that this is what the market wants (see Carmona, 2001a).

Finally, PPG3 grappled with the issue of housing affordability. DETR Circular (6/98) on planning and affordable housing was not superseded by PPG3 and the key mechanisms for extracting affordable housing from the planning process (using obligations or making planning exceptions) remained in place. However, the guidance emphasised government's support for socially mixed communities through the integration of market and affordable housing. It also suggested that 'indicative estimates' for affordable housing should be included within RPG, and that there should be greater onus on local authorities to assess need using robust methods. Consequently, local plans should include a figure for affordable housing that should be required as part of any development. The failure by a developer to propose sufficient affordable homes 'could justify the refusal of planning permission', and hence PPG3 reiterates affordable housing's status as a material planning consideration.

PPG3 (DETR 2000a) represented a broadening out of official attitude towards the role of planning with regards to housing land. Originally conceived as a mechanism for releasing adequate land for house building, planning was now called upon to deal with far more areas of concern and carry much wider aspirations in terms of environmental protection (from particular types of housing development), the efficiency of land-use, the design of homes, and equity of housing access.

political machinations underpinning local debate have been discussed at length by Murdoch and Abram (2002).

Planning for Communities of the Future represented an attempt by government to set out its stall with regards to planning and housing. In it, government articulated a strategy for house building in England: one that was to be in part challenged and in part supported by the UTF of the following year (Box 4.2). Some but not all of this earlier thinking (on recycling and the efficient use of land) found its way into the revision of Planning Policy Guidance Note 3: Housing (Box 4.3). And two years later, a more fundamental overhaul of the planning system heralded by the PPS (an update of the previous year's Planning Green Paper: see Box 4.4) looked set to bring about a step change in house building and planning for housing, and led into the Communities Plan of 2002/2003 (Box 4.5). Each of these documents is briefly summarised in Box 4.1 to 4.5. The CP and the entire notion of framing housing debate in the idea of 'sustainable communities' provides the focus for Chapter 8.

In the next part of this chapter we consider some of the key debates introduced above in greater detail. Indeed, much of the policy debate carried forward into the new millennium centred on a small number of key issues and themes. Some of these related to where and in what form housing is developed: the emphasis being on previously used sites and building at higher densities. There was also a persistent concern over the affordability of new homes and the part planning plays in relating the needs of different social groups to the profile of new housing built: there was also a parallel concern for the way in which affordable housing could be secured through the planning system using a framework of obligations (see Chapter 5). Projections of household growth – which have provided a driving force behind recent policy debate – also raised the broader question of future housing supply and the role that the planning system could and should play in ensuring that good quality housing was delivered within a reasonable timescale. Reform of the planning system in 2004 was grounded in a belief that planning has under-performed in relation to house building, to the detriment of both consumers and the house building industry. The next part of this chapter extends our broad introduction in respect of:

- brownfield development, and the advantages thought to accrue from the redevelopment of previously used sites;
- the perceived advantages of building at higher densities and the case for urban intensification: this issue is examined in far greater length in Chapter 5;
- the affordability of new housing and the means by which planning can deliver a greater social mix and balanced communities. The delivery of affordable housing through the planning system provides part of the focus of chapter 5;
- the calculation of household growth and the wider land for housing debates surrounding the issue of future growth and its presumed scale.

Brownfield good, greenfield bad

The current planning agenda outlined above (and the breakdown of views summarised in Box 4.6) reveals a growing concern for land recycling and the emergence of a 'brownfield good, greenfield bad' tone to planning debate. The Town and Country Planning Association has warned that 'the current debate about planning and housing is dominated by dogma which places an infinite value on saving greenfields regardless of the social consequences and simply assumes that higher densities will reduce car dependency and congestion' (TCPA, 2000).

Box 4.4 Planning Policy Statement – 2002 – and planning reform

A principal thrust of the 2002 Planning Policy Statement – which expanded on the earlier Planning Green Paper – was the move to replace Unitory Development Plans (UDPs)/Local Plans and Structure Plans with LDFs (ODPM, 2002b: Para. 33). The intention was to move to a faster planning process, with LDFs creating more certainty for house builders by employing criteria-based policies. A Select Committee looking at the government's proposals argued that LDFs might provide less detail and certainty than development plans, slowing down development because of the requirement for constant review and modification (House of Commons, 2002a: 44). But government maintained that the frameworks would accelerate development by reducing delays at the planning stage, hence resulting in the faster delivery of new housing.

PPG 3 (DETR 2000a) called on planning authorities to be more proactive at the development site level (affordable housing, density and design). The Planning Policy Statement of 2002 suggested that this could be achieved by introducing a hierarchy of action plans that provide authorities with the means to establish aspirations. Government had already proposed that such action plans would include area master plans, neighbourhood and village plans, design statements and site development briefs (DTLR, 2001c: 15).

Government also indicated its support for handling targets and delivery contracts on major housing developments, with authorities agreeing new targets for dealing with applications and appeals. Again this was a move designed to accelerate the planning process and ensure that new housing schemes – whether urban extensions or major land recycling developments – were kept on track and made a timely contribution to meeting housing need. But a key problem with major applications is that small disagreements between housing developers and planning authorities can become magnified through the planning process if they are not dealt with at an early enough stage. For example, developers need to know how a particular approach to layout (and design) will be received by the Highways Authority or if a particular mix of affordable housing types will be welcomed by partner RSLs. In order to ensure that such issues do not become sticking points in the house building process, the government looked to regularise procedures for pre-application discussion, again as a means of speeding up the planning process by ensuring that different stakeholders engaged early on development issues.

One of the more radical moves contained in planning reform was the proposed move away from planning obligations (as the norm) and the introduction of a system of structured tariffs as a means of extracting gains from the development process. The intention was to expedite development by avoiding prolonged and fraught negotiations on a site-by-site basis. But the scrutinising Select Committee argued that 'tariffs would replace one form of complexity with another' (House of Commons, 2002a: 46): it was suggested that time spent on negotiating individual obligations would suddenly be spent on establishing the basis 'for tariffs around the country, authority by authority, at the forward planning stage'. The committee argued that the change would bring few benefits in terms of speed and clarity: tariffs would also break the link (the 'necessity test') between the development of sites and on-site gains, with authorities free to spend the tariff on anything, anywhere in the local area.

Box 4.5 The Communities Plan – 2003

Government's Communities Plan is examined at length in Chapter 8. The CP has offered a broad statement on the housing and planning challenge facing England: essentially an over-heating market in the south and a steadily weakening market further north (notwithstanding local market peculiarities). In introducing the plan, the then Deputy Prime Minister – John Prescott – argued that housing challenges are rooted in both economic and demographic change, and that this change has resulted in a serious shortage of homes in London and the south east, balanced by housing abandonment in the north and the Midlands. The CP was a broad statement of intent, following on from the previous year's Ministerial Statement (Box 4.4), accompanied by a consultation on proposed revisions of PPG3 (ODPM, 2003c; 2003e) and preceding the arrival of the new Planning Act in 2004. It built a case for revised planning and housing policy arguing that:

- greenfield sites had been developed too hastily in the past, with insufficient consideration of alternative options;
- future development should be targeted to brownfield sites, though efficient use of greenfield land must not be ruled out (at a minimum density of 30 dph; ibid., 11).

These were of course familiar themes, though slightly less familiar was the new focus on the 'long term planning of communities', which incorporates good design and sustained effort to ensure that planning creates places where people really want to live. The south-east remains a key focus of the CP: in order to deal with the housing shortages in this part of the country, government identified four growth areas (established initially in RPG9; GOSE, 2000): Thames Gateway, Milton Keynes/South Midlands, Ashford, and the London–Stansted–Cambridge corridor. London and these four growth areas are said to have the potential to accommodate 200,000 new homes (in addition to those already included in regional planning guidance), but if this potential is to be realised, major infrastructure investments will be needed. The government committed itself to make available up to £446 million for the Thames Gateway (see Chapter 8) and £164 million for Milton Keynes/south Midlands and Ashford (ODPM, 2003a: 41–42). Some transport improvements have since been approved, including extensions of the Docklands Light Railway and an initial phase of a new transit system in East London (ibid.: 44). However, there was some concern that these investments would not be sufficient to provide high-quality access to and from the new centres, making them less attractive to homebuyers and reducing the enthusiasm of investors – including major employers – to relocate to the centres.

While there were, and are, serious housing shortages in some parts of the country, this is balanced by the problem of apparent oversupply elsewhere. The north–south division mentioned above seems to suggest a population gain for southern counties at the expense of the north and some parts of the Midlands. However, 'these movements are not part of a general migration to the South, rather [movements] from conurbations to suburbs and rural areas that are considered more attractive' (ODPM, 2003a: 11). Across England as a whole, there were 730,000 empty homes (in 2003): 3.4 per cent of total stock. Many of the northwest's 135,000 empty properties were concentrated in areas of market failure, where prices had fallen rapidly since the bust of the early 1990s and where there was little indication of any subsequent recovery. In response to this problem, the government identified nine 'Market Renewal Pathfinder Areas' (ibid.: 24), all of which were in the north and the Midlands. Five-hundred million pounds of funding was set aside to address the structural, physical, economic and social problems afflicting these areas. In a further attempt to bring long-term empty properties back into use, VAT was reduced to encourage the renovation of such properties (ibid., 32).

The way the planning system works is critical to achieving a solution to the problems identified in the CP. The Plan itself reinforces the need for many of the reforms first introduced in the Planning Green Paper (DTLR, 2001c) and subsequent Policy Statement (ODPM, 2002b) and is closely allied to the Planning and Compulsory Purchase Act 2004 as we will see in Chapter 8.

Box 4.6 Where to build?

Supporting continued green building

Supporting greater development on brownfield sites

- The **builders** want more land to bank for future building. Green development is easier, cheaper, more profitable and until now politically popular. They want further green land releases as long as land is there. Green land will run out.

- The **NIMBYs** argue that building destroys the countryside, not just for country dwellers, but for urban migrants too. They oppose further green development.

- The **'affordable housing' lobby** wants enough homes for all and a proportion of affordable homes in all communities. New greenfield estates should include affordable homes.

- The **pro-city, pro-urban lobby** sees countryside and cities being destroyed by current patterns, and wants to use all the gaps and spaces in existing built-up areas.

- The **'affordable movers'** cannot access reasonable housing In popular inner-city neighbourhoods. They reject poorer, urban neighbourhoods where affordable housing is available but where social conditions are unfavourable. Green development offers a low-cost quality option.

- The **environmentalists** want to safeguard the natural environment as our prime responsibility. Greenfield development is pro-car and damages a much wider environment. If we recycle land and buildings we will need less green land. More environmentally friendly, less traffic-dominated cities attract people.

- **Smaller cities and towns and small non-urban local authorities** often support some new greenfield development so as not to stymie growth or drive investors away.

- The **social environmentalists** support pro-city policies as the only way to reverse social polarisation and make city environments attractive again to a broad cross-section of the population.

Source: Rogers and Power, 2000: 181

But brownfield development was seen as critically important if many inner cities were to be regenerated and if urban areas were to avoid the 'Manchester syndrome' mentioned earlier in this discussion. Constraining green-field consumption ensures that the 'countryside is better preserved' (Balchin and Rhoden, 2002: 58) while also directing development interests to the most deprived areas. This, at least, was and remains the theory. Government also remains committed to a belief that development within the existing urban foot-print is inherently more sustainable (see discussion of PPG3 and Communities Plan in Boxes 4.3 and 4.5 above) because such locations are tied into existing public transport networks and therefore reduce car use and commuting. According to Balchin and Rhoden (2002), higher densities were also thought to result in a new urban vibrancy: more people in cities leads to greater investment in public and private services.

But the arguments in favour of continued greenfield development seemed equally persuasive. In many areas there were insufficient brownfield sites (e.g. in many southern English counties) but these were also the areas of highest growth: constraint here could have wider economic repercussions. It was also the case that most new housing built on brownfield sites in attractive inner-city locations (e.g. in London) was unaffordable to all but the most affluent households: green-field schemes were relatively more affordable. There was also an argument that inner cities should not become a dumping ground for new development or subject to low quality 'town cramming': though in the rush to meet housing need, the risk of cramming in development was very real, with the urban poor bearing the brunt of this problem. Developing brownfields (particularly conta-minated sites) could be inordinately expensive with sites consequently unable to carry planning gains in the form of affordable housing. In contrast, greenfield sites are generally cheaper to develop and highly profitable, making it easier to extract gains from such developments. Large sites may also be able to 'carry' larger planning gains, an argument used by the supporters of many larger, strategic, greenfield allocations (see Chapter 6). Though not strictly equating with green- and brownfield development, Crook et al. (2001) revealed that affordable housing elements on urban sites between 1992 and 2000 averaged out at 1.51 per cent compared with 4.25 per cent on rural sites.

Despite the delicate balance of arguments, government remained com-mitted to its 60 per cent target for land recycling during this period. In 2002, announcing the government's Planning Policy Statement, John Prescott stated that government had surpassed this target, building 61 per cent of new homes on brownfield land (figures for the ten-year period 1992–2002 are set out in Table 4.2). Shadow Planning Minister Eric Pickles repudiated this claim, noting

Table 4.2 New dwellings and residential land from previously developed land: 1992–2002[1] (In per cent)

	1992	1993	1994	1995	1996	1997	1998	1999[2]	2000	2001	2002	Aver-age*
New dwellings on previously developed land including conversions[3]	56	56	54	57	57	56	58	59	61	63	64	61
New dwellings on previously developed land	53	53	51	54	54	53	55	56	58	60	61	58
Land area changing to residential use that was previously developed	46	47	44	47	45	45	46	48	49	55	56	50

* 1998–2002 in per cent

1 Information relates to map changes recorded by Ordnance Survey as at the end of 2002, where the year of change has been estimated by surveyors from available information.

2 1999 estimates subject to some uncertainty due to incomplete data.

3 Conversion of existing buildings estimated to add 3 percentage points (source: ODPM, 2003f).

that new house building had fallen to an all-time low and arguing that 'frankly, 60 per cent of not very much is still not very much' (Hansard, 2002: July 18, Column 443). There was some suggestion in the early years of this decade that the government was 'cooking the books', constraining greenfield development so as to ensure they could meet their brownfield target. This would seem to be a dangerous game to play in the light of the impending housing shortages outlined earlier.

Density and design

Achieving higher density development is sometimes likened to rocket science: difficult to achieve for all but the most adept planners and house builders. But developers regularly increase housing density in order to maximise profits from a site. Research by Short *et al.* (1986) in Berkshire 20 years ago found that builders who acquired land with outline planning permission would often push for higher densities, changing the economics of a site in their favour. But the willingness of developers to build at higher density has its limit and this limit is determined by what homebuyers are perceived to want. PPG3 (DETR, 2000a) revealed that more than half of new housing development in the late 1990s was built at a density of below 20 dph: the average was 25 dph (average density figures by region and by previous land-use are noted in Table 4.3). This probably represented what the typical purchaser of a Redrow, Wimpey or Beazer (major UK volume house builders) home traditionally wanted, conditioned of course by the marketing strategies of these respective volume builders.

It appeared that there was a need to 'de-condition' buyers and thereby establish a market for a different type and density of housing development. It has since been generally agreed that a move to medium to high densities (30 to 50 dph: see ODPM, 2003a) will need to be accompanied by higher design standards. The case studies presented in Chapter 5 demonstrate that in policy guidance at least, government has prioritised design quality as a more important part of the planning process. This was confirmed by PPG3, which extended LPA powers in relation to design: 'in determining planning applications, local planning authorities should reject poor design particularly where their decisions are supported by clear plan policies and adopted supplementary planning guidance' (DETR, 2000a: para. 63). But Bateman (1995) argued that such a course of action would drag planners into a 'minefield' that could create significant difficulties within the development process: 'Most planners are not qualified to talk in detail about design and yet it will be in their hands to give greater weight to it' (ibid., 28). Developers tended to be very critical of design guidance issued by

Table 4.3 Density of dwellings built, by previous use (1998–2002 average), average expressed in dph

Government Office Region	On previously developed land	Not on previously developed land	All land dwellings per hectare
North-east	29	21	24
North-west	28	21	25
Yorkshire and the Humber	23	21	22
East Midlands	26	21	23
West Midlands	31	22	26
East of England	23	22	23
London	55	32	52
South-east	25	23	24
South-west	29	24	26
England	28	22	25

Source: ODPM, 2003f

planning authorities and voiced their anger at the inconsistencies existing between different authorities (Hooper and Nicol, 1999). There was growing frustration from developers that by involving planners in design issues the likelihood of planning delay would be significantly increased, particularly when planners are perceived to throw out proposals 'for absolutely no good planning reason except that they dislike it' (Bateman, 1995).

There was growing consensus, towards the end of the 1990s, around the need to (a) ensure that planners were adequately trained in design issues, and (b) that plan policies set out a clear design agenda on a site-by-site basis and (c) that consumers are made aware of the benefits of both good design and higher density. And yet, both low- and high-density housing development has its merits and drawbacks (Table 4.4), making it difficult to cast definite judgement on the density issue at a national level.

Table 4.4 Implications of density for sustainable housing

Type	dph	Advantages	Disadvantages
Low density	10	• Renewable energy can readily be exploited • Rainwater and grey water systems can be employed • Food production in gardens • High biodiversity • High tranquillity	• Poor land utilisation • Infrastructure costs high • High transport energy costs • High building energy costs unless renewables used
Medium density	30	• Renewable energy can be exploited • Some local foods and energy crops can be grown in gardens • Movement by bicycle viable • Community grey water systems viable	• Public transport will need large subsidy • Careful design needed to exploit renewable energy • Neighbour disputes can occur over waste or recycling initiatives • Poor urban form
High density	60	• Compact forms are energy efficient • Supports mixed use development • Most journeys on foot, bicycle or public transport • Good urban design • Good microclimate	• Crime and vandalism can be a problem • Anti-social behaviour undermines community spirit • Low tranquility • Good design essential • Costs can be high per unit

Source: Edwards, 2000: 132

Affordable housing and planning

Affordability dominated the house building debate during the early 1990s when government first put in place the formalised systems for extracting a contribution of affordable homes from development permissions (Gallent, 2000a). Since that time, it has maintained a high priority on the planning agenda, but has been joined by numerous other concerns, including housing design and the more efficient use of land. A fuller discussion of the affordability debate is provided in Chapter 5 but some general points are introduced here.

First, in the early part of this decade, Holmans (2001) projected that more than a third of new households forming between 1996 and 2016 would require some form of affordable housing built with either a land or direct (financial) subsidy. The proportion may change as more housing is built and the balance between supply and demand shifts: though overall the one-third figure is based on projected losses of affordable housing (through the Right to Buy and Right to Acquire – see Chapter 3) and the un-affordability of much new housing, particularly in the south-east and in London. More recently, Bramley and Karley (2005), have noted that the need for affordable housing varies significantly between the English regions, but generally, the shortage of affordable housing annually (the backlog of need plus newly arising need) appears to be in line with Holman's estimates (ibid., 710).

Second, in the past, it was suggested that government would need to develop an immediate strategy for providing this affordable housing, probably by extending the powers of and funding to RSLs. Planning's contribution to affordable housing (through the use of obligations and exceptions today, and possibly tariffs in the future: Whitehead, 2002) is likely to be limited. Government suggested that 15,000 affordable homes can and are being provided through planning each year, though Crook *et al.* (2001) contend that 4,000 is a more realistic figure. This means that planning will contribute, at most, 100,000 affordable homes during the period 1996 to 2016, leaving an additional 1.5 million to be provided by other means. The crisis of mathematics introduced earlier extends to affordable housing: it is extremely difficult to see how government and the voluntary sector (i.e. RSLs) will provide for this need without a massive injection of capital funding and a huge programme of house building, the likes of which have not been seen since the immediate post-war period. However, the move to an 'affordability-led' approach to planning for housing (seeking new market equilibriums: see Chapter 7) is one possible way forward.

Another headache for government, relating to affordability, was how to achieve mixed tenure developments: that is, developments – building into coherent communities – that mix market and social housing. PPG3 stated that 'local planning authorities should encourage the development of mixed and balanced communities: they should ensure that new housing developments help to secure a better social mix by avoiding the creation of large areas of housing of similar characteristics' (DETR, 2000a: para. 10). The thinking behind this policy was that mixed communities have clear social benefits: the creation of a more inclusive society, inter-generational and inter-social support (including 'role model' effects), and the avoidance of concentrated poverty blamed for past urban crises. However, many critics, including house builders, argue that the better off want to live apart and that tenure mixing is an unsustainable form of social engineering (DEMOS, 1999) that will be rejected by communities. Indeed, Allen *et al.* (2005) have demonstrated that the 'role model' effect is limited, though mixed-tenure policies may promote social stability in some instances. It is also the case that developers are often keen to offer councils money to build social housing elsewhere (in the form of commuted sums), rather than run the risk of lowering the value of a potentially prestigious development. Government, for its part, has pushed for social mixing by requiring developers to provide on-site contributions of affordable housing in new market schemes. But does the move towards tariffs (initially abandoned following consultation on the 2001 Planning Green Paper, but which may be resurrected) or 'Planning Gain Supplement' (PGS: see Chapter 7) mean that government, in the future, might abandon this strategy and regularise the growing practice of accepting commuted sums in lieu of contributions?

There has been, and continues to be, great uncertainty over how affordable housing will be secured through planning and also over whether the strategy will contribute, in the future, to social mixing. There is more certainty, however, over the inability of current mechanisms to deliver enough affordable housing to meet existing and future need. These issues are returned to in Chapters 5 and 7.

Housing numbers

Housing numbers have been central to the house building debate: we look more closely at this issue – in the context of regional planning – in Chapter 6. Here, the aim is to outline the process for arriving at housing numbers in regional planning as it has developed in recent years. This is the 'status quo' that may now evolve in the context of the 2004 Barker Review of Housing Supply (Chapter 7). The regional politics of this 'objective process' is dealt with later on.

Government has engaged in the business of forecasting population change since the 1920s when it first became concerned with social security payments: indeed, 'one of the main uses of these earlier projections [produced by the Government Actuaries Department] was in connection with the long-term financial estimates under the Contributory Pensions Acts and other schemes of social insurance' (Office for National Statistics, 1999: 3). In the 1950s, the procedures for forecasting became more formalised as government came to recognise the importance of translating population change into household change and hence setting a target for future housing provision (ibid.). Population projections were made each year between 1955 and 1979, and then every second year until 1991. Since then, projections have been calculated using 1992-based, 1994-based, 1996-based and 2003-based mid-year estimates. In recent times, population and subsequent housing demand predictions have become more scientific and now define a 'formal set of relations between the various tiers of government – central, regional, county and district – and were used to ensure that local government [housing] designations meshed with national requirements' (Murdoch and Abram, 2002: 67). As we noted in the last section, providing for future household growth is one of the most fundamental planning activities of government and involves the translation of population projections into household projections. Murdoch and Abram provide an overview of how this is achieved (ibid., 66 to 69) and a summary, gleaned from official sources, is set out in Box 4.7.

The two key methodological elements of this process occur at Stages 1 and 5 in Box 4.7: the first involves the use of a 'growth composition' approach to project changes in the base population; the second involves the calculation of the proportion of household 'representatives' within the base population, as a means of transforming population projections into household projections and thereby arriving at base figures that can be cascaded to the regions, the counties (where appropriate) and ultimately to local planning authorities. The calculation of growth composition involves breaking a base population down into age cohorts and dividing the cohorts by gender. Historic trend data – concerning birth rates (affecting women of childbearing age), death rates and in/out migration rates – are used to project what the base population will look like in a year's time. Projections are then made year-on-year, with the original base population (and each of the component cohorts) changing as assumptions are made regarding the impacts of key trends on the cohorts. The calculation of 'representatives' involves deciding who, in the population structure, 'heads' or 'represents' a household. Recent thinking stipulates that there are five types of household – married couples, cohabiting couples, lone parents, other types of multi-person households, and singles – and that all individuals in a population either head or do not head a household. By calculating the proportion of 'heads' (or representatives), it is possible to transform a population into a household projection divided into five household types. This process is explained in more length by Gallent (2007).

Box 4.7 From population to household projections

Stage 1: The Government Actuary's Department (GAD) projects the resident population at the national level, on the basis of assumptions regarding mortality, fertility and international migration. This is then broken down for sub-national areas by the Office for National Statistics (ONS).

Stage 2: The marital status of the population is projected by GAD. This is an assessment of legal (*de jure*) marriages cross analysed against whether or not couples are cohabiting. The proportions cohabiting in 1991 and 1992 were estimated by the Office of Population Censuses and Surveys (OPCS) and projected for future years by GAD.

Stage 3: The institutional population is projected by the DETR. This is the population resident in residential care homes, nursing homes and long-stay hospitals.

Stage 4: The institutional population is subtracted from the total resident population to leave the private household population.

Stage 5: Within each age/gender/marital-cum-cohabitational status category, household membership rates are projected from historical data derived from Censuses and (at national level) Labour Force Survey (LFS) data. These rates are then multiplied by the appropriate private household population projection.

Separate household projections are made independently for individual projection areas (DETR, 1999b: 55), which enables estimates to be converted into housing requirements (Adams and Watkins, 2002: 99) expressed as regional and county figures. This is explained diagrammatically by Breheny (1999: see Figure 4.1). Stages 1 and 4 in Figure 4.1 have already been discussed briefly; the procedures for arriving at population and household figures for individual regions and counties are part of the same approach. In the 1990s, the national projections (based on the underlying 1996 population) suggested that the total number of households in England would rise from 20.2 million in 1996 to 24.0 million by 2021: a rate of about 150,000 households per year. This was the 'trend figure' for household growth (the more recent trend figure – 209,000 between 2006 and 2026 – was highlighted in Chapter 1).

Corresponding trend figures are produced for the regions. For example, DETR figures suggested that the number of households in the north-west would

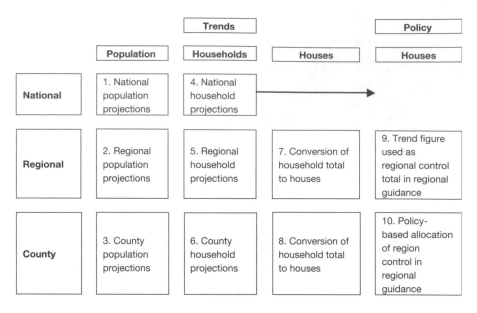

Figure 4.1 Local housing allocations in regional guidance
Source: Breheny, 1999

increase from 2.812 million in 1996 to 3.016 million in 2016: an increase of 249,000 households (DETR, 1999b: 40). This is converted into a trend figure for the region: in this case, a formation rate of 12,450 households per year. In Regional Planning Guidance for the North West (RPG13) (GONW, 2003), this regional control figure was not set out explicitly. However, it was stated that the 'guidance takes a realistic and responsible view of future housing require-ments, within the context of an up-to-date projection of household growth' (ibid., 68). What this meant in reality was that the guidance put 'forward a level of housing provision slightly higher than that given by the projections [i.e. 12,790 compared with 12,450], allowing for economic growth rates, household formation and migration rates slightly in excess of those incorporated in the projections (ibid., 68). Hence we move from a trend-based figure (Stage 9 in Figure 4.1) to a policy-based allocation of regional control within regional guidance (Stage 10).

Adams and Watkins (2002: 102) explain that the 'primary aim of the RPGs [and Regional Spatial Strategies in the future] is to provide a framework for development plans, which must be taken into consideration by local authorities in the preparation and review of structure plans, or in metropolitan areas, the unitary development plans'. Housing allocations are an important component of this framework as we show in Chapters 5 and 7.

However, the same authors highlight a number of methodological deficiencies relating to the broad projection process that moves from a base population estimate through to projections of year-on-year population change, and which is then translated into a projection of household growth (ibid., 103–109). Essentially, a process of splitting base population into gender and age cohorts means that changes in cohort membership can be projected on the basis of assumptions regarding mortality, fertility and inward and outward migration affecting individual cohorts. This results in an ability to make forward projections of population changes with diminishing degrees of statistical confidence as the projection horizon becomes more distant. The projection is trend-based. These population projections are then transformed into household projections not simply by dividing the population by average household size, but by making various assumptions regarding the type and sizes of households that will form, again using past trends as being indicative of future patterns.

Adams and Watkins suggest, first, that there are inherent shortcomings of an approach that is 'backward looking' and trend-based. Trends – including the propensity of more people to live alone – often decelerate or accelerate, but the rate of change may not be reflected in periodic social statistics. Some commentators have argued that this can imply that projections tend to over-estimate future growth. (Holmans (2001) however, suggests that projections made in recent decades have in fact underestimated the importance of reductions in household size and contended that more households would form in the period ending 2021 than official figures suggested.) Second, Adams and Watkins note that the projections are not consistently in-step with economic realities. Changes in the economy may influence the rate of household formation and consequent levels of housing demand (see Bramley *et al.*, 1997). There is a case, therefore, for factoring economic indicators (including unemployment levels or interest rate forecasts) into the household projections (or moving to a system where the market has a bigger influence in land allocation). Third, it is suggested that the projections themselves are 'self-fulfilling': 'the provision of housing to meet expected demand ensures that further demand occurs, and this in turn leads to increased future projections' (Adams and Watkins, 2002: 104). This suggests that either households form more rapidly where housing is readily available (i.e. availability drives formation) or households migrate to those areas to which housing is being directed (i.e. availability provides an impetus for migration, especially when coupled with greater job opportunities: see also Bramley and Watkins, 1995). Finally, serious doubts are raised over the reliability of data pertaining to both domestic and international migration flows. For domestic flows, greater accuracy can be achieved for those years immediately preceding a census; at other times, figures are less reliable. For international flows, there are considerable discrepancies between Census estimates and estimates derived from the

International Passenger Survey (IPS), which reduces confidence in the reliability of both these potential sources.

Generally, there is a view that the limitations noted above all result from too great an emphasis being placed on the national perspective, justified because of the relative weakness of local data, the need for control totals and political dilution of responsibility at the local level (see Cullingworth, 1997). Clearly, the national perspective is important, but more weight might be placed on the local perspective if more robust data were available on local market conditions (again, see Chapter 7), on migration patterns, housing needs and on existing building stock. The systematic collection of these types of data locally would, it is suggested, provide a firmer foundation for forward planning. The crudeness of national projections is a recurring criticism, and there is a widespread belief that a failure to take account of economic considerations (at a more fine-grained level) or the realities of local housing markets reduces the chances of the system 'delivering dwellings of the required type and size or in the appropriate locations' (Adams and Watkins, 2002: 106). Indeed, the Barker Review has recently concluded that planning needs to make 'better use of information about prices and preferences' (Barker, 2004: 6) to ensure a quicker and more flexible response to changing market conditions. We return to the issue of housing numbers and to regional planning's role in housing delivery in Chapter 6.

Conclusion

In this chapter, we have sought to define the parameters of recent housing and planning debate. We have only made brief reference to the Planning and Compulsory Purchase Act 2004 and to the Barker Review (of housing supply) also appearing in 2004. These milestones in recent policy development are dealt with in more depth in Chapters 7 and 9. However, it is perhaps worth saying something about the recent Barker Review as this reflects on many of the issues introduced in this chapter. The Treasury's review (undertaken by Kate Barker) of housing supply in England and its links with the wider economy points to many problems that persist despite changes to the context for house building since Labour came to power in 1997. Government has attempted to promote additional land recycling; it has set in motion policies and practices that might ensure a faster and more efficient planning system; and it is actively promoting additional housing supply through its CP (Chapter 8). But the Barker Review (which is examined in Chapter 7) points to a clear failure: a failure to build the right number of homes in the right locations, and a failure to ensure universal access to the housing market. We noted in the last chapter that the smooth operation of the housing market has become of critical concern given that a single-tenure, single-sector market has now fully eclipsed the former mixed-tenure, mixed-opportunity housing system of the 1970s. It is crucial that the private sector is allowed to deliver and is not impeded by planning or by politics, preventing the delivery of sufficient homes. Barker argues that both of these impediments remain and that an unresponsive housing market – resulting from a slow and inefficient planning system – threatens necessary labour mobility, the workings of the macro-economy, and the life-chances of many households (to access decent homes and quality jobs).

Many lobbying groups – including the homeless charity Shelter and the Town and Country Planning Association – have joined Barker's call for more house building in England. More particularly, it is felt that housing supply should be more market-responsive with additional housing delivered where affordability targets are not being achieved. Government is investigating this option but a consultation draft of a new PPS on housing, discussed earlier in Chapter 1, suggests that the market will play a bigger part in future planning for housing.

Our examination of the house building debate began with a rejection of the notion of a single 'house building' question and with the argument that all too often political debate focuses on stark choices, presenting highly polarised and politically motivated solutions to the country's present housing crisis. Murdoch and Abram (2002) have argued that there are two competing ratio-nales in the way we plan for housing – developmental and environmental – and the differences between the two seem intractable. But sitting between these extremes are a number of other questions, relating to the quality of housing to be provided, its possible location and, above all, its required quantity. Of all the statistics in the public domain in recent years (concerned with land recycling targets, desired densities, housing numbers and the speed of planning decisions) the most alarming is that of absolute household growth. In less than 15 years' time, there will be more than 2 million extra households in London and the rest of the south. At the beginning of this decade, it was calculated that the building rate had fallen to just under 76,000 dwellings per year: and in southern England this was around half of what was actually required. [Holmans *et al.* (2000) calcu-lates a housing completion rate (1996 to 1998 average) of 146,000 units for the 1990s. Of this, London's share was 9 per cent and the rest of the south 43 per cent. These equate with completion averages of 13,140 and 62,780 respectively – or just below 76,000.] During the 1990s, just over 2 per cent of all new dwellings were affordable units provided through planning. The total proportion necessary to meet need is estimated to be 37 per cent (provided with a combi-nation of land and grant subsidy). Is it possible to double the building rate nationally and reverse the huge losses in affordable housing over the last 20 years? Or is the deepest housing crisis England has ever faced now inevitable? These are questions we return to toward the end of this book.

Chapter 5
Planning intervention
Housing design, density and affordability

Introduction

A number of central planning for housing themes were introduced in the last chapter. Among them were housing design, the density of housing development, and the attempts made by government to secure affordable housing through planning mechanisms. We also looked at housing numbers and how these are derived. Housing numbers are considered again in Chapter 6, in the context of regional planning. In this chapter, we focus on planning's local role in housing delivery: how it intervenes to facilitate particular outcomes, influencing the quality and form of development, and the affordability of new homes. These issues have been sown together in the planning guidance issued to local authorities in recent times, with authorities called upon to make considerable improvements to design (avoiding the standardised pattern-book designs that became common-place in the 1980s and now account for the negative attitude to new residential development, especially in the countryside), to look at ways of using land more efficiently (by promoting higher densities), and to use planning as a tool to promote housing access and hence the creation of more balanced communities. This chapter is concerned with the powers of local authorities to address the concerns of the current 'policy context' described in the last chapter. Like the previous chapter, it examines the period pre-Barker and before the 2004 planning Act.

Density and design

The role of planning in influencing residential densities and increasing the design quality of housing is, as Carmona (2001a) points out, one of the major planning debates of our time. Good design is seen as critical in the context of future household growth (see Chapter 4): the negative environmental implications that this growth could bring, were design standards not raised and rigorously enforced, is a driving force behind planning's recent attempt to reinvent itself as a 'design discipline'. Design innovation and variation is a key debate in its own right and has received a considerable amount of attention from both academics (see

Goodchild, 1996; Carmona, 2001a; Grant, 2005) and practitioners (CABE and DETR, 2001a; 2001b; CABE, 2005). There has been a move away from seeing design purely as a part of the development process and as a technical aspect of building construction, and a move towards viewing better design as a central policy objective. Government has paid increasing lip-service to housing design (together with density), with policy makers keen to distance themselves from the low-density standard development models of the 1990s (Hooper and Nicol, 1999) and aligning themselves with much of the 'new thinking' on design and innovation that has been led by the UTF (1999: see Chapter 4) among others. Hence, much government literature is garnished with images of design innovation, and with futuristic eco-tech visions that might have been considered outlandish only a decade ago.

A central part of the current design debate is the link to wider urban regeneration concerns and to issues of land recycling and higher residential densities. The link between density and design provides the main focus of the first two parts of this chapter. After looking broadly at some of the general design issues emerging in recent years we turn our attention to:

- The current housing density debate and the arguments for and against higher or lower residential densities; before moving on to look at.
- Why density – whether high or low – must be wedded to higher design standards; this third section of the chapter elaborates on the premise that neither low density nor high density housing development will be assisted by a continuation of the low design standards prevalent throughout the last 20 years.

These opening sections dealing with the power of local authorities to influence housing design and density conclude with a brief overview of how various barriers to achieving higher housing quality might be overcome.

Housing design

> I cannot emphasise enough the importance of quality and design when it comes to new developments. Good design shouldn't be the preserve of expensive buildings. We can't repeat the mistakes of the past and build ugly places where no one wants to live.
>
> (Keith Hill MP, 17 July 2003; ODPM, 2003g)

A concern for design quality in residential development is not new: many of the model settlements of the nineteenth century – places such as Bournville, a product of the philanthropy of the Cadbury family (see Chapter 2) – sought to showcase the social and economic benefits of providing high quality homes in settings where essential services were close to hand. Garside (2000) traces some of the history of the Sutton Model Dwellings Trust, founded in 1900, and its contribution towards housing a range of poorer tenants in the run-up to the Second World War. According to Garside, the Trust was committed to providing housing 'of advanced design' for its tenants (ibid., 742). But in an age of twentieth century mass-housing production, design standards sometimes took second place to overall delivery targets. Nowhere is this problem more clearly illustrated than in Hulme, an inner-city neighbourhood of Manchester. In the nineteenth century, Hulme comprised a dense network of grid-iron streets:

> The layout supported a wide range of human activity: living, shopping, education, employment and all the elements of urban life that constitute working neighbourhoods. It was a classic example of what we are now beginning to refer to as a sustainable urban village. Within a 5 to 10 minute walk of any dwelling most of the facilities necessary for the sustenance of an urban settlement were to be found. In many ways Hulme 100 years ago was the essence of a sustainable community.
>
> (Mills, 2000: 96)

But within 50 years the entire area, with the exception of one or two pubs and churches, was razed to the ground as Manchester embarked on a post-war programme of slum clearance. The area was redeveloped around five large estates centred on prefabricated buildings and 'severed from the rest of the city by elevated and subterranean pedestrian routes, and sunken arterial road systems' (ibid., 96). The central features of the redevelopment were four deck-access concrete 'crescents'. The crescents were isolated from the rest of the city; they also represented a move away from the high density grid-iron pattern of the Victorian period: despite being 'high-rise' and large scaled, the new estates housed 75 per cent fewer people than the Victorian terraces they replaced (ibid., 98). Their unpopularity with families and the dangers posed by elevated decks meant that within a few years, the area was devoid of families and children and home only to a few students and a concentration of economically disadvantaged groups. The City Council's housing scheme had been an unprecedented disaster, largely because what was an essentially integrated and 'organic' residential layout had been replaced by a wholly disconnected, inorganic and unattractive development. The Hulme experience holds important lessons for planners and designers alike.

One fundamental lesson is that good design can be thought of as a break away from the 'commoditisation' of homes sustained through real-estate markets or, in the case of Hulme, through an over-reliance on institutional power to impose residential solutions without significant recourse to the people and communities that will have to live in the houses and places that are created. Good design seeks to integrate human experience and needs with urban form. It is essentially more 'organic' and integrative: inorganic form and organic experience are non-integrative (as was the case in Hulme's post-war redevelopment) while organic form and experience (building for people) are inherently integrative. This argument is summarised by Steinberg (2000: 265–278), and was a philosophy taken forward in Hulme's redevelopment, which began in 1992.

Similar arguments regarding the way housing and design solutions are taken forward are explored by Power (1999) in relation to other high-rise housing developments across Europe after the Second World War. Power questions whether it is indeed possible to 'reorder' society through physical changes to the urban environment (ibid., 139). High-rise European housing estates were, at least in part, a design failure. But added to this design failure were the inadequacies of organisational frameworks for managing new communities. This particular design solution had been 'top down', based on a belief in the virtues of institutional power and capacity to re-shape communities without recourse to those communities themselves (this is an important lesson for the delivery of Sustainable Communities as we see in Chapter 8). Estate renewal in the late 1980s and 1990s represented a move away from this paradigm and recognition of the need for a communicative, people-focused approach to dealing with past mistakes: again, the post-1992 Hulme redevelopment (which we return to later in this chapter) is an excellent example of such a strategy. The critical point is that high-rise development itself was not the source of failure: rather, it was the institutional (power-based) approach to planning such developments and imposing such solutions that failed.

It appears that 'good design' cannot be achieved through the imposition of solutions or by ignoring the fact that people will have to live (with all that living entails) in the places created by planners, architects and developers. Therefore, good design has a social value, while bad design has a social cost. The Commission for Architecture and the Built Environment (CABE) has attempted to quantify the social value of good urban design (CABE 2001), alongside both its environmental and economic benefits. As part of its remit to advance design standards, it has tried to sell the virtues of design to private development interests by arguing that better urban design adds both an economic and a socio-environmental value to new development. The latter is perhaps more relevant in relation to residential development. Indeed, the study looked at a number of different types of development and concluded that the social value of better urban design lies in:

- The creation of well connected, more inclusive and accessible places. This includes connection to the wider urban system and beyond, making it more organic in the sense highlighted by Steinberg (2000).
- The delivery of mixed environments with a broad range of facilities and amenities open to all. This provides people with a place in which they can live, socialise and work.
- The delivery of development sensitive to its context, and thereby providing a context that is neither socially nor environmentally displaced.
- An enhancement of the sense of safety and security within and beyond developments. This is an attribute never achieved by the post-war Hulme redevelopment.
- The returning of inaccessible or run-down areas and amenities to beneficial public use. This is a special value that can be achieved through well-designed redevelopment: the recent Hulme redevelopment (see Mills, 2000) has sought to overcome the problem of limited accessibility by reconnecting Hulme to different parts of the City of Manchester: to the universities (through employment), to the city centre (through a revised road and pedestrian walkway system) and to the renaissance being experienced in the Castlefields area of the city (again, physically and by attempting to blur the division between Castlefields and Hulme through common design principles).
- Boosting civic pride and civic image. The same issues of pride and image can be restored within local neighbourhoods, particularly through the creation of a sense of quality and unique place.
- Creating more energy efficient and less polluting development. This might be viewed as an environmental value, but is also a social gain if better design results in reduced car use and a cleaner environment for families and for children.
- By the revitalisation of urban heritage. A fundamental social value of better design must be the restoration of decaying inner-city cores and their historic heritage. This is part of the wider urban renaissance, intended to halt the flow of people away from inner-city areas and so reverse the trend of falling population density and the under-use of services.

The benefits of good over poor or indifferent urban design have been widely agreed upon and the UTF (1999) has separated this agreement into ten design commandments (ibid., 71) relating to:

- site and setting;
- context, scale and character;
- public realm;
- access and permeability;
- optimising land-use and density;

- mixing activities;
- mixing housing tenures;
- building to last;
- sustainable buildings;
- environmental responsibility.

It has been suggested that better planned housing schemes will address each of these concerns, and it is the role of planning and planning officers (in partnership with architects and developers) to ensure that none of these concerns are neglected. Indeed, innovations and quality in housing design have been viewed as part of the much-debated New Urbanism rhetoric, which is sometimes heralded as the successor to (and perhaps a respite from) the modernist tradition thought to be behind the type of post-war housing development typified by Hulme's crescents. Bohl (2000) for example looks at the manifestations of New Urbanism in the United States, arguing that New Urbanist type housing design principles have been adopted for many recent inner-city housing projects: similar principles – including flexibility and organic growth – can be identified in British schemes, including Hulme (Mills, 2000) and the much-publicised Greenwich Millennium Village (Derbyshire, 2000). Carmona (2001a: 141–142) provides a comprehensive list of such principles and offers some explanation of their practical application (see Box 5.1).

According to Carmona, these 17 principles reflect and draw upon the evolution of thinking on housing design. They encompass issues that are 'spatial' and 'contextual' (relating to landscape, surrounding environment and the existing context of built form), issues that are 'morphological' and 'visual' (relating to connectivity and urban space), issues that are 'perceptual' and 'social' (relating to social interactions and a sense of place) and issues that are 'functional' and 'sustainable' (relating to flexibility, adaptability and personal security). If housing and residential neighbourhoods display an appreciation of all these concerns, then they are likely to reflect the principles of good design with all the potential added-value highlighted earlier. But Bohl (2000: 801) argues that good design alone – and adherence to all the principles set out by Carmona – is not in itself a solution to the broader housing problems encountered by nations or by neighbourhoods. Rather, certain forms of development and design can complement wider efforts towards social, community and economic development. Better designed neighbourhoods can provide the canvas on which to set out new policy directions and strive towards broader social, environmental and economic goals. This is an issue returned to in Chapter 8 in the context of delivering Sustainable Communities.

Box 5.1 Principles for housing design quality

1 **Context**: the need to adequately respond to established urban design, landscape and architectural context and to what is distinctive about the site and its surroundings.

2 **Sense of place**: the need to establish a sense of place in new developments and, where appropriate, in their constituent parts.

3 **Community**: the need through design to encourage the creation of a sense of community through the integration of physical and social foci and a well-used public realm.

4 **Urban space**: the need to establish a coherent network and hierarchy of well-defined individual urban spaces and a visually interesting townscape layout.

5 **Legibility**: the need to create legible, easily navigable environments.

6 **Connectivity**: the related need to create well-connected permeable layouts that are fully integrated into their surrounding environment.

7 **Movement**: the need to create a pedestrian friendly public realm designed for walking, for child play activities and to encourage social intercourse.

8 **Car dominance**: the need to cater adequately for vehicular access, but to reduce the dominance of cars in the design of urban space by designing for reduced vehicle speeds and reduced parking standards.

9 **Security**: the need to create well used, well 'surveilled' streets and spaces.

10 **Innovation**: the need to build to last through high quality materials and detailing and, where appropriate, through innovation in architectural design.

11 **Flexibility**: the need to create spaces and buildings that are resilient and adaptable, which can be used flexibly and, in the case of houses, extended if necessary.

12 **Choice**: the need to offer variety and choice in building sizes, types and tenures.

13 **Landscape**: the need to integrate fully and address positively public open space, to invest in high quality hard and soft landscaping (including trees) and to provide ample opportunity for private landscape display.

14 **Sustainability**: the need to respond to the sustainability agenda by conserving land and material resources, integrating energy-efficient technologies, designing for ecological diversity, for less car travel and greater use of public transport.

15 **Mixing uses**: the need to move beyond strict zoning by designing developments with all appropriate facilities and services, and by mixing housing with other uses when appropriate and feasible.

16   **Functionality**: the need to create buildings and environments that function successfully allowing for sun, light and fresh air penetration, reduction and exclusion of noise and pollution, for economy in use (and in purchase), for good accessibility, and for appropriate maintenance and servicing as required.

17   **Homeliness**: the need to create buildings and environments that offer peace of mind through privacy and individuality, which are safe and secure, which carry for their users a sense and meaning of home, and which offer reasonable scope for personalisation.

Source: Carmona, 2001a: 141–142

Housing density

The question of housing density was also touched upon in the last chapter where we alluded to a prevailing mindset of 'high density good, low density bad'. This philosophy is closely related to government's desire and objective of ensuring that the majority (at least 60 per cent) of all new housing is directed to brownfield sites. Given that there is a scarcity of such sites in those regions where there is greatest housing demand (including and dominated by the south-east), there will be a need to maximise the use of available brownfield land by building at higher densities. There is a natural assumption that the higher the housing density, the greater the need to adhere more strictly to the principles of better design, particularly if developments are to retain their functionality, their sustainability, their social value and their sense of place. In other words, higher densities must be accompanied by housing quality and not result in town cramming. As policy makers grapple with the question of how to deliver more homes, they must deal more specifically with the critical link between density and design.

The case for building at higher densities has been a subject of intense debate for a decade and has been summarised by Hall (2001) who suggests that there is 'a bad reason and a good reason for more compact urban development' (ibid., 101) and hence for building at higher densities in some instances:

> The bad one is to save rural land. It is bad because there is no reason to do so, either now or in the foreseeable future. About 10 per cent of the land in South East England, in 1995, was in EU set-aside, growing nothing but weeds. EU farm policies are undergoing the most fundamental shake-up in their forty-year history, and the outcome is still undecided, but it is certain that agricultural subsidies will be slashed, so if anything the problem of surplus agricultural land will rapidly get worse.
>
> (ibid., 101)

Hall adds that there is a pressing need to find new land-uses and activities to replace farming in many rural areas and that additional urban development may be one of these new uses in some instances. The good reason for urban compaction and higher density relates to sustainability and the fact that 'denser cities use less energy for travel, perhaps appreciably so'. The same justification is offered by Banister (1997) who points to the link between urban form and residential density, and travel patterns. He argues that reductions in the need to travel (and hence urban congestion) can only be achieved by examining the impact that density and settlement size can have on urban sustainability, and that this would involve an appraisal of housing allocations across the UK and perhaps a reallocation of housing in some instances. The case for doing so appears to be strengthened by findings from Stead *et al.* (2000: quoted in Hall, 2001) who suggest that higher population densities mean:

- a widening of social interactions without constant resort to motorised transport;
- the maintenance of a wide range of local services;
- a reduction in average journeys between homes, services, employment and other opportunities and hence reductions in travelled distances;
- a strengthening of public transport systems (which favour higher densities) and a reduced reliance on car ownership and use.

The attributes of higher density appear to fit well with the principles of good housing design. Higher density addresses the principle of car dominance; it appears to be inherently sustainable; it may promote a mixing of uses as homes, services and employment are brought closer together. It may also help nurture a sense of place and a sense of community as people find social interaction is not hindered by the barrier of physical distance. High density, if coupled with better design, also holds the promise of more secure and safer places to live.

However, Carmona (2001b) questions whether such a simple link can be drawn between higher densities and better, more sustainable, housing design. He argues that urban 'concentration [through higher density development] is perhaps the least straightforward of the design principles' (ibid., 184). Higher densities might well contribute to greater levels of congestion and pollution, and result in the destruction of existing urban heritage. There is also a view that higher density living offers only a technical solution to the question of residential sustainability, and may prove individually unacceptable over the longer term. A study of the London Boroughs of Brixton, Hackney, Hammersmith, Croydon and Newham by Burdett *et al.* (2005) illustrated that attitudes towards higher density development is complicated by other, 'non-density' issues:

- Other factors override density in the judgement as to whether a particular urban area is positive or negative. Satisfaction is judged against:
  - access to public transport, 'proximity to large and safe open spaces';
  - and also good access to shops and social facilities;
- Where dense neighbourhoods are viewed as poor or failing, this is often a result of overcrowding or deprivation, factors that are not directly linked to density.
- But high densities can lead to a lack of parking, and this may be viewed as a problem.
- Concentrations of high density social housing can cause a negative disposition towards higher density.
- Views towards high density tend to be mixed: vibrancy and social mix are among the most valued characteristics of densely populated areas.
- 'Higher density areas are capable of sustaining very different social and community dynamics: places with significantly different demographic features can operate.'

The fact that some residents apparently reject urban living and display a preference for areas that are less densely developed is one argument used against enforced 'densification' as a general principle (though Burdett *et al.* demonstrate that negative perceptions of places are sometimes wrongly attributed to density). However, Robertson and Walford (2000) emphasise 'the error' of assuming that higher density living has popular support: their study of young people and school children indicated a desire to see 'greater provision for well-planned low density housing' (ibid., 239) over the next 20 years, and a parallel concern and pessimism over the future of cities. There is also a persuasive economic and social case against 'urban intensification' (as the push towards higher densities is sometimes labelled). Burton (2000), for instance, looks at the question of whether higher density urban forms promote greater social equity. She argues that in medium-sized cities, higher densities bring both positive and negative social consequences. They may result in improvements in public transport, reduce social segregation and increase access to facilities (as Banister, 1997; Stead *et al.*, 2000 and Hall, 2001 contend). But on the other hand, the same densities will also lead to reduced living space and a lack of affordable housing. On balance, however, she concludes that social equity is best served by higher urban densities.

But the question of affordability – dealt with later in this chapter – is a critical one. Balchin and Rhoden (2002: 58) argue that 'most new housing units developed in the inner city would be unaffordable to new households, and even if they became affordable (possibly as an outcome of subsidised regeneration), many new households would prefer a detached house in the country to a flat in the city for the same price'. This problem has had greatest effect in London in recent years (Hamnett, 2001) and has resulted in a poor experience of higher density urban living by a large number of low- to middle-income households who find it difficult to buy their own homes or occupy anything but the most basic and cramped accommodation. Indeed, demonstrating that quality, high density urban housing can be affordable will be a key step to reversing the types of attitudes highlighted by Robertson and Walford.

Arguments in favour of compaction and higher densities continue to rest on the issues of (a) land-take and (b) the support of urban living (Carmona, 2001b: 185). Hall has suggested that the latter argument should command greater respect; first, because vast swathes of agricultural land are essentially redundant and that there is a strong case for putting at least some of this land to residential and development use as a response to the rising tide of household growth and housing need; and second, because there is empirical evidence to support the wisdom of higher densities with regards to urban sustainability.

But this argument does not close the door on lower densities in some situations. Indeed, Edwards (2000a) has suggested that all densities can be made 'more sustainable' and all densities suffer a range of potential drawbacks (see Table 4.4). With regards to high density (defined as having 60 dwellings per hectare in this instance) energy efficiency and a mixing of uses are viewed as critical attributes.

However, housing costs can be high and affordability low (see again, Burton, 2000). Similarly, different forms of antisocial behaviour can be a feature of some higher density developments. In older housing blocks, for instance, noise transmission is a recurrent problem and past design faults have led landlords to insist that tenants or leaseholders carpet their homes and do not use hard floorings. This type of problem highlights the critical importance of better design in future high density development. With regard to what Edwards terms 'medium' densities (30 dph), many aspects of sustainable living are retained and there is no sudden reliance on private transport. Private gardens may offer a source of food production. On the downside, public transport is weakened and may need supporting, and medium densities can constitute 'poor urban form'. The lowest densities discussed by Edwards (ten dwellings per hectare) can offer significant advantages in terms of sustainability by providing the potential to use renewable energy sources and by promoting higher levels of biodiversity (a pattern of low density housing and attached gardens has far higher biodiversity than a landscape of intensive agriculture: London Biodiversity Partnership, 2005). However, transport energy costs are lower and land utilisation is judged by Edwards to be 'poor'. Edwards' assessment is for the most part quantitative and objective, except when he makes judgements regarding 'urban form'. Here, his assump-

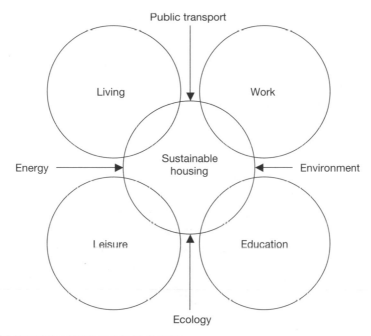

Figure 5.1 Key relationships in sustainable housing
Source: Edwards, 2000b: 35

tion is simply that compaction or concentration has clear benefits over dispersion. These benefits accrue from the fact that compact cities bring together all
the supposed ingredients of sustainable living (see Figure 5.1).

It is inevitable that future house building will take place in a vast range of
different settings and that many different density standards will be applied.
Edwards highlights the great importance of bringing together high density and
good design. But if lower densities run the risk of being less sustainable (or
having fewer sustainable attributes and more drawbacks), then the need to apply
higher design standards to these developments is at least as great as the need
to apply them in dense inner-urban areas. Good design will be the essential
ingredient in all future house building, irrespective of density.

Planning intervention in density and design

The responsibility for delivering better design rests with the private sector,
though public policy will influence design standards as well as the density of new
housing development. More than 80 per cent of new housing is now produced
by speculative builders (Hooper and Nicol, 1999) who tend to employ standard

house types across the country. House builders see clear advantages in adopting standard types:

- This strategy provides business security: standard designs are tried, tested and sell.
- Standard designs result in efficiencies for the building industry in terms of costs and skills.
- It is easy to maintain a 'portfolio' of designs and amend and revise this portfolio over time and in response to market appraisal.

However, Leishman and Warren (2006) argue that house builders are coming round to the view that the market is demanding more than the standard pattern-book designs and are looking at ways of incorporating 'customisation' into their products. We looked at the broad contents of planning policy guidance in the last chapter. In relation to design and density, it:

- Places greater emphasis on improving the quality of new housing development and making more efficient use of land through promoting mixed use schemes, increasing densities and improving design. PPG3 stated that 'local planning authorities and developers should think imaginatively about designs and layouts which make more efficient use of land without compromising the quality of the environment' (para. 54).
- Supports initiatives such as VDS, suggesting that shared visions between stakeholders and communities should be developed.
- Poor design should become a critical factor in refusing planning applications: 'In determining planning applications, local planning authorities should reject poor design particularly where their decisions are supported by clear plan policies and adopted supplementary planning guidance, including village design statements' (para. 63).
- Increase the efficient use of land, by increasing development density: 'Local planning authorities should avoid the inefficient use of land. New housing development in England is currently built at an average of 25 dwellings per hectare but more than half of new housing is built at less than 20 dwellings per hectare. That represents a level of land take which is historically very high and which can no longer be sustained' (para. 57). Efficiency is to be enhanced by:

  1 reviewing all existing standards for car parking and road layouts;
  2 avoiding maximum density standards;

3 avoiding developments of less than 30 dwellings per hectare;
4 encouraging an increase in densities to 30–50 dwellings per hectare.

The messages contained in PPG3 were elaborated upon in *By Design: Better Places to Live* (CABE and DETR, 2001b). *By Design* set out planning's role in ensuring that housing schemes have a sense of character and identity, and thereby move beyond the monotony that plagued some post-war and more recent housing developments. It argued that planning should also seek continuity and enclosure, distinguishing between public and private spaces. Planning also has a role in promoting quality in the public realm, in facilitating ease of movement (to and through the new development) and in making places 'legible' (design parlance for easy to understand and move around). And finally, planning should promote both adaptability and diversity: that is a place that can evolve with needs and that offers a diversity of housing choice.

How these objectives may be achieved is now examined through two brief case studies: the first looks at the 'codification' of design principles at Hulme in Manchester, and the second at the development of design skills and building consensus around the need for greater housing quality, using the example of Stratford-upon-Avon in Warwickshire.

Codifying design principles: Hulme, Manchester

Under the auspices of City Challenge, a programme of demolition and reconstruction began in Hulme in 1992. The redevelopment was to provide a broad range of housing types while achieving a minimum density of 30–35 dwellings per acre (74 to 86 per hectare). A master-plan provided by a team of architects was supported by an intentionally prescriptive Hulme Design Guide, adopted as SPG by the City Council. The guide was viewed as important in the light of the low densities and qualities being achieved elsewhere in the city centre at this time. The guide itself was based on:

> Simple rules with respect to hierarchy, permeability, and integration [. . .] translated in the Design Guide into strategies and technical dimensions for defining how streets, open spaces and urban blocks [were] to be formed.
>
> (Mills, 2000: 99)

The Guide (Hulme Regeneration Ltd/Manchester City Council, 1994: quoted in Carmona, 2001a: 243) aimed to:

- redevelop Hulme in an incremental, organic fashion, as a distinct residential quarter, physically and socially integrated once more into Manchester;

- encourage development which is both human in scale and urban in nature;
- encourage a diverse range of economic and social activities and uses within the area;
- nurture a quality public realm;
- create a clear urban framework that produces streets, squares and buildings of variety and quality at a density that can sustain the local economy, be robust enough to last, but still be able to accommodate change over time.

Between 1992 and 2000, 13 different firms of architects were involved in the scheme representing an 'ethos of variety' thought to be essential given the domination of Hulme's post-war development by a single architectural style and scale. Parts of the scheme were built at significant density – 54 dwellings per acre in the case of Rolls Crescent (CABE and DETR, 2001b: 97) – and at this density, the key design principles were addressed in the following ways.

In relation to 'character and identity', a central concern was with the foot-print of buildings and with legibility (below). The new character and identity of Hulme was to be based on variety (of building styles and materials) in response to the monotony of design inherent in the former crescents. A sense of identity was also established through the creation of co-operatives to oversee some sections of the redevelopment (moving away from the imposed solutions described by Power, 1999). The Homes for Change (HFC) and Homes for Work (HFW) co-operatives (comprising residents of the former crescents) directed the development of a high density, mixed use building. Retaining a mix of lifestyle, culture and diversity within Hulme was seen as an important means of retaining and promoting neighbourhood identity and, again, to avoid the problem of 'soulless' imposed solutions. However, Carmona (2001a) notes that Hulme has been criticised for its homogeneity, a problem that stems not from the Design Guide, but from an 'early decision to sell off the land to relatively few players' (ibid., 245).

In the case of Rolls Crescent, greater 'continuity and enclosure' was aided by the fact that the 'building line is behind a two-metre deep buffer zone, which provides space for rubbish, storage, meter boxes, cycles, and allows for personal-isation. This design also reinforces the public/private divide' (CABE and DETR, 2001b: 96). But common with many higher density developments, private and communal gardens are small and often overlooked. There is a 'buffered' conti-nuity between spaces, though communal outdoor space comprises 9 per cent of the overall land budget compared with 30 per cent for roads, footpaths and parking. The 'public realm' also occupies a relatively small land-take; a feature also common to many higher density developments. The aim therefore in Hulme has been to create interest and a sense of place from what public realm there is.

Plate 9 A view of the Hulme redevelopment (Manchester, 2003)

The Design Guide places no restriction on the height of buildings with a foot-print of less than 100 square meters. This has enabled the use of 'varied building heights' and 'enhanced corner treatment' (another issue raised in the Design Guide) to help 'create positive focal points along both sides of the street' (i.e. in Rolls Crescent, ibid., 96). With regard to 'movement and legibility' the Design Guide emphasises the need for both permeability and hierarchy. These principles were taken forward in the context of the master plan which set out how people would flow through the new Hulme. To a large extent, Hulme has been recon-nected to the rest of Manchester and some of these connections (including the 'Hulme Arch') have become focal points in Manchester's wider public realm (see Plate 10). Finally, 'adaptability and diversity' have been key goals of the Hulme regeneration. In the case of the HFC building, the dwellings vary from one-bedroom gallery flats to four-bedroom apartments. Mills claims that this variation means:

> people whose social circumstances change are not forced into leaving the building and living elsewhere, they can simply move to larger or smaller accommodation within the basic structure.
>
> (Mills, 2000: 101)

Whether this happens in reality is another issue, yet the principles of adaptability and diversity (of housing choice) are clearly embedded within the design rationale of the HFC building. Choice and variety – as noted above – are also more general features of Hulme's changed character, and will hopefully be a key strength of the area in the years to come.

In a denser urban setting – and one where there is a history of social and physical decay – the Hulme example illustrates the importance of:

- Clear leadership from the local planning authority in setting an agenda for change (through the use of Design Codes and Guides) and driving that change over the life of the project: in part, this was achieved in Hulme through the secondment of planning staff members to the regeneration company (Mace *et al.*, 2004).
- The role of master planning in developing the design agenda and setting out how the broad principles will be translated into actual development.
- The need to involve hitherto 'disenfranchised' groups in the planning and design process. This was achieved in Hulme through the setting up of

Plate 10 Reconnecting Hulme – the Hulme Arch (Manchester, 2003)

co-operatives in some instances, and hence the delivery of Power's (1999) 'people-centred' solutions.

• The importance of avoiding monotony in dense urban settings by bringing in a range of complementary design ideas: arguably, the Hulme experience shows, on the one hand, the benefits of sectioning areas off to different architects but also the problems, on the other, of involving a small number of volume builders in large regeneration schemes.

Design skills and consensus: Stratford-upon-Avon

Research by Carmona *et al.* (2001) demonstrates that Stratford-upon-Avon District Council has been developing an active and integrated approach to the use of design Guidance. Stratford upon Avon is a largely rural district in the south of the county of Warwickshire. It has one major settlement – Stratford itself – and several smaller villages and market towns including Kineton, Shipston on Stour and Wellesbourne. It also has a scattering of smaller villages and hamlets, all of which are potentially sensitive to new housing development but which have been subject to significant housing pressure in recent years. Stratford upon-Avon District borders Cotswold District to the south and many of its villages are attractive to people commuting to nearby Warwick, Leamington Spa and Stratford, or further afield to Coventry and Birmingham. Some residents make use of the M40 (completed in 1990) and commute the 90 or so miles to London. There is, as a consequence of commuting patterns, significant pressure for new housing across the District. Adherence to strict design principles are viewed as essential if villages are to retain their existing character and not be swamped by the type of standardised volume house building that has already radically altered the characters of many of the district's villages.

Rural housing schemes are not inherently low-density. *By Design*'s highest density case study was a scheme of 62 dwellings on a 0.35 hectare site in Kendal (equating to a density of 177 dph) in the largely 'rural' Lake District. The intention here is to focus not on the fact that many of Stratford's recent developments have been at relatively low density, but on how planning authorities have grappled with the design agenda at a strategic level given the accusation that planners are poorly equipped – in terms of training and resourcing – to take forward design issues.

Following the publication of *Quality in Town and Country* (DoE, 1994a), the local authority embarked on a programme designed to address what it viewed as critical omissions in its design strategy. The first step was to establish the post of Design Officer, whose role it would be to coordinate the preparation of stra tegic guidance and to negotiate higher design standards at a site level. Within five years, the authority had developed a suite of design guidance including a district-wide guide, individual VDS (see discussion of PPG3 above) together with Town Design Statements. As well as setting out the aspirations of the planning authority, the hierarchy of guidance also drew on consultation with communities (again, aiming towards Power's 'people centred' solutions) and on the input of development interests. There was a view – confirmed by Government in the Planning Green Paper of 2001 – that the public sector should draw on the design expertise of private industry, given that a design skills gap had developed within local government. This was part of the rationale of stakeholder consultation. Another part of the rationale was to ensure that design policies were widely accepted and would not be aggressively challenged once planning applications were submitted.

Development interests tended to welcome the production of the various design guides, suggesting that they offered greater clarity in terms of the authority's expectations from particular sites and places. It was also agreed that principle-based guidance rather than prescription brings greater rewards: an element that Stratford's Design Guide shares with that of Hulme; both set out issues and principles but do not present solutions.

Consultation in establishing a design agenda proved to be crucial: this seemed to be true at all levels. Five hundred copies of the District Design Guide (2000) were sent out for consultation. At the level of VDS, the authority used funding from the Countryside Agency to establish pilot projects in three villages, overseen by a single project officer. Again, the process is one of people-centred solutions. The VDS are produced by members of the community, guided and assisted by the project officer: they identify and describe the distinctive character of a village and its surroundings at three levels: landscape setting, shape of the settlement and the nature of buildings. The objective is to establish forward looking principles based upon existing local character (see Carmona *et al.*, 2003).

But the attempt to make design a more central component of the planning process is not without its difficulties. Experience in Stratford suggested that design guidance is only effective if planning teams possess the knowledge and understanding necessary to implement and enforce policy. Developers were of the view that policy designed by those with limited design training tends to be whimsical, grounded in the personal views and tastes of individual officers (echoing the view of Bateman, 1995; see Chapter 4). Many authorities accept that design skills in the planning professional are lacking, but would argue that they have done as much as possible – in the context of resource constraints – to bring planning teams up to speed with regard to design issues. Stratford-upon-Avon, for example, runs regular Continuing Professional Development (CPD) sessions within Development Control to ensure that the policies set out by design specialists are understood by non-specialists. A similar programme of training has been extended to planning committee members. Experience in Stratford revealed that:

- Design solutions need to be built on broad consensus, taking on board the views of those communities that must live with planning decisions, and drawing on the expertise and experience of those who work in the housing industry. Design principles must fit the needs of users, and perhaps to a more limited extent, providers.
- Design skills have been in short supply within some local authorities (ODPM 2003a). A limited number of design specialists often have to work with and alongside colleagues who have limited experience of design issues. This is a general weakness in current planning practice, and one that the government has sought to remedy in recent years.
- Design Guidance can represent a first step in establishing broad principles, which are then expanded upon in a wider hierarchy of policy.

Overall, the Stratford example suggests that planning's role in design is largely about setting an agenda and reflecting aspirations established through consensus. The degree of influence that planning wields over design standards on the ground will depend on the robustness of planning control and enforcement and upon the skills of local authority planning staff.

Planning for density and design

There is broad consensus on what constitutes quality in housing design; there is also – albeit more fragmented – agreement on the need to build at higher densities for the sake of greater urban vitality and in order to support the paraphernalia of 'urban living'. But there is less support for concentrating population, enforcing particular lifestyles or 'needlessly' promoting urban intensification. Higher densities help breath life into existing urban areas, promote energy efficiency in new urban extensions and foster greater social interaction in all sorts of neighbourhoods. But irrespective of density objectives (even 'high' density developments vary significantly in terms of land budgeted for dwellings or in terms of the exact 'dph' figure), there is a clear need to embrace issues of housing quality.

Many planning authorities have come together with housing providers, communities and wider interest groups, and established broad principles for promoting good design. These tend to draw on the established design commandments agreed by government in *By Design: Better Places to Live* (see p. 123), and are local interpretations of principles that have evolved over a number of years. The codification of these principles into local policy is based on public sector

Plate 11 New semi-detached housing – real improvements to housing design? (Stratford-upon-Avon, 2001)

aspiration and on the type of development that authorities want and believe will emerge in designated areas. But ensuring that development meets aspirations has often proven difficult. Some of the challenges faced by planning teams emerge from the local examples presented above and these include:

• the need to build consensus around design principles and aspirations;
• the view among developers that standard products reduce risk, and therefore the unwillingness of some builders to innovate;
• the hijacking of the design agenda by NIMBY interests as a means to block development;
• the lack of a wide design skill-base within local government leading to a view that planning cannot effectively influence or manage the design agenda and therefore a lack of public and professional trust in planning's role in design.

Added to these problems, Carmona (2001b: 187) argues that the design agenda sometimes hits a range of barriers, including:

• entrenched patterns of living including a reliance on private modes of transport: this may lead people to reject lower parking standards, making developers caution about accepting certain design principles;

- entrenched aspirations towards high consumption, low density lifestyles;
- a lack of political will to embrace the design agenda when the overarching priority is either to block new housing development or prioritise quantity (of dwellings) over quality;
- a lack of vision (in either the public or private sectors) to innovate and move beyond established practices;
- selfishness, with different groups seeing design and the environment as someone else's problem.

In the context of planning reform and the Planning and Compulsory Purchase Act 2004, it is likely that design will figure prominently in Local Development Frameworks with principles or 'codes' (Carmona *et al.*, 2006) and consultation playing bigger parts in future housing and residential design. However, many of the problems identified above will take time to overcome. Planning's initial task is to take forward a pro-quality agenda, bringing people on board, and building consensus around the need – in many instances – to live differently and reassess lifestyle choices. But this must not be based on limiting personal choice. The quality agenda may well involve promoting new density solutions, but it should not be about imposing such solutions.

Affordable housing

Controls over density and design have become an important part of planning's interventionist role in the delivery of new housing. Another power, which has evolved and developed over the last 30 years, is the extraction of more indirect planning gain, in the form of affordable housing, and it is to this power that attention now turns. In earlier chapters, we drew a distinction between ensuring general affordability in the housing market (to ensure the market's smooth operation), and the use of the planning system to generate a supply of 'affordable homes' built with a land-value subsidy extracted via planning. In the remainder of this chapter, we concentrate on the latter (with the former receiving attention in Chapter 7). We begin by looking at the operation of this system and its evolution; we end by considering its value and future operation.

Planning and affordable housing

Within local development plans, planning authorities may include policies that indicate an intention to seek an element of affordable housing on suitable sites – that is, 'both low-cost housing and subsidised housing, as both will have some role to play in providing for local needs' (DETR, 1998b: 3). Such policies must be grounded in rigorous assessments of local need. And having established a need for affordable housing, authorities can specify the number of affordable units required in the plan area and set 'indicative targets for specific suitable sites'. Plan policies will then indicate an intention to negotiate for the inclusion of such dwellings within sale housing schemes or – in rural locations – the intention to grant exceptional planning permissions as outlined in an Annex to PPG3 (DETR, 2000a). The affordable housing mechanisms set out in 2000 are re-endorsed in the consultation draft of PPS3 (2005) but not elaborated upon. There is an emergent view, however, that the need for local intervention will be determined by sub-regional level market assessment (ODPM, 2005a: para. 23). Again, we return to this issue in Chapter 7.

'Exceptions' and 'site quotas' (Box 5.2) extract an indirect subsidy from total land costs. In the case of exceptions policies, authorities have been able to use their powers to grant planning permission on land not allocated for housing in the local plan (DETR, 1998b: 8). Owners of small rural 'non-allocated' sites may be encouraged to release such land – which may have a limited agricultural value – at a negotiated price between agricultural and full development value. Hence, affordable units are built at a lower cost (as the land price element is reduced) and controlled for local occupation using Section 106 (Town and Country Planning Act 1990) controls. Nationally, the contribution of exception sites is limited though their role in serving community needs in some rural areas can prove useful (Gallent and Bell, 2000; see also DEFRA, 2006; JRF, 2006).

'Site quotas' – and the treatment of affordable housing as just another planning gain – in contrast, are more ubiquitous and central to the government's stated aim of providing a 'reasonable mix of and balance of house types and sizes to cater for a range of housing needs' (DETR, 1998b: 1; this message is also re-iterated in PPS3: 'it is important that a broad mix of housing suitable for different household types is provided for', para. 21). It was noted above that within the local plan, the LPA will outline where new housing development (during the plan period) will be permitted and set indicative targets for the number of affordable units it will 'require' from developers. It is then left to developers to deliver a 'contribution' of affordable housing that will satisfy this 'public requirement' and ensure the development will proceed.

With such contributions, it is sometimes the case that the developer will provide affordable housing directly for sale to an RSL (exactly how this is to be done, and how many units are to be provided, will be written into the Section 106 Agreement – some options are listed in Box 5.3). In these instances, the agreed unit price will be set at a level where no SHG (see Chapter 3) will be required. The developer cross-subsidises this discount sale with the profit made from the market housing, though ultimately it is the landowner who has shouldered the

---

Box 5.2 Planning and affordable houslng

General approach

The negotiation of contributions from developers of affordable housing within market housing schemes, usually on the basis of Section 106 (Town and Country Planning Act 1990) Agreements. Under the general approach, affordable housing is treated as a planning gain and usually specified as a requirement within Section 106. The inclusion of affordable housing is an obligation imposed on the developer. Sometimes, the developer builds these units (a specified number or proportion) and then sells them at discount to a RSL. The government believes that RSLs are best placed to ensure than such units remain for the use of low-income groups in perpetuity. The general approach means that social housing is provided as part of a mixed-tenure development and is funded through planning gain, private sector borrowing and public subsidy. Gain – generated at the expense of landowner/developer profit – often replaces some, or all, of the public subsidy.

Exceptlons approach

The granting of planning permissions for housing on land not allocated for that particular use within a local authority's development plan. The initiative aims to reduce land value and therefore housing unit costs by establishing a framework whereby developable land can be acquired at below full development value. This approach is only to be taken in rural areas, and is to be used for the procurement a small number of units within or adjacent to existing settlements. It is hoped that landowners can be encouraged to part with land at a price nearer agricultural than full development value. However, the approach will only work where a comprehensive development plan is in place and where a LPA has a reputation for adhering closely to plan policy. Research has shown that where there is uncertainty over a planning authority development strategy or its intentions for a particular site are unclear, owners will hang onto all land in the hope that one day, it may be earmarked for market housing.

---

subsidy burden by accepting a price for the land fettered by the Section 106 Agreement. So in many instances, these unit contributions from the developer may cut out the need for capital grant funding altogether. Similarly, cash contributions from the developers (either directly to the RSL or via a local authority) may be sufficient for the RSL to progress a new scheme without grant funding. Hence the planning system – whether planners employ an exceptions strategy

---

Box 5.3 Type of developer contribution

1   The developer sells space or dwellings on the site at full market price for another organisation to provide affordable housing on the site.

2   The developer provides a form of affordable housing himself. This is either (a) smaller dwellings but sold at full market price for their size, (b) dwellings sold at a discount against market price, or (c) dwellings sold under shared equity with the developer retaining partial ownership.

3   The developer sells land or dwellings to a registered social landlord who purchases them with the maximum amount of SHG and private finance permitted by the Housing Corporation's grant rate framework.

4   The developer sells land or dwellings to a RSL who purchases them without any SHG input (but with private finance).

5   The developers sells land or dwellings to a RSL at a nominal price.

6   The developer makes an off-site contribution.

Source: Whitehead, 2002: 13

---

or developers contributions – are circumventing some of the need for government grant in order to deliver affordable housing (see Carmona *et al.*, 2003).

Recent policy development

This policy has evolved over a number of years. The potential of extracting gains from planning permissions was first recognised in the 1970s (Jowell, 1977), and there were some early experiments, but also fears that authorities would be perceived to be 'selling' planning permissions and that this might undermine the integrity of the planning system. Government Circular 22/83 attempted to tie gains explicitly to planning permissions, stating that requirements from developers should be closely related to a proposed scheme to the extent that a development 'ought not to be permitted without it' (Barlow *et al.*, 1994: 3; see also Barlow and Chambers, 1992). But the arrival of 'exceptions' policies in the 1980s caused additional confusion (Clark, 1984) with authorities apparently pursuing 'off plan' housing schemes not restricted by formal planning procedures, and bringing planning into an era of uncertainty (Heap and Ward, 1980). Rhodes (1988) was an early advocate of the need to clarify the powers and responsibilities of the local state in respect of planning and housing.

Some clarification arrived with the first PPG on housing in 1988 (DoE, 1988), but this was primarily concerned with planning's basic function of ensuring a supply of building land (extending Circular 15/84; DoE, 1984), It also talked about planning's enabling role (see Chapter 3), though gave little indication as to how the uncertainties surrounding planning and affordable housing might be resolved. Uncertainty persisted for another year: a redraft of PPG3 in 1989 displayed greater concern for design (see above) and for the extraction of planning gain, with a new reference to 'low cost housing for local needs' (DoE, 1989b: para. 25–30). But the new PPG3 was not made official until 1992 (DoE, 1992). In the meantime, the first Circular (7/91; DoE, 1991) on affordable housing was published, which created the system described in Box 5.2. The new Circular gave universal endorsement to the practice of extracting planning gains in the form of affordable housing, but noted that gain should be negotiated on a site by site basis, and its extraction would be dependent on site economics and the 'carrying capacity' of an individual housing scheme (a view that is today contradicted by the setting of a blanket affordable housing target in London).

There were a number of studies of the early effectiveness of these policies. Williams *et al.* (1991) looked at the operation of exceptions schemes in rural districts. Bishop and Hooper (1991) undertook a more general appraisal of on-site negotiation. All such evaluations tended to talk of the policy's local importance but inability to deal with general affordability concerns. Indeed, Bishop and Hooper concluded that 'manipulation of the planning system will never be a substitute for an appropriate level of public subsidy' (ibid., 36). This sentiment was echoed in the Joseph Rowntree's Inquiry into Planning for Housing (1994). A view developed that planning's role in delivering affordable housing should be viewed as ancillary to wider efforts to ensure general affordability (see Chapter 7), and the need for direct funding for 'social housing' where necessary.

Arguably, a more coherent strategy for extracting affordable housing from planning permissions was prompted by household projections (see Chapter 4) in the mid 1990s, which forecast a dramatic rise in the number of households forming in England in the years ahead (see Holmans, 1995; DoE, 1995a; DoE, 1996b) and a continuing need for affordable homes (accentuated by the sale of public housing – see Chapter 3). In this context, a tighter system was introduced in 1996 (Circular 13/96; DoE, 1996a) in which a requirement to provide affordable housing would be 'triggered' by certain development size thresholds. The thresholds were intended to promote certainty but prompted inevitable debate (with the private sector arguing they were too low, and the public sector too high). This debate obscured the real question: was the system delivering enough affordable housing? The new Labour government joined the debate and lowered the thresholds (in a revised Circular, 6/98), a move that failed to satisfy most planning authorities (Housing and Planning Review, 1998: 3).

Apart from PPG3 (DETR, 2000a), and the more recent consultation draft of PPS3, which does not elaborate upon the mechanics of the gain mechanism, there have been no further developments to this system since 1998. However, there are currently expectations of change. Government ran two consultations in 2005 on affordability and housing supply and on housing in rural areas. These have since fed into a consultation draft of PPS3, but which switches emphasis to general affordability rather than affordable housing achieved through local intervention. An issue that has been on the back-burner since the appearance of the Planning Green Paper in 2001 is that of 'development tariffs': should government move away from planning gain (via Section 106 agreements) and towards a system of fixed-cost tariffs (with developers paying a tariff in 'exchange' for development permission, calculated on the basis of proposed development size)? This proposal was first set out in a document accompanying the Green Paper (DTLR, 2001b), but it received a lukewarm reception with a Transport, Local Government and the Regions Select Committee suggesting that 'tariffs would replace one form of complexity with another' (House of Commons, 2002: 46). It was suggested that time spent on negotiating individual obligations – and contributions of affordable homes – would suddenly be spent on establishing the basis 'for tariffs around the country, authority by authority, at the forward planning stage'. The committee argued that the change would bring few benefits in terms of speed and clarity: tariffs would also break the link (the 'necessity test') between the development of sites and on-site gains, with authorities free to spend the tariff on anything, anywhere in the local area. It would amount to a formalising of the practice of accepting commuted sums in lieu of on-site gains. It could mean that less affordable housing might be generated through planning, as authorities prioritise other policy objectives and use tariff money for other purposes.

But the idea of fixed tariffs was not lost. Instead, government has introduced the idea of a 'twin-track' approach or 'optional planning charge'. The Planning and Compulsory Purchase Act 2004 awards the power to ministers to introduce an optional planning charge to the development system. Developers would be given the choice to continue to negotiate contributions (under section 106 agreements) or to opt to pay an upfront charge levelled according to set criteria. The most recent Circular on planning obligations (05/2005) does not make reference to such charges, though there is an expectation that government may move on this issue once ongoing consultations on various aspects of the Barker Review are complete (and more recent debate has focused on the Planning Gain Supplement Mechanism favoured by Barker: see Chapter 7). Perhaps the most important aspect of Circular 05/2005 is its restated support for planning and affordable housing policies, which should be 'in line with Local Development Framework (LDF) policies on the creation of mixed communities'. The use of the planning system to deliver affordable homes looks set to remain. The policy represents a planning power that is distinct from the setting of tariffs which may ultimately break the link between development and 'planning contribution'. In the remainder of this section, we consider the efficacy of recent policy.

Delivering affordable housing through planning

Gain and exceptions mechanisms have provided an inherently uncertain amount of affordable housing and have only a minor impact on the overall level of actual housing need. We have noted, at several points, in Holmans (2001) estimate that an additional 3.5 million households would form in England between 1998 and 2016. Much of this will result from a surge in single-person households: 68 per cent of the net increase will stem from a rise in never-married households. Net inward migration will also play an important part in increasing housing demand, adding 95,000 persons to the total population each year with migrants initially heading to London and the south-east, and so accentuating housing pressure in this region (Barlow *et al.*, 2002: 4). Again, more recent projections point to an acceleration of this growth. These demographic pressures will combine with problems in the existing housing stock (the need for replacement and demolitions or the mismatch between supply and demand caused by second homes) to further heighten the need for more housing and more affordable housing. By 2026, there will be nearly 21 million households in England: a rise of nearly 5 million on the 2003 base.

In this context, what contribution can planning and affordable housing make towards meeting current and future needs? Barlow *et al.* (2002: 7) have tackled this question directly, arguing that:

> too much weight is being placed on the additional affordable housing that can be expected to be made available through section 106 agreements. While the use of planning agreements for socially beneficial purposes is to be welcomed, it cannot on its own deliver a sufficient amount of affordable housing to meet current and emerging needs.

The authors quote figures from Holmans *et al.* (2001) suggesting that the maximum contribution that can be expected from planning agreements is in the order of 15,000 homes per annum, not all of which may be 'additional'. They may not be additional because there may be no tangible 'gain', with no true land-subsidy or some of the 'affordable homes' simply being smaller market units deemed affordable by planning authorities wishing to publicise their efforts to meet local need. The way in which affordable homes are provided on-site is an issue returned to below.

General supply constraint is of course central to the issue of affordability (Barker, 2004): as fewer market homes are built, the scarcity value of housing increases, thereby pushing up the theoretical need for more affordable homes (as fewer households can secure sufficient mortgage advances to purchase more expensive housing). Even if 15,000 affordable homes can be secured through planning each year (a figure derived from official HIP returns), the future deficit against future need is likely to be significant and will grow each year as new need arising is added to the growing backlog. If the HIP figures were correct, then planning would have added 300,000 units to the affordable housing stock between 1996 and 2016, with more than a million needing to be provided through other means. Crook *et al.* (2001) suggest that figures on recent provision through the planning system (derived from HIPs) hugely overestimate the contribution made by planning agreements and rural exceptions schemes (ibid., 6–7), so the future shortfall may be even larger than anticipated.

Arguably, government overestimates the role that the planning system can play in delivering affordable housing through the mechanisms described in this chapter. But it should be remembered that the role of planning in extracting gains from development permission is viewed as ancillary to its wider purpose of facilitating general housing supply and, in so doing, ensuring general affordability and thereby decreasing the need for indirect interventions. Government has become increasingly concerned with general supply and the operation of the planning system since the publication of the Barker Review in 2004, and this is an issue that we return to in Chapter 7. But even with a more efficient planning system, the emphasis on private provision and on homeownership (see Chapter 3) is likely to result in localised patterns of market distortion, where house prices become inflated and many households face access barriers. This is an issue that we look at in the next chapter, and is also a concern that government is grappling with through the proposed implementation of 'affordability targets' (i.e. the linking of house-building rates to market signals and hence to measures of declining affordability). It is likely that planning will continue to be called upon to deliver affordable homes through gain mechanisms and therefore, a need remains to understand how the system might be improved with a view to making it more efficient.

Whitehead (2002) has listed the top ten reasons why planning and affordable housing policies may not deliver an optimal number of affordable homes (see Box 5.4). The biggest problem seems to be the 'clarity' of the existing framework.

Developers believe that it is too difficult to factor planning obligations into land transactions because there is little certainty as to what will be required once they begin negotiating with planning authorities. On the other hand, authorities believe that the national framework does not give them the certainty and hence power to request clear contributions from developers. The second biggest obstacle is the concern that mixing different tenures on a single site will undermine the marketability of private housing: consequently, developers resist the provision of affordable homes. The third biggest issue is the 'difficulty judging what the developer can afford to provide'. This can mean that authorities are over-cautious and will ask for too little in case they scare off development interest: this, of course, reduces the overall contribution of the system to affordable housing supply. Additional barriers are listed in Box 5.4, and others might be added to this list: land supply in some rural areas (Gallent *et al.*, 2001); lower land values in the north of England (Crook *et al.*, 2001); 'hope value' on potential exception sites (Gallent and Bell, 2000); a reticence among planning authorities to dedicate resources to complex Section 106 negotiations (House of Commons, 2002); the quality of supporting 'needs' assessments (Tewdwr-Jones *et al.*, 2002); and the political and community barriers hindering general house building, which is the source of Section 106 contributions (Holmans, 2001).

Box 5.4 Problems of securing affordable housing through the planning system

Factor	Rank
Clarity of national planning and affordable housing policy framework	1
Resistance to the mixing of tenure/income groups on a single site	2
Difficulty judging what the developer can afford to provide	3
Definition of affordable housing too broad	4
Insufficient land supply for housing	5
Insufficient social housing grant available	6
Competing priorities for planning obligations within local government	7
Lack of clarity over what developers should provide: land or dwellings, cost or subsidise	8
Imposition of site thresholds is not appropriate	9
Remediation costs on brownfield sites limit the capacity to secure affordable housing	10

Source: Whitehead, 2002: 6

These difficulties conspire to reduce the effectiveness of providing afford-able homes through the planning system. But even if these difficulties were to disappear, government estimates that planning could supply only 20 per cent of total need. But this fraction assumes that the current barriers to securing market housing (i.e. elevated prices) were to remain and therefore many households will require future assistance. We have already noted that, since the Barker Review of 2004, attention has focused on general supply and general affordability (seeking to regulate house price inflation). It is impossible to predict, with any certainty, future changes to housing supply, but it is inevitable that any change will impact on the need for affordable housing. Government remains convinced of the need for a planning policy relating to the specific provision of affordable homes and this is restated in Circular 5/2005. In 2003, it consulted on the future of PPG3 setting out a number of favoured revisions, which included: bringing down the trigger thresholds (again); linking local housing polices with regional and sub-regional agendas; a requirement that all planning authorities should have stated affordable housing policies; and the allocation of sites for affordable housing only in some rural areas. However, given that the consulta-tion draft of PPS3 is more concerned with general market process, it looks likely that in the future government will focus on systemic affordability, relegating local affordable housing policies behind a desire to control house price inflation. We return to this issue in Chapter 7.

Conclusions

In this chapter, we have been concerned with the role of local planning in influ-encing the type of housing that is delivered by the private sector. Our primary concern has been with local intervention: addressing the contemporary concerns of design, density and the provision of affordable homes. Arguably, less contro-versy surrounds local planning's role in setting design and density standards, though some concerns remain over how well qualified planners are, to judge the aesthetics of building or residential design. Since the UTF report in 1999, there has been growing concern over the need to equip the planning profession with the skills needed to take forward the new 'spatial planning' agenda. Spatial plan-ning – a term that we focus on in later chapters – seeks to broaden the land-use focus of planning. Increasing concern for design and affordability over the last 30 years has been indicative of planning's broadening role in housing provision, marking a departure from Circular 15/84's narrow focus on land release. Planning's broader role is perhaps accepted by the vast majority of interest groups, though uneasiness remains, for a number of reasons. For developers, a wider role for planning can be equated with a bigger list of 'public test' barriers, extending the planning process. For planners, it creates a need for a broader skills base, which may be difficult to secure, and for social housing providers, it suggests a substitution of public funding with planning gain, which has delivered an uncertain and unpredictable supply of affordable housing (CIH/RTPI, 2003: 5) over recent years.

But there is clearly a bigger picture that may be obscured by planning's local role in housing provision. Design (and related density) issues are clearly important whenever housing is built. But the same is true of affordability. This is not an 'add-on' concern based on an assumption that most housing will be unaffordable and that the state must – invariably – intervene to protect the interests of an economically weaker minority. Rather, affordability is a general concern that affects the entire operation of the housing market. If young people or first-time buyers cannot enter this market (and are confined to 'social housing') then the processes of trade-up and intra-market movement will stall. The market needs through-flow: the big question, therefore, is not how to provide alternatives for a minority, but how to bring this minority into the fold, and more specifically, whether 'existing mechanisms [for land release] will in practice deliver the necessary supply of homes to meet emerging economic and social needs' (Barlow *et al.*, 2002: 24; again, see later chapters for a possible answer).

Local interventions in the way that new homes are provided assume that the market does not always place a social value on housing quality and on the most efficient use of land. It is far more concerned with profitability. Local authorities, as gatekeepers, can influence both affordability and quality and this role will be maintained in the context of new Local Development Frameworks. However, the planning system also faces more general challenges in relation to the delivery of 'sustainable communities' and general supply. And yet, the mechanisms discussed in this chapter will remain relevant in the context of these broader debates.

Chapter 6
Responding to strategic and local housing pressures

Introduction

Previous chapters have dealt with general concerns: we began this book by establishing that the key issues in planning for housing relate to general housing supply and affordability, and to sustainability, which embraces the issues of design and density. In Chapter 4 we presented a broader picture of key housing debates and introduced the issue of 'housing numbers', how these are calculated and why they are viewed as important. In the last chapter, the focus was placed on the power of LPAs to influence housing design and density, and to procure affordable housing through the development control process. We have alluded to different scales of concern – to the calculation of housing demand at the national and regional levels; and to the exercising of development control powers at the local level. There has also been some reference to issues that are more critical at different levels or that affect urban or rural areas differently. The purpose of this chapter is to provide a more detailed 'spatial' account of these various issues, centring on strategic and local housing issues. Concerns centring on housing numbers, density and design, and affordability are revisited in the context of three case studies, and concerned with debates and events pre-dating the Barker Review and the 2004 Planning Act.

The first case study deals with regional housing, and particularly with the production of housing numbers and their translation into land allocations. In Chapter 4, we examined housing numbers in broad terms, dealing with the question of methodology (how projections are made and how 'trend figures' become 'policy figures' and finally allocations). Here we focus on the politics of housing numbers and how regional debate may influence the figures adopted in regional planning guidance or in regional spatial strategies. These issues are addressed in the context of two regions that exemplify current housing debate in England, and the division between growth and low-demand agendas set out in the Government's Communities Plan (ODPM, 2003a). Indeed, the regions selected – the east of England and the north-west of England – exemplify the dual poles of recent planning policy in relation to housing provision: avoiding over-supply in the north of England and delivering managed growth in the south.

The second case study shifts the focus to a more local level. It looks at the question of planning for housing on a strategic local site. The focus is on a green-field 'extension' site – adjacent to Stevenage in Hertfordshire – and the debate between land recycling and the option of developing sustainable urban extensions. The case study deals with the need for housing development of a strategic nature (identified at a regional and county level) in order to meet future need; acceptance or rejection of new housing and the political and local pressures present in new housing development; ensuring sustainability and securing afford-able housing through the planning system; the planning of large strategic housing sites over extended timescales, including issues of design and density; the question of developing greenfields given government's emphasis on land recycling; and the underlying rationale of recent reforms of the planning system. This urban case study focuses on national issues and debates that have been ongoing for a number of years, but which are illustrated by experience at the strategic-local interface in Stevenage.

The final case study is also concerned with local housing, but this time in the wider countryside. It uses Pembrokeshire (the Unitary Authority and National Park) in Wales as an area able to exemplify many of the current concerns relating to housing demand and supply in 'remoter' rural areas. In such areas, housing debate is framed rather differently. Here, the principal concerns relate to the socio-economic pressures faced by rural communities, the impacts of migration (into and from these communities) and competition (for housing), which might place inflationary pressure on house prices and cause the displace-ment of local households (Hoggart, 2003). Bevan *et al.* (2001) have suggested that of primary concern in the countryside is the ongoing 'social exchange': the replacement of local communities with wealthy incomers, leading to a fear that communities in the countryside are becoming socially unbalanced. We introduce the Pembrokeshire case study by discussing broader rural housing concerns: the peculiarities of rural housing markets; migration patterns; planning's current housing role, as defined in planning policy guidance and through legal prece-dent; and planning's dilemma, examined in terms of the desire of planning authorities to assist local communities relative to the unforeseen consequences of planning intervention in the housing market. The case study itself is primarily concerned with recent experience of planning intervention in the housing market. All three examples take the form of narratives, intended to show how some of the big debates in planning and housing end up as more 'local stories'.

Regional housing

This case study is primarily concerned with what happens to household projec-tion figures – examined in Chapter 4 – at the regional level, and as they trickle down to local development planning. It is concerned with the value attributed to the projections and household growth figures among different parties, and with the balance struck in decision making between technical considerations (again, introduced in Chapter 4) and political priority. Striking this balance is particularly difficult in the UK where local planning policies and decisions draw as much on interpretation of guidelines as on fixed legal requirement (Reade, 1987). The system allows regions, counties (where they exist and retain planning powers) and local authorities to weigh technical considerations (i.e. the Government Actuary's Department's calculations of growth) against local matters that may be prioritised for political reasons, including assessments of local economic growth or the weight of objection against strategic allocations. Such a system is inevitably less 'certain' and dilutes the emphasis on technical criteria (Cronin, 1993: 17). To some extent, the issues addressed in this section are unique to England and its discretionary planning system, which may act to free decision makers from the inflexibility of rules (Booth, 1996: 110). But across Europe, all nations are grappling with inter- and intra-regional population movement; with growth and local resistance to that growth; or with decline, low demand and shrinkage (Mace *et al.*, 2004).

In Chapter 4, we looked at the production of 'trend figures' for household growth, derived from calculations of future population change. The story begun in Chapter 4 is picked up again at the point where these trend figures are scrutinised at the level of regional planning. The questioning of trend figures (i.e. those grounded in technical considerations and 'free' of the more local political considerations) provides the critical focus for this section: the standing committees comprising local authority representatives together with the regional assemblies and development agencies introduce broad assumptions regarding economic growth and regional capacity to arrive at a policy-based allocation. It is at this stage that divisions between local and national considerations become apparent, and policy and political priorities may clash (Baker and Wong, 1997). This is illustrated using recent experiences in north-west England and in the east of England. Because we look at past experience, we deal primarily with the pre-2004 planning system, which is in a state of transition, instigated by the Planning and Compulsory Purchase Act of 2004. This has resulted in RPG (a non-statutory framework for Structure and Local Planning) being replaced with Regional Spatial Strategies (RSS: a statutory framework for local planning incorporating sub-regional components) and an end to the Structure Planning function in County Councils. Another 'technical' consideration in future allocations might comprise sub-regional market assessments, and this issue is examined in Chapter 7. However, the debates occurring in the case study regions is likely to be replicated in the future, albeit in the context of a new planning framework for the regions.

The north-west and east of England compared

During the EIP of draft RPG13 (during spring of 2001), considerable debate focused not on the RPG's Core Strategy, but on the housing figures. Draft Regional Planning Guidance had been published in July 2000 by the North West Regional Assembly (NWRA, 2000) in which it was argued that 'a higher level of growth than that which underpin[ned] the government's figures' was anticipated, resulting in faster rates of household formation and migration. Hence, the draft RPG made provision for 343,000 additional households (357,400 after adjustments for vacancy rates, or 17,150 units per annum; NWRA, 2000: 30). Following the EIP, a Panel Report, and a number of required changes from the Secretary of State, a revised Public Consultation Draft of RPG13 was issued in March 2002 (GONW, 2002a). Planned housing provision for the region had now fallen to a policy-based allocation of 12,790 units figure: the level set in the final RPG published exactly one year later. The debates that shaped this revision pre-dated the 2000 draft of the Guidance and can be traced back to the Regional Housing Forum with its membership comprising representatives from the HBF and a number of environmental interests including the CPRE, the Royal Society for the Protection of Birds (RSPB) and local groups such as Friends of the Lake District. Consensus among the environmental lobby was that the economic growth card was being over-played, backed by the house builders and accepted by some local councils whose interests lay in projecting an image of healthy growth rather than conceding the likelihood of economic uncertainties ahead.

Arguably, the arrival of a new PPG3 in 2000 gave environmental interests the upper hand. King (1999) has suggested that 'while in the 1950s and 1960s the balance between providing homes and protecting the environment appears to have been tilted in favour of homes, from the 1980s onwards the balance has tended to tilt more in favour of protecting the environment' (ibid., 10). With the environment in the ascendancy, groups opposed to control figures higher than the trend-based allocation were able to use national planning guidance to portray draft RPG figures as being out-of-step with government thinking (particularly in respect of land recycling and building re-use). Inevitably, both the economic arguments and the environmental concerns were overstated and it was left to the EIP Panel to force a compromise. A key problem here is that through the process of regional brokering, an 'objective' calculation of household formation (see Chapter 4) can quickly become a highly subjective housing allocation, determined not by real demand or need but by the agendas of competing political groups. Environmental pressures are likely to have greatest impact in those areas and sub-regions viewed as more 'sensitive'; hence Shire counties may end up with smaller allocations than metropolitan boroughs whereas the original trend-based figures pointed to the need for a more even spread of new homes. However, there was little evidence of this occurring in the north-west: between 2000 and 2003, the *relative* allocation to the Mersey Belt and to the rest of the conurbations fell by two percentage points, while the relative allocation to the Shire counties rose by the same amount (NWRA, 2000: 30; GONW, 2003: 69). The *absolute* downsizing across the region was fairly evenly distributed.

A schedule of the amendments to the original Draft of RPG13 was published by the Government Office for the North West (GONW) in May 2002. This revealed that the EIP panel broadly agreed with the housing provision figures set out in Draft RPG13 (GONW, 2002b: 120), but that the Secretary of State took a very different view. Indeed, the Secretary overruled the Panel's broad agreement with the original policy-based allocation and annualised figures, stipulating a 'reduction of 15 per cent on the draft RPG figure' (ibid., 121). The need for the reduction was attributed to lower economic growth rates than anticipated two years earlier, a high reported incidence of low demand in the region and a need to promote 'more sustainable patterns of provision'. The detailed explanation given was as follows:

> The draft RPG level of housing provision significantly exceeds the 1996-based household projections. It has as its economic basis a 'high (maximum) growth' scenario, which utilises the 1996-based household projections and applies to them a high (2.5% annual growth in GDP) growth rate and a reduced rate of unemployment. Actual growth to date is nearer to the draft RPG's 'moderate growth' scenario, suggesting necessary housing provision would accord with the 1996-based household projections (249,000 dwellings by 2016). In the Secretary of State's view, the draft RPG level of housing provision also pays insufficient regard to vacancy rates and the incidence of low demand. Accordingly, the Secretary of State proposes the annual average rate of provision to be based upon a total provision of 256,000 dwellings over the period 1996–2016. Whilst this is a reduction of 15% on the draft RPG provision, it is still in excess of that implied by the 'moderate growth' scenario.
>
> (GONW, 2002b: 125)

The growth scenarios referred to by the Secretary of State derived from work undertaken for GONW by Manchester and Liverpool Universities in 1999/2000 (DETR, 2000b). Three scenarios were devised, relating migration and household formation to low, moderate and high economic growth forecasts. GONW and its regional partners chose to select the high growth scenario to guide the policy-based allocation; the justification for this decision could of course be questioned, especially in light of the low demand issues referred to by the Secretary of State. However, central government's own preference for the moderate growth scenario was based on economic performance figures for only

24 months of the full projection period: this was perhaps another questionable justification. The choices made are of course politically motivated: the Regional Assembly's (RA) draft figures reflected the preferences of the house building lobby and local councils. The Secretary of State's objective was to secure the government's target for re-using previously development land.

The particular narrative behind the eventual 'adoption' of a policy-based allocation in the final version of RPG13 (GONW, 2003) was not dissimilar to the story behind all nine sets of RPG in England. Central government pays lip-service to the need for local ownership of the figures (Adams and Watkins, 2002: 102), but eventually, these are issued by government itself, which will demand that the level and proposed distribution of provision accord with its own policy aims. In the case of regional guidance in north-west England, this meant a net figure that was extremely close to official (trend-based) projections of household growth.

Arguably, the close relationship between the Secretary of State, the Government Office (GO) and the RA, acts to limit potential discord surrounding the regional control figures. There is scope for far greater disagreement between the Counties and LPA, on the one hand, and the RA (which has the task of preparing draft RPG), on the other. This was certainly the case during the preparation of Regional Guidance for the East of England. A draft of RPG14 was 'banked' with the Secretary of State in March 2004 and a final version was scheduled for publication early in 2006 (but is now subject to further review in the light of the 2004 Planning Act). The context for regional planning guidance in the east of England is very different from the context in the north-west. Government was extremely keen that housing provision figures set in RPG14 (and RPG11 (south-east England)) should accord with its Sustainable Communities Plan (ODPM, 2003a): this meant setting policy-based figures in excess of the 1996-based projections. In a letter to the East of England Regional Assembly, a government Minister set out the official position:

> You [referring to the Chairman of the East of England Regional Planning Panel] asked me for an indication of what level of growth should be considered for the LSC [London–Stansted–Cambridge] Growth Area and I indicated that I would be looking for your assessment of what would be required to get to 40,000 above current RPG levels by 2016 – with 35,000 as a minimum, compared with a base of around 90,000 in existing RPG (for the LSC area including Peterborough and the Cambridge sub-region). This is consistent with the scale of potential we referred to in the Sustainable Communities Plan. For comparison, the Milton Keynes/South Midlands Growth Area has submitted growth proposals for 44,300 on a base of 89,000 in existing RPG.
>
> (source: www.eelgc.gov.uk/eelgcDocs/
> scannedlordrooker.doc accessed 29 March 2004)

The government's agenda across the south-east and east of England is to push up planned allocations, thereby attempting to stave off a future crisis in housing provision (see also Chapter 8). This led to unease among the regional bodies and local authorities, who, first, shared concerns over how infrastructure could be provided to sustain such growth, and second, worried that many communities might vociferously reject the inflated allocations. Indeed, the Chairman of the Regional Planning Panel called the 'step change' in the allocations 'ambitious' and pointed out that it is 'one which has not been universally welcomed throughout all parts of the region' (hwww.eelgc.gov.uk: accessed 29 March 2004). Acknowledging the importance of infrastructure in securing a settlement, the Chairman also conveyed his hope that regional technical studies would assist government in securing the 'best possible infrastructure settlement for the East of England in the [. . .] 2004 Spending Review'. Making sure the necessary infrastructure accompanied the revised allocations was described as crucial to obtaining local political support; the RA expressed doubts as to whether headway could be made on the preparation of regional guidance without this support. This infrastructure debate is revisited in Chapters 7, 8 and 10.

In the months leading up to this exchange between Government and the RA, a number of east of England authorities voiced concerns over potentially inflated allocations. The draft of RPG14 set a regional target of 478,000 additional dwellings between 2001 and 2021 (EERA, 2004: 109): in Hertfordshire (the eastern parts of which fall into the London–Stansted–Cambridge Growth Area), an interim target of 72,000 units (3,600 annualised) was set. This was 'interim' partly because the figure was likely to be affected by technical studies of additional capacity in the London-Stansted-Cambridge–Peterborough corridor, and partly because:

> In Hertfordshire, the dwelling figures reflect an initial view of distribution in the county [. . .] pending an assessment of urban capacity, options for greenfield development, principally urban extensions, and appropriate density assumptions for use in assessing potential housing supply. A further study is to be undertaken to investigate the appropriate scale and density of potential housing supply from previously developed land, sustainable development options for possible greenfield development (including possible Green Belt releases), and mechanisms for ensuring that a sequential test can be applied to prioritise the supply from previously developed sources versus greenfield development.
>
> (EERA, 2004: 112)

This and earlier statements from The East of England Regional Assembly (EERA) prompted a joint response from the County and District councils in

Hertfordshire. Late in 2003, and prior to the issuing of a first draft of RPG14, Hertfordshire's local authorities became aware that the RA was likely to call upon them to allocate land for an additional 20,000 homes across the county above a 66,000 allocation already proposed by EERA. Under the direction of the RA, the authorities were asked to look at five growth scenarios (A to E), the highest of which would lead to 86,000 extra homes in the county during the projection period to 2021 (HertsDirect, 8 October 2003a). The initial reaction of the county was to point out the potentially negative impact of this additional allocation, in terms of both the loss of greenfield sites, and the repercussions for local communities. By November, the County's Executive Member for Environment was calling on the RA to give greater consideration to infrastructure needs, and the potential loss of both greenfield sites and green belt land (HertsDirect, 10 November 2003b). Criticisms of the RA's approach, and its lack of realism, became more defined with the County and districts raising the following concerns:

- Even with the lowest growth scenario (A, with 66,000 additional households), there would be a need to build on significant areas of green belt and on greenfield sites.
- The 'particular pressures on Hertfordshire' had not been recognised.
- The timescale given for the submission of district level figures had proven to be inadequate and did not allow 'for the proper development of robust figures' which could stand up to sustainability appraisal and public examination.
- Some districts did not have the capacity to meet their own housing needs.
- There was a need to ensure that a consistent methodology (for arriving at district figures) was followed across the region.
- The figures (i.e. the regional policy-based allocations) varied greatly depending on what assumptions were made (e.g. the amount of people expected to move into the county over the next twenty years).

(HertsDirect, 10 November 2003; www.hertsdirect.org/
environment/plan/eoferesponse, accessed 30 March 2004)

The local perspective differs greatly from the regional and the national one. For the county and districts, the 'pressures on Hertfordshire' related to the loss of greenfield sites and given the priority to defend such sites, the inability of some districts to find enough land to meet the housing needs of local people. The timescale for feeding into RPG was held to be particularly problematic as was the lack of consistency in arriving at district figures (there was at least a suggestion that districts in different counties dealt with capacity issues in different ways). Key among the criticisms contained in the joint response was that although Hertfordshire's authorities had been obliged to submit local figures, the rush to get these out and lack of a consensual strategy has meant that 'they [had] not agreed their own preferred locations for new housing and numbers [had] therefore been estimated'. Crucially, the figures were not viewed as a

> true representation of where houses can be accommodated, but are the result of a mathematical exercise in order to respond to pressure from the Regional Assembly.
>
> (HertsDirect, 10th November 2003)

The national perspective is somewhat different. In a joint response from the National Housing Federation (NHF) and Chartered Institute of Housing (CIH) to the 2003 consultation exercise leading up the banked draft of RPG14, it was argued that 'many parts of the East of England, particularly those influenced by the growing London Travel to Work Area, are subject to severe housing pressures' (NHF/CIH, 2003: 1). The biggest pressure facing the east of England – and Hertfordshire – resulted from 'migration from equity rich or income rich Londoners' moving into the region and fuelling house price rises (ibid.: 3). Because of this, local household formation was suppressed and past housing allocations had been inadequate to accommodate growth or meet needs. Hence, the key pressure facing Hertfordshire was not RPG14's inflated allocations, but past historic shortfalls in housing supply, which it might be argued, had prompted the response outlined in the Sustainable Communities Plan and the Barker Review of Housing Supply undertaken in 2004. The county and the districts viewed a recent slowing of household formation in Hertfordshire as license to resist higher control figures in RPG14; however, the NHF and CIH argued that:

> the slowdown in household formation [was] symptomatic of current market pressures and not a long term fundamental change. We therefore think Scenario C is unlikely to be correct and RPG14 must plan for a higher dwelling provision than the current RPG, as indicated by the other three scenarios. Our best estimate would be that the annual dwelling requirement is likely to be somewhere between scenarios B and D.
>
> (ibid., 4)

With Scenario 'A' representing the base level of growth and 'E' representing an 86,000 dwelling target, the first draft of RPG14, as we noted earlier, set an interim policy-based allocation of 72,000 units. This was below the recommendation of the NHF and CIH, but was likely to be subject to later revision. Debates over the level of growth throughout the east of England are unlikely to subside. Local resistance to higher allocations have shaped political debate in Hertfordshire at least since the publication of the county's Structure Plan in 1998, and the strategic allocation at Stevenage West (see p. 153). In the context of these local and regional concerns, it is easy to lose sight of the household projections as they become obscured by, and frequently relegated behind, the local controversies that embroil new housing provision. Within Hertfordshire, there was – and continues to be – a belief that an emphasis on the mathematics of provision has resulted in too little attention being given to local outcomes, and to questions of infrastructure, affordability, local need, environmental capacity, and the actual types of homes that should be built. Preparations for a revised RSS for the east of England are currently at an early stage and although debates are presently focused on housing numbers, much is going on behind the scenes to address these concerns.

Planning for housing in England at this regional level is an overtly political process. The clearest political interventions occur when the trend-based figures discussed in Chapter 4 are translated into allocations; each tier of planning and government has its own agenda and its own motivation. This might

Plate 12 The Hertfordshire landscape, which is perceived as 'under threat' from housing development
Source: UK Aviation NavAids Gallery

suggest that the projections themselves lose much of their initial potency as they become just one factor among many 'framing' the debate. Indeed, the first draft of RPG14 neglected to even mention the projections when setting out the factors that needed to be taken into account when planning future housing provision in the region: PPG3 (DETR, 2000a) priorities, the Sustainable Communities Plan, and the region's own Economic Strategy and Spatial Development Framework were all key considerations, but the projections were not listed as a guiding concern (EERA, 2004: 108).

One possible means of addressing concerns over the politicisation of the projections process, and the centralisation of control, was brought forward by Kate Barker in 2004 whose proposal to establish independent regional advice units for scrutinising housing figures met with a cautious welcome among local and regional actors. Government has recently responded to key recommendations from the Barker Review relating to the future of housing and planning in the regions (ODPM, 2004b). This response focused on Barker's call for Regional Housing Boards and Planning Bodies in England to be merged, and for the creation of Regional Planning Executives (advice units) to advise the merged bodies with independent advice on housing numbers. While government accepted the case for merger (ibid., 3) on efficiency grounds and because it accorded with its own objectives of streamlining the planning system and promoting 'joined up thinking' while avoiding added expense and bureaucracy (ibid.: 18), it rejected the idea of separate regional executives, arguing instead that a 'national unit will be a stronger centre of expertise, ensure greater consistency, allowing cross-regional issues to be addressed more efficiently' (ibid., 3).

The sub-text is that government wants to retain consistency with its own CP, and fears that independent think-tanks in the regions will further encourage departures from the national strategy. The single 'advice unit' proposed by the ODPM would have a broad remit: ensuring consistent regional methodologies for arriving at housing targets; integrating housing objectives with other regional targets; and assisting with the setting of regional affordability targets (incorporated into Public Service Agreements) (ibid., 20–21) discussed in the next chapter. But to what extent will government use this national policing service to ensure compliance as opposed to consistency, potentially strengthening its hand in regional affairs?

This must be a major concern for the English regions: the Secretary of State is already the most powerful player in regional planning. The regions and local authorities have been called upon to manage demand, to feed local intelligence into regional housing debates and to avoid the 'predict and provide' mentality of the past. Recent events in the east of England have suggested that authorities are keen to engage with government on housing provision issues, but many feel that Whitehall continues to railroad them along a preordained path: government has *predicted* growth and it remains their responsibility to simply *provide* for it. Government has staked its political future on the success of the CP, and this plan will need driving from the centre, perhaps undermining its own 'plan, monitor and manage' approach to housing provision.

The local level: strategic allocation

The east of England and Hertfordshire received some attention in the last section. The intention now is to shift scale and focus on the issues surrounding a large-scale strategic housing scheme within Hertfordshire, emerging from the context of regional and county-level strategic planning. The allocation of housing at Stevenage West dates back to the Structure Plan adopted in April 1999 but the idea of extending Stevenage west of the A1(M) had been around since the 1960s and can be traced to the original master plan for Stevenage New Town. During the preparation of the Hertfordshire Structure Plan, a variety of options for accommodating housing need within the county were considered, in light of the regional housing figures published in RPG9 (South East England: DoE, 1994b; revised and re-issued in 2001 by the DETR (DETR, 2001c)) before Hertfordshire moved into the RPG14 area in 2001. Stevenage West – as an option – was promoted by the County Council as being the most sustainable way forward. Alternatives considered included dispersal across a large number of scattered greenfield sites within the county or the development of other strategic locations elsewhere in Hertfordshire.

The concentration of development in a single location was thought to have a number of clear advantages: first, because there was thought to be a potential for such a settlement to enjoy a degree of self-containment in terms of employment and necessary shops and facilities. Second, there was also an expectation that more affordable housing could be procured on a single larger site. If smaller sites were developed, some might be below the trigger thresholds (see Chapter 5) and would not therefore yield affordable homes. Generally, it was considered that on a larger development, there would be greater potential to lever planning gains through obligations, including the provision of additional school places and other social infrastructure. Therefore concentration seemed to offer the potential for greater social gains compared to that which might be extracted from a number of smaller development sites.

The Stevenage West site was also considered to have more particular advantages. First, the site to the west of the A1(M) between Junctions 7 and 8 was located very close to Stevenage town centre and the main-line railway station. The centre itself is positioned at the western edge of the existing settlement so any extension westward of the A1(M) would balance out what is presently a 'lop-sided' town. People living in the extension would therefore live as close to the centre as Stevenage's existing residents. Second, Stevenage is already well connected by main-line rail links and by motorways to London, Cambridge, Peterborough and the English north-east. Third, the Examination in Public Panel (for the Structure Plan) considered evidence from a number of environmental consultees including statutory and local interest groups. It concluded that there were no in principle objections to developing the site on environmental or ecological grounds. While the site itself consists of relatively high-quality agricultural land, the Panel – following advice from The Ministry for Agriculture, Food and Fisheries (MAFF, now Department for the Environment, Food and Rural Affairs (DEFRA) – concluded that it would be impossible to avoid building on agricultural land anywhere in the county and that the Stevenage West site was at least not among the highest grade agricultural land in Hertfordshire.

In April 1998 the principle for the allocation was established in the Structure Plan (Policy 8): for 5,000 homes with 3,600 to be built before 2011. The site itself (280.96 hectares) is located across two local planning authorities: Stevenage Borough to the east (1,000 dwellings on 93 hectares in the opening period) and North Hertfordshire to the west (2,600 dwellings on 187.96 hectares). Following the allocation in the Structure Plan, the two local authorities along with the County Council and a consortium of developers (initially Persimmon, Taywood, Bryant and Garden Village Partnerships (comprising Leech, Redrow and Wilcon)) held a series of public events culminating in a consultation session on a draft master-plan in 1999. In parallel, the local authorities commenced pre-application and scoping discussions involving the developers, statutory consultees and other public agencies in order to establish the technical and detailed aspects for the planning applications. Six core topic groups – covering transport and access, infrastructure and resources, environment, social infrastructure, settlement planning and design, and development processes – were established, each with a remit of engaging in pre-application discussions; preparing chapter material for the two local development plans; and preparing the master planning principles document, subsequently to be adopted as SPG. Hence the local authorities embarked on the process of translating a Structure Plan allocation into more tangible development frameworks within the context of the local development plans.

In theory, it appeared that the structures and procedures were being established to bring forward a coherent development scheme. But in practice, the process was already being undermined by a number of unforeseen events alongside political uncertainties and differences. These included, first, a by-election in 1999 after which political power within the County Council shifted in favour of those opposed to the Stevenage West allocation. Newly elected conservative elements within the council sought to withdraw the Structure Plan, but were unable to do so because of legal impediments. However, determined to scuttle the development, the County Council began an early review of the Structure Plan as a first step to the potential deletion of the allocation. Second, the arrival of a revised PPG3 in March 2000 called into question the appropriateness of larger greenfield housing allocations, and gave the opponents of such allocations the excuse to back away from the Stevenage West development. Third, members of North Hertfordshire Council had consistently opposed the allocation through the Structure Plan review process. The publication of PPG3 in 2000 was jumped upon by the council who, on the basis of legal advice, withdrew their local plan. At the point of withdrawal, North Hertfordshire were already preparing their development plan and were about to insert a chapter on Stevenage West. When PPG3 arrived, it was decided that the planning authority should undertake an urban capacity study before committing itself to the allocation. It was further decided that the plan should be abandoned and re-written once the results of the capacity study were known. In neighbouring Stevenage, the District Plan was retained with the council choosing to carry on with their plan review (prior to second deposit) and to undertake a capacity study in tandem with this process. The withdrawal of the North Hertfordshire plan was a turning point for the Stevenage West development.

These events undermined the process in a variety of ways. First, the development consortium no longer had the certainty it needed to commit itself fully to the process. This caused severe problems later in the planning process because initial technical work on the application had not been as thoroughly undertaken as it might have been had the developers felt more confident that the principle of the development would not be called into question. Second, although joint working continued at an officer level, the relationship between the county and the district authorities became increasingly strained. Internally, officers within North Hertfordshire and the county were obliged to continue the detailed technical work required by the development, but were, at the same time, aware that councillors were completely opposed to the principle of the development. This in turn meant that working relations between the developers and the county and North Hertfordshire became ever more fraught.

Another complicating factor affecting the Stevenage West development was the level of organised public opposition built around the Campaign Against the Stevenage Expansion (CASE). Its impact on the development has been indirect, galvanising and giving additional weight to some of the political opposition at the county level and within North Hertfordshire. Following the close of the Public Inquiry into the development at Stevenage West (in May 2004) there was a period of silence from government, with a decision expected on the future of the development late in 2005 or early in 2006. During this period, CASE refocused its attention on the East of England Plan (which proposes the development of 478,000 houses in the region), which it is bitterly opposed to. However, this opposition has, arguably, never effectively challenged the principle underpinning the development at Stevenage West or the fact that household growth needs to be accommodated within the district of North Hertfordshire, the county and the region.

These concerns provide the backdrop for this development and we now turn to the planning of Stevenage West. A master-plan covering the entire site was prepared by the development consortium during the consultation process (above) and then submitted as part of a planning application in August 2001. Again, the plan cut across the two LPA areas. Both authorities were obliged to assess the development as a whole: they worked jointly and aimed to arrive at compatible conclusions on the technical aspects of the proposal where possible, notwithstanding their opposing views on the principle of the development. With regards to the issue of affordable housing, for example, to be delivered on site, the authorities jointly appointed a consultant to negotiate the level of affordable housing and the method of provision for the site as a whole. This principle of joint working was extended throughout negotiations with the developers and in relation to issues such as housing density and design. However, the relationship between the planning authorities (with one supporting and one opposing the development in principle) meant that although it was possible to reach broad agreement on some issues at the early stages, once the detail was fleshed out, there were regular disagreements between the authorities, often because North Hertfordshire were looking for reasons for refusal, while Stevenage were keen to see the development proceed.

At a practical development planning level, local officers faced a number of difficulties in planning a development of this scale phased over such an extended period of time. Some of the most intractable difficulties related to design, to the long-term nature and phasing of the development, to its sustainability and to the negotiation of affordable housing. We now look at each of these issues in turn.

A key challenge at Stevenage West has been how to agree on a process that will ensure consistent quality of design throughout different phases of the development. There was found to be a need to ensure an intermediary stage between outline application (in the case of Stevenage the outline application was accompanied by a master plan and a Development Principles and Design Guide (West Stevenage Consortium, 2001) establishing a broad design framework – see Chapter 5) and the many small-scale reserved matters applications, commonly from a number of different developers and involving small numbers of new homes. An intermediary stage was considered vital if the planning team were to effectively relate broad master-planning and design principles to specific areas within the development site and set a practical framework for detailed small-scale applications. Another challenge – common to all such strategic development – is the long-term nature of the build programme. Stevenage West has an antici-pated build programme that will stretch over a period of at least 15 years. The challenge for planners at the beginning of the programme is to ensure long-term responsiveness to changing standards (particularly given the ongoing revision of planning guidance) and expectations from development as new phases come on-line. The local planning teams recognised that this would necessitate a phased approach to the planning of the development, with the development framework and design guidance being linked closely to the phasing of the development and mechanisms put in place now for the future review of planning obligations. Designing such a process would also ensure that the development adheres to changing construction standards into the future: phases appearing in a decade's time should, for example, be able to reflect new innovations and standards as agreements and principles are renegotiated. A third challenge has been to ensure sustainability. Despite the rhetoric of sustainability found in much planning guid-ance, the planning system remains constrained in terms of what it can achieve: it can, for example, aim to reduce the need to travel through the promotion of mixed uses and by ensuring higher density development in areas accessible to public transport. It is more difficult for the planning system to guarantee high levels of energy efficiency in building design or influence the quality of public transport provision. In Stevenage West there was a great deal of uncertainty as to whether the local authorities could reasonably impose a variety of condi-tions aimed at securing the sustainability aspirations set out in the application documentation: for example, whether conditions could require all new homes to achieve an 'eco-homes' rating of 'excellent'. Although English Partnerships frequently impose a covenant to this end through their role as landowner (they own 28 hectares of the Stevenage West site), a planning condition of this type has not been tested through the appeals process. Therefore, experience at Stevenage West has revealed the limitations of the planning system in directly delivering more sustainable forms of development. Despite the sustainability aspirations expressed in planning guidance, planning conditions and obliga-tions still have to meet the relatively restrictive tests set out in Circulars 11/95 (conditions) and 1/97 (obligations), now updated in Circular 5/2005 (ODPM, 2005k).

Another critical challenge has been the proposed procurement of afford-able housing. The capacity of Stevenage West to deliver affordable housing through the use of a Section 106 Agreement was a key supporting argument for its allocation as opposed to the allocation of a large number of smaller sites throughout the county. However, securing affordable housing through the planning process and securing a mix of housing types and sizes (originally consistent with PPG1 and PPG3 and, in the future, with PPS1 and PPS3) has not been without its problems. On the issue of affordable housing, the two authorities jointly commissioned a housing needs assessment from Fordham Associates in 2000, which informed a specific affordable housing policy for Stevenage West within the Stevenage District Plan (an identical policy would have been inserted into the North Hertfordshire plan had this not been withdrawn following the publication of PPG3). The policy required at least 20 per cent affordable rented housing and a further 5–10 per cent 'other tenures'. This meant that the local authority set a 25 per cent negotiation threshold for affordable housing. Citing Circular 6/98 and its emphasis on tenure neutrality, the developers argued that the site could support no more than 20 per cent affordable housing, and that the local authority should not call for a specific tenure mix or – by implication – require the involvement of RSLs. A particular sticking point was the confusion over the relationship between planning gain and housing corporation funding (Social Housing Grant) for RSL developments. Progress was slowed by questions over funding mix, how much SHG would be required and how much subsidy would be delivered by the developer or how much of the cost of delivering affordable housing would be passed to the landowners. Further confusion centred on the issue of 'additionality' (see Chapter 5): how affordable housing would actually be delivered and how much gain would be extracted directly from the development consortium. On the second and wider issue of securing a mix of housing sizes and types, there was considerable disagreement between the developers and local authorities. Although promoting a balance of housing types is a stated policy objective of the planning system (PPG3, and now also Circular 5/2005 on Planning Obligations and PPS3 on housing), it is difficult to define what might be deemed an appropriate mix at different development scales. At Stevenage West, disagreement centred on whether 'appropriate mix' should be an objective set for the development as a whole or whether it should be an objective attached to smaller development parcels, and if so *how* small. In practice, the developer argued that in the context of individual parcels, the mix of homes built should be determined purely by the prevailing market and not defined by local planning. Such an approach was felt to have both strengths and weaknesses. A prescriptive approach by the planning teams may have resulted in a less flexible development framework, unresponsive to changing needs and market demands, especially if the mix were defined well in advance of the developer going on-site. However, without greater control by the planning authority, there remained a risk that the developer would build to the upper end of the market, delivering executive-style homes in the hope of greater profit. This issue was taken up during a 2004 Public Inquiry.

The development at Stevenage West has now been sucked into broader 'Sustainable Communities' and 'Growth Areas' debates initiated by the publication of government's Sustainable Communities Plan (ODPM, 2002b; 2003a). In November 2004, the Inspector at the Stevenage West Public Inquiry submitted his report to John Prescott and an interim decision emerged in late 2005 when the Deputy Prime Minister indicated that he was 'minded to approve' at least the first phase of the development (see Chapter 10). At the same time, work was underway by the East of England Regional Assembly aimed at transforming the 2004 draft of RPG14 into an East of England Plan (a Spatial Strategy, as required by the 2004 Planning and Compulsory Purchase Act). A recent draft of this plan (tested in front of an independent panel at an EIP commencing in September 2005), proposed that 478,000 additional homes need to be built in the region: 79,600 in Hertfordshire, of which 15,800 will be sited in North Hertfordshire. In relation to Stevenage, the plan proposed 8,500 dwellings to the north and west of the town within North Hertfordshire District, and a further 6,400 within Stevenage Borough. In the context of its Communities Plan (see Chapter 9), government wishes to add a further 18,000 houses to the regional total, another issue to be discussed at the EIP. Within the emerging policy context, it appears that the urban extension at Stevenage West will eventually go ahead. But the planning process has proven to be a significant source of frustration from the point of view of the development consortium. The developers went from a position of having the certainty of a Structure Plan allocation in 1998 through the uncertainty of a politically motivated Structure Plan Review two years later, to the current situation in which government, keen to promote the principle of 'Growth Areas' looks likely to exert the pressure needed to ensure that the development gets the green light. Perhaps the greatest hurdle facing the Stevenage West development in the early part of this decade was the apparent contradictions and inconsistencies between the two levels of strategic (county) and development (district) planning. The two-tier planning system generated considerable tension, from the point of view of the consortium, and probably from the point of view of many of the planners involved in this process. This tension also resulted in a reluctance to commit the necessary resources to the planning of the scheme, and therefore the issues of design, the phasing of the development, and the need for affordable housing have all been put on a back-burner until John Prescott and his successors move from being 'minded to approve' the proposal to giving it formal endorsement.

Experience at Stevenage arguably provides a supporting case for government's decision to abolish Structure Planning and to create a system of statutory regional planning. It also illustrates the tension between greenfield and brownfield development, a tension that is particularly pronounced in southern England where the government's CP will inevitably mean some building on greenfield, and green belt, land. Indeed, Barker's *Review of Housing Supply* (2004) seems to add further support for the types of strategic development that Stevenage West represents. Debates centred on urban extensions are unlikely to disappear in the years ahead, and it seems more likely that the Stevenage story will be repeated in other towns and cities.

Local housing in the countryside

The effect of migration into and out of the countryside is perhaps the critical issue that the planning system has been called upon to address in rural areas. It has resulted in conflicts that primarily centre on local housing markets and on access to housing among those groups considered 'local'. In any housing market, the 'powerful' (wealth and income rich) find advantage at the expense of the 'weak' (wealth and income poor). But the weak may endure particular difficulties in accessing housing where there is more intensive competition for a limited housing resource. This is the situation in many rural areas where planning has sought to restrict housing supply (on environmental and landscape grounds) while housing demand (among those seeking to retire to the countryside, or those looking to buy second homes: see Gallent *et al.*, 2002) has increased. The dual pressures exerted by planning and migration are often viewed as the key ingredients of the rural housing problem. These are briefly introduced below before we consider how planning has sought to respond to this pressure – and the consequent problem of housing access experienced by some local groups – drawing on experience in Pembrokeshire, a rural area comprising a National Park and a Unitary Authority, in south-west Wales.

In the countryside, local housing markets are often constrained by a planning system that has, since 1947, prioritised urban containment. This priority is implicit in the designation of Green Belt, National Parks, AONBs and so forth, providing such areas with anti-development protections. More generally, PPG7 (now Planning Policy Statement 7) has restricted the development of new housing in the open countryside and general planning principles seek to limit development to within prescribed boundaries within and around existing settlements. Hence, there is little scope for growth within many rural communities. However, government has accepted the need for some growth in the countryside and has adopted a strategy of directing development to 'key rural settlements', handing some centres the task of absorbing growth and meeting the wider needs of other smaller settlements within their hinterland (see Cloke,

1979: the same strategy, repackaged as the 'market towns initiative', re-emerged in the Rural White Paper of 2000; DTLR, 2000). Wellesbourne (in Stratford-upon-Avon district – see Chapter 5) has, for example, enjoyed the dubious honour of being a key settlement for more than 30 years. While other villages in its immediate vicinity have retained their 'rural character', Wellesbourne has grown at a phenomenal rate, tripling its population since 1976 and absorbing several thousand new houses since the early 1980s.

But outside the key settlements, growth is heavily constrained by the planning system: this is manifest locally in a desire to protect rural settings and communities, and nationally, by the objective of containing urban growth and maintaining environmental quality. Central to the problems that rural areas face is the fact that they exist under the same market conditions as other areas, but with the added complication of tight restraint. This means that where demand for housing is strong (as is the case in many, but not all rural areas: see Bevan *et al.*, 2001: 57), the impact on house prices and housing affordability may be pronounced. In 2005, the newly formed Commission for Rural Communities (CRC) published an affordability index for the English regions. The index 'represents housing affordability based on the expected monthly mortgage payment on the basis of the mean house price compared to the median monthly household income by area classification' (CRC, 2005: 44). Index figures – shown in Table 6.1 – reveal that housing is less affordable in villages and hamlets than in towns or in urban areas with populations exceeding 10,000.

Table 6.1 Affordability index for English regions, 2004

Region	Hamlet and isolated dwellings	Village	Town and fringe	Urban >10k
East Midlands	5.4	5.0	3.9	3.7
East of England	6.7	5.6	4.7	4.6
North-east	5.0	4.2	3.3	3.4
North-west	5.8	4.9	4.0	3.5
South-east	8.2	6.9	5.3	5.6
South-west	7.5	6.4	5.4	4.8
West Midlands	6.8	5.7	4.4	3.9
Yorkshire and the Humber	5.3	4.9	3.8	3.4

Source: Commission for Rural Communities, 2005: 44

Generally, the housing market functions in rural areas in much the same way is it does elsewhere: however the setting is more restrictive and the potential for the market to absorb growth (and balance supply with demand, thereby stabilising prices) is far lower. The combination of migration pressure and planning constraint may place inflationary pressure on both the cost of new and existing housing. Allied with low rural wage levels – and the loss of social housing through privatisation (see Chapter 3) – this can have important implications for housing access. Median gross wage levels in rural areas of England in 2004 were £318 per week compared with almost £370 per week in urban areas (CRC, 2005: 77). It is also the case that average wage figures in the countryside are often inflated by a concentration of commuting households who derive their income from urban jobs: wages in the 'agricultural' or tourist economy may be far lower than the median. In this context of disadvantage and limited housing access, planning's role in rationing land supply might be viewed as inherently negative. But it is often only viewed as problematic when coupled with migration pressures.

Champion (2000) has argued that the movement of people from urban to more rural areas is driven by a 'trilogy' of factors, categorised under the headings 'flight', 'quest' and 'overflow'. He argues that the term 'flight' suggests a one-way movement away from cities by people pushed by negative urban drivers. Although this may happen in some instances, rural–urban migration is not all one-way traffic though as the 1991 and 2001 censuses revealed, there is a trend among 'professional and managerial workers' residing in larger conurbations to move out to the shire counties. Champion further agues that rather than seeing movement as 'flight' (driven by 'urban negatives'), it may be more accurately conceptualised as 'quest' with people seeking a different lifestyle or particular residential qualities on which they place a personal premium. Hence, various studies have pointed to the 'lure of the countryside', which may offer some of the qualities that people seek. But the quest may involve more than one step (or may not just result in a straightforward urban–rural movement). Some quests may lead people to the suburbs, the urban fringe, or to larger towns: although in some instances, these moves may represent staging posts on the journey to the countryside. Champion conceptualises this quest as a counter-urbanisation cascade (ibid., 14). The final process in Champion's trilogy is that of 'overflow': here, a lack of room in cities results in a natural drift away from urban areas. This third process also sits squarely with the concept of a 'cascade', with population gravitating to satellite towns or locations further afield.

The Commission for Rural Communities (2005: 17) points out that 'migration to rural areas has been a key feature of net, area-to-area population movement in England for over 20 years'. Indeed, the urban to rural shift based on

Plate 13 New village housing in Powys – notice how well the red-brick terrace blends with the traditional detached Welsh stone-cottage to the right . . . (near Welshpool, 1993)

internal migration estimates (from the Office for National Statistics), was 103,700 for the year July 2002 to July 2003. Migration pressure in the countryside may derive from a range of sources including: retirement and the succumbing of ex-urban households to the aforementioned 'lure of the countryside'; commuting, with households moving out of urban areas either in search of a better quality of family life or simply more space (a trend that might be accelerated by the current drive to greater urban compaction and higher density living); alternative lifestyles, with some people looking to 'escape the rat race' (Champion, 2000: 19) and choosing to take up new professions in the countryside or opting for careers that allow them to 'telework' (Clarke, 2000); second home purchasing (for recreation), with those living in cities deciding that they want/need somewhere to escape to during weekends or during holidays (Gallent *et al.*, 2005); second home purchasing (for investment), sometimes by people who are forced to rent in pressured urban markets (i.e. London) but want 'a place of their own' somewhere where they can afford to buy; and finally, the seasonal pressure from those occupying holiday homes: not a 'true' migration pressure, but a pressure on the housing market if properties are removed from the market for this purpose.

It has been acknowledged that many of these migration pressures (with the exception of commuting) frequently concentrate in the most attractive rural areas, where landscape value is at its highest and planning constraint at its most rigorous (Schmied, 2002: 20). Thus, the National Parks have been placed under particularly significant pressure from those retiring from cities and those buying second homes. This concentration has long concerned both those in the planning profession and academics: Shucksmith's (1981) study of housing pressure in the Lake District and his subsequent analysis of the long-term effects of planning intervention (1990) are especially noteworthy. It is often in these areas that planning is pro-active in trying to formulate an effective response. This response is sometimes positive – promoting the use of planning polices to procure affordable housing – and sometimes negative in the sense that it seeks to restrict the use of housing to those households deemed 'local'. In many areas, new housing is needed (if communities are to develop in the future), but there is a fear that additional house building will act as a catalyst for further migration. Hence planning can become even more restrictive than the general policy context dictates. We looked at the use of 'planning exceptions' to procure affordable housing in the last chapter, but these have rarely generated enough housing to meet local need (Gallent and Bell, 2000; Hoggart and Henderson, 2005). Hence, planning authorities regularly face a dilemma in rural areas: how to respond to migration pressures (resist it or manage it?) while addressing local needs. We now look at this dilemma in the context of Pembrokeshire.

In response to acute migration pressures of the type outlined above, The Pembrokeshire Coast National Park Authority (PCNPA) inserted a policy into its Draft Joint Unitary Development Plan (JUDP: joint with Pembrokeshire Council) in January 2002. This policy – essentially an occupancy condition applied to all new housing in designated Sustainable Communities (which covered most of the attractive and deeper rural parts of the county) – limited the use and future occupancy of all new housing to 'local need'. In the Park, migration pressures have combined with limited environmental capacity (to carry new housing) and low local wage levels, to cause an overheating of the housing market to the detriment of local first-time buyers and other disadvantaged groups. External housing demand in the Park is frequently expressed by retiring households and by those purchasing second homes (Tewdwr-Jones *et al.*, 2002). These combine with other trends to present the planning authorities with a particular Pembrokeshire problem.

For example, Pembrokeshire has a rural economy that lacks diversity: it is strongly reliant on a handful of sectors including farming, fishing and tourism. It also suffers from high levels of unemployment (particularly seasonal employment tied to tourism) and wage levels are low. There is also considerable pressure to limit future house building and a belief that a continuation of past rates of housing completion would have a detrimental impact on the landscape of the Park. Landscape protection is assigned high priority because it is felt that any erosion of environmental quality could impact on visitor numbers, bringing economic consequences. The area also has an ageing population profile, generated by a loss of young people (who leave in search of jobs) and an influx of retired households; it also has a seasonal population comprising second-homeowners who may affect the use and viability of local services. These trends have implications for housing in the National Park: second-homeowners have purchased almost a third of all new housing coming on the market in recent years; there are limited new-build opportunities given the environmental sensitivities noted; and an increase in house prices has been attributed to externally derived housing demand, though the underlying cause is land scarcity and planning constraint.

This context is not unusual and many of the same conditions and trends are found in many remoter rural areas, especially those with high landscape value, across Britain. And Pembrokeshire's response to this challenge is not unique: i.e. the introduction of the 'local needs' policy outlined above. Indeed, the National Park Authority remarked in 2001 'that many of our National Parks seem to be at different times recognising quite similar issues, i.e. the scarcity of housing land, the predominance of second homes and retirement homes

Plate 14 Dale, Pembrokeshire National Park – one of the 26 designated 'sustainable communities' (Pembrokeshire, 2002)

and the consequential displacement of local demand' (Pembrokeshire Coast National Park Authority Evidence for Housing Policy, 2001: para. 57). It added that 'the Lake District was first to tackle the issue'. Indeed the Lake District Special Planning Board (LDSPB, established in 1974) introduced a similar policy in 1977 designed to 'restrict completely all new development to that which can be shown to satisfy a local need' (LDSPB, 1977; see LDSPM, 1980). In the remainder of this case study we look at Pembrokeshire's response to its current housing pressures, exploring possible implications with reference to earlier experience in the Lake District in the north-west of England.

We have already noted that the Pembrokeshire policy sought to restrict housing occupancy to 'locals', requiring that all new housing must be occupied only by persons meeting specific residency criteria. This was 'Policy 47' in the Joint Unitary Development Plan, and is the re-manifestation of an approach that has made several appearances in local plans in recent years. The similarities in the purpose and intent of the Lake District's 'local needs' policy (1977) and that originally outlined in PCPNA's draft deposit JUDP were striking. Like Pembrokeshire Coast's policy, it was designed to ensure that remaining development sites were used for local needs housing: a response to land scarcity. Indeed, the LDSPB argued that there was a pressing need to ensure that 'the diminishing number of sites where new housing will be acceptable are used to maintain rural life' (LDSPB, 1978: 22). And like Pembrokeshire Coast's policy, the LDSPB's approach faced immediate scrutiny. In the panel report from a 1981 EIP it was argued that:

> planning is concerned with the manner of the use of land, not the identity or merits of the occupiers. Planning permission for a particular use of land otherwise suitable for that use cannot appropriately be refused simply because the planning authority wishes to restrict the user.
>
> (DoE, 1981: 10–11: quoted in Shucksmith, 1990)

These same views were reflected in the Welsh Assembly Government's objection to Policy 47. The Assembly Government argued that 'land allocated in UDPs as housing land should be available to all applicants and not allocated specifically to meet the needs of particular sections of the community' (WAG, 2002: 5). Moreover, there was concern over the wider impacts of such a policy on the operation of the housing market in the Park: impacts that are now examined in more detail.

Attempts in rural areas to protect 'local interests' through planning policy are problematic: Pembrokeshire's policy tried to prevent new housing from being built for migrants to the county and National Park, including retiring households

Plate 15 Derelict cottage, Musslewick, Pembrokeshire – reinstatement to residential use would be subject to the planning authority's Policy 47 on 'housing within the National Park'. (This particular cottage has since been rebuilt) (Pembrokeshire, 2002)

and second-home buyers. The policy was to be applied in 26 so-called 'sustainable communities'. One problem with such restrictions is that attractive areas remain attractive irrespective of planning restrictions. If no new housing is available then demand will tend to focus on existing housing stock, causing a concentration of demand pressure in that section of the market. Alternatively, some pressure may refocus to nearby settlements, pushing 'market distortions' elsewhere, but not preventing them. Hence, such restrictive policies may have a number of unforeseen consequences: they may impact on new housing development, reducing supply, and on the second-hand market, intensifying competition. Those locals who should, if reality had followed intent, have benefited from the policy often end up as the biggest losers.

On the issue of development impact Shucksmith (1990) notes that builders in rural areas are often building specifically for an external market. If this market is restricted, then it cannot be assumed that they will simply start building for local needs; many may decide to focus on projects in other areas, where no restrictions apply. In the Lake District, the local needs policy impacted on the supply of new housing as 'builders ceased speculative residential developments, partly because of the uncertainties raised by the new policy, but principally because of the greater difficulty of acquiring suitable land with planning permission' (Shucksmith, 1990: 122). The combined effects of the policy on both housing demand (reducing the potential market within certain areas where the policy applied) and housing supply (limiting the size and number of developments by changing the environment for house builders) meant that the policy itself had no discernible impact on the price of new homes. Its biggest impact was on the second-hand market, leading Capstick (1987: 144) to conclude that it 'did more to assist existing homeowners than it did to assist new homeowners'.

This is a key problem with 'restrictive' planning policies in rural areas. Planning can seek to influence new building and the occupancy of new homes, but it has no control over the second-hand market. Hence, restrictions in the new-build market may have a more general impact on the wider housing market. The supply of houses already built and occupied tends to be insensitive to changes in house prices: people decide to move not in response to the changing value of their homes but because of changing household circumstances and needs. Shucksmith (1990: 123) argues that this reality makes the supply of existing dwellings very 'price inelastic'. This means that prices in the existing market will only even out relative to demand if there is a sudden surge in people putting their homes on the market (and hence an increase in supply to balance out demand). Because this is unlikely, restrictions on the occupancy of new housing, and hence a re-focusing of aspiration and demand on existing housing, will mean that property values in areas subject to occupancy restriction are likely to surge upwards.

In the Lake District, a substantial increase in property values (in the market for existing housing) deterred some outside buyers from seeking retirement or second homes in the National Park. This was applauded as a success. However, South Lakeland District Council claimed that this led buyers to focus their attention outside of the Park and resulted to an inflation of house prices both in South Lakeland itself and elsewhere on the Park's boundary. Because prices may rise in Pembrokeshire Coast, they may also rise throughout south-west Wales as the market is affected by Policy 47. This inflationary pressure (caused by restricting new supply and the intensification of competition for existing housing) may reduce the affordability of housing more generally.

Clearly, this is not good news for lower income local households. In very general terms, planning restriction tends to increase the scarcity value of housing in the countryside (Hoggart, 2003), pushing up market prices. Occupancy restrictions, because of their potential to influence house building activity, may accentuate this general planning impact. However, an important lesson from the

Lake District and one that is relevant to the situation in Pembrokeshire is that restrictions on the occupancy of new market housing are likely to depress land values. This may enable RSLs to more effectively compete for development land, stretch grant subsidy, and build more affordable homes. Because of higher prices in the market for existing housing and a reduced supply of new market homes, lower income groups in Pembrokeshire are likely to be more reliant on social housing and so handing associations a small degree of competitive advantage could be beneficial.

This leads to another important point: the reliance on market solutions to housing affordability issues in most rural areas. It is very difficult to create the conditions in which one group ('newcomers') are excluded from the market while another ('locals') enjoy relative advantage. The market favours profit maximisation and so will chase those with most spending power. This is true in both the second-hand market and in the market for new build. Existing home-owners seeking to move will sell their homes to outside buyers who have seen the property advertised by a London estate agent or on the Internet. Only rarely will a local vendor sell for 25 or 50 per cent market value to a local buyer. Similarly, private developers and their shareholders are unlikely to accept a drastically squeezed profit margin by providing for local needs, unless they are motivated by social concerns. Such concerns are central to the operation of registered social landlords. Despite the recent history of rolling back public and social housing provision (see Chapter 3), there is a clear role for RSLs in the countryside. Planning can effectively hand social housing providers some competitive advantage (see above) enabling them to provide more affordable homes for rent, or for shared-equity schemes perhaps on land earmarked solely for social housing. This was one recommendation emerging from a Housing Forum Report published by the Joseph Rowntree Foundation in 2006 (p. 4). But planning restrictions are increasingly tied to market housing solutions that suffer the problems outlined in this case study.

A policy of restriction remains within Pembrokeshire's JUDP, and the Park Authority looks set to defend the policy within the courts if the need arises. But despite the rhetoric of protecting local interests, the clearest immediate impact of the policy is likely to be environmental. Restrictions within the sustainable communities will result in fewer housing approvals and therefore a reduction in house building. Because of this, it could be reasonably argued that Policy 47 is really a device for reducing – and diverting – development rather than for helping to meet local needs, a conclusion reached by Shucksmith in relation to the Lake District. This returns us to an issue introduced in Chapter 1: the inherent tension between 'developmental' and 'environmental' agendas in planning. This tension is central to the housing problems faced in many rural areas. In some instances, an anti-development agenda is promoted by newcomers who expect their adoptive communities to remain unchanged: they have 'bought into' a preconceived idea of what rural living is about, and refuse to see this modified by further housing or other forms of development. In other instances, it is existing communities (or often the homeowners within those communities), who – allied with political representatives – lead the crusade against social or affordable housing, which they perceive to be an inappropriate 'urban' housing solution. But above these local concerns sits a broad and pervasive environmental agenda which places great premium on protecting the British countryside. For more than 50 years, planning has been its most potent weapon, used with regularity for halting new housing development despite overwhelming evidence of need. The DEFRA's Rural Housing Commission maintains that planning must continue to play a crucial role in finding solutions to rural housing problems (DEFRA, 2006: 20). But restriction alone – for whatever purpose – cannot deliver decent homes for all within rural areas.

Conclusions

In this chapter we have offered three inter-related stories. The first dealt with planning's regional dimension and the way in which political debates shape the adoption of housing numbers targets within regional planning guidance – now Regional Spatial Strategies – and their allocation within development planning. The second story was concerned with a 'strategic allocation' that exemplifies current debates over housing on green or brownfields, together with the issues of design, density and affordability. These first two narratives were concerned, in part, with southern England and with government's promotion of housing growth and 'sustainable communities'. For the third story – dealing with housing in the countryside – we were obliged to look further afield, and refocused on the County of Pembrokeshire in Wales. The Pembrokeshire case study exemplifies many of the debates that regularly run in more rural areas: debates over migration pressure, housing quality and the tension between environment and development. It was also concerned with 'sustainable communities', a term that has entered the nomenclature of UK planning but can mean a wide range of different things. This is a theme we return to in Chapter 8.

None of the three stories set out in this chapter are complete. At the regional level, all the various government offices and regional assemblies are busying themselves with the task of transforming regional planning guidance into spatial strategies, and all are looking again at housing numbers in the light of government's CP. At Stevenage, a decision over the future of the western urban extension is expected shortly, but the planning of Stevenage West is likely to be complicated by the arrival of a finalised Planning Policy Statement 3, some time in 2006. And in Pembrokeshire, the JUDP went to public inquiry in 2004, and the Park Authority is currently working on amendments to Policy 47 (which are unlikely to affect the substance of the Policy) which it hopes to fully implement successfully in the near future, though what success will actually mean in practice is unclear.

In planning, there are few completed stories at the present time. Policy is in a state of transition, with many narratives caught between two systems and a number of competing agendas. In the remaining chapters of this book, attention turns to the changing shape of planning policy as it relates to the delivery of decent homes. Of particular concern from this point onwards are the broad, perhaps more fundamental reforms that may affect future housing supply and affordability (Chapter 7) within the context of government's stated desire to deliver Sustainable Communities (Chapter 8).

Chapter 7
The new market agenda in housing supply

Introduction

Housing demand and consequent supply is, quite obviously, a central concern of this book. We have already touched on this issue at several points, introducing the need to balance greater affordability (and access) with more sustainable patterns of development, in the opening chapter. These same issues were examined in greater depth in Chapters 4 and 5, and again – in the context of different settings – in the last chapter. The purpose of this current chapter is to provide a focused analysis of current supply debates in the light of the 2004 Treasury-sponsored 'Barker Review' (Barker, 2004). Our analysis is set in the context of apparent undersupply: the planning system has not released sufficient land for new house building in recent years despite considerable acceleration in the rate of household formation driven, to a large extent, by a fall in average household size. The most recent household projections, published in March 2006, suggest that an additional 4.8 million households will form in England between 2003 and 2026 and that the number of persons per household will decline from 2.34 to 2.10 during this same period. The apparent scale of undersupply – if planning continues to 'permit' current levels of house building – was set out in the first chapter: by 2016, the mismatch between what has been built and what is 'needed' will be in the order of 1.5 million homes. Government has become increasingly concerned with this apparent mismatch: no administration wants to preside over, or be seen as the architect of, the biggest housing crisis since the mid-Victorian era. In the introduction to the draft of Planning Policy Statement 3 (ODPM, 2005a), the minister responsible for planning argues that:

> for too long, the housing market has not responded sufficiently to housing demand. Over the last 30 years, we have seen a 30% increase in the number of households, but a 50% drop in the level of house building. Some areas have seen strongly rising demand with little increases in supply and rising house prices as a result, and others have struggled with problems of low demand.
>
> (Yvette Cooper, Foreword to Consultation on PPS3, ODPM, 2005a)

This is the context for this chapter. Put simply, the 'housing market' has not been able to respond to demand because of the way the planning system operates. This same argument was aired in the Planning Green Paper in 2001 which initiated a programme of rolling reform aimed at streamlining the system and making it more responsive to business (including house building) interests. But the new PPS3 – as discussed in Chapter 1 – is not simply concerned with achieving greater systemic efficiency: rather, it points to the need for an entirely new rationale for housing land release. The ultimate aim of this chapter is to analyse this new rationale. The Barker Review of Housing Supply published in 2004 argued strongly for a break from the past practice of allocating land for housing at a fixed point in the planning cycle and then restricting supply to designated sites irrespective of shifting market conditions. Barker suggested an 'affordability led' system of land release, with planning responding to 'market signals', releasing additional land for housing where house prices come to exceed median wage levels by a particular factor. This chapter focuses on two key questions:

1   How has planning traditionally responded to housing demand, including projections of future household formation?
2   How might planning respond to demand in the future, perhaps by moving to an 'affordability-led' model of land release?

In the first of the next two sections we examine existing demand responses and consequent supply concerns. In the second section, we examine the affordability-led model, and its possible implications for future housing supply in England. Beyond a general discussion of key issues – in relation to the status quo and possible movement to a market model – we focus on the current situation in the south-east of England and ongoing debates relating to housing supply and its consequences.

Housing supply – the status quo

The current system of housing land release is dominated by the 'plan-led' ethos. As noted in the introduction, land for housing is generally allocated at the beginning of the planning cycle, though some allowance is made for 'windfall' sites becoming available during the life of a plan (i.e. land that was not initially available, but which becomes available, and by virtue of it being previously developed, may help a local authority achieve its land recycling aspirations). The central importance of a plan-led approach to housing – and all other land-use regulation – was emphasised in the Planning and Compensation Act 1991, which asserted that a local plan, once adopted, becomes the primary consideration in development control: local authorities must adopt a plan and they must adhere to its policies to the letter of the law. At the current time, there is some concern that any departure from this approach (to an 'affordability-led' model) to land release will create uncertainty in the planning system. In a recent submission to an ODPM Select Committee on Affordability and Housing Supply, the RSPB (one of government's statutory consultees) noted their 'concern about the degree to which the allocation of housing land will [in the future] be market-driven rather than driven by the interests of good planning and sustainable development' (Planning, 2006a: 8). There is a belief that the 'plan-led' system gives planning greater control over eventual outcomes and that any weakening of this system might result in more haphazard development that is unable to fulfil community or environmental objectives. The government's existing – 'status quo' – view on the need for the system to follow-though on initial plan policy was emphasised by the Joseph Rowntree Foundation in 1994:

> The Government sees the role of the planning system in relation to housing provision as principally to ensure that sufficient residential land is allocated for building in accordance with policies set out in local authority Development Plans.
>
> (Joseph Rowntree Foundation, 1994)

In relation to housing supply, planning must concern itself with sufficient land release for a five-year housing supply (trickling down from the national and regional projections of household growth): it must also ensure predictability, maintaining control of what is built and where; and it must ensure that permissions for new housing reflect broader policy objectives, including the aspirations relating to density, design and affordability discussed at some length in Chapter 5. These principles can be illustrated in any local plan. For example, Mole Valley District Council in southern England began a review of its existing plan in 1993 in the context of the Planning and Compensation Act 1991. By April of 1994, it issued its first consultation draft. A revised version of this draft was put on deposit at the end of the same year, and in 1995 a Public Inquiry was held into objections and representations. The version that was finally adopted in 1996 contained three key housing policies: HSG4, the designation of housing land; HSG6, 'reserve sites' in case the HSG4 site allocations proved inadequate; and HSG9, a general policy noting the authority's intention to negotiate affordable housing on residential development sites within the built-up area (e.g. in towns such as Dorking). The relationship between the policies and the plan – the 'proposals map' – is shown in Figure 7.1. In this instance, there is some commitment to flexibility. The local authority recognised that needs may change during

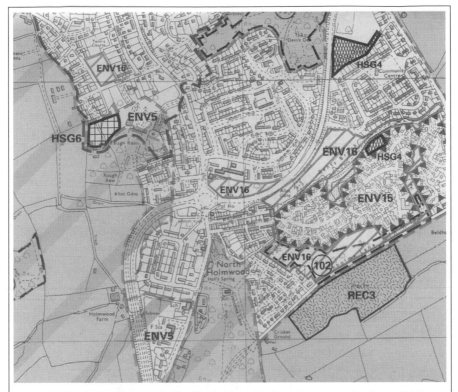

HSG6: RESERVE HOUSING LAND 'The District Council will continue to monitor the availability of housing land. If it is satisfied that land is required in addition to that allocated in Policy HSG4 [. . .] consideration will be given to the release of one or more of the following sites, as shown on the Proposals Map'.

HSG9: AFFORDABLE HOUSING IN THE BUILT-UP AREAS 'The Council will seek to ensure that a proportion of new dwellings provided during the period of the Plan are made available to people on lower incomes [. . .]. On sites of 0.4ha or more, the Council will negotiate with developers and landowners to ensure that a proportion of the dwellings proposed are in the form of affordable housing [. . .]'.

Figure 7.1 Housing policies in Mole Valley in 1996 (Mole Valley District Council, 1996)

the life of a plan and that planning must be in a position to respond. The general system of land release, in response to demand, is summarised in 7.2.

Figure 7.2 shows, in a much-simplified form, the steps that exist between acceptance of household projections and their conversion into regional dwelling requirements (i.e. the demand for housing) and consequent local plan preparation and site development (i.e. the supply of new housing). The movement from projections to allocations was examined at some length in the latter half of Chapter 4 (under the heading 'housing numbers') and in the opening section

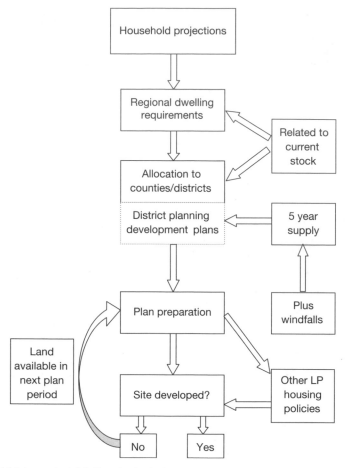

Figure 7.2 A 'status quo' model of housing land release
Source: Adapted from original unknown source

of Chapter 6 (regional housing). Essentially, 'trend figures' derived by government are translated into 'policy figures' for regional planning purposes; the amount of new housing that can be 'created' through conversion is subtracted from the total and a re-allocation is made to the incumbent planning authorities who must then ensure a 5-year land supply (making an allowance for windfalls) in accordance with the 1991 Act. Plans are prepared with this requirement in mind and land for housing is allocated in line with government policy on recycling and infill. Plans acknowledge other policy objectives, including the need to negotiate for affordable housing, and planning permissions are granted subject to these policies. At the end of a plan period, a site may or may not have been

brought forward for development (if it has not, there will still be a strong likelihood that a potential developer has bought an 'option' on the land and may
develop it in the future). Essentially, this is the standard approach for measuring
demand (priority is given to demographic forecasts, modified to some extent by
local intelligence) and for supplying new housing (up front, at the beginning of
the 5-year cycle). It is very much a 'predict and provide' approach that the current
UK government, at the time of writing, has tried to move away from (or, rather
merely distance itself from) since coming to power in 1997. Planning Policy
Guidance Note 3, published by the Department for Transport, Local Government and the Regions (DTLR) in 2000, was at the heart of this system and
stressed the central role of planning in delivering sufficient housing:

> One of the roles of the planning system is to ensure that new homes are provided in
> the right place and at the right time, whether through new development or the conver-
> sion of existing buildings. The aim is to provide a choice of sites which are both
> suitable and available for house building. This is important not only to ensure that
> everyone has the opportunity of a decent home but also to maintain the momentum
> of economic growth. Economic growth should not be frustrated by a lack of homes
> for those wishing to take up new employment opportunities: but to promote sustain-
> able development, the need for economic growth has to be reconciled with social and
> environmental considerations, particularly those of conserving and enhancing the
> quality of our environment in both town and country.
>
> (DETR, 2000a: para. 3)

At all levels (in regional bodies and within local authorities) government
called on planning to take responsibility for understanding demand and planning
for new housing in relation to environmental and physical capacity. The
relationship between housing supply and the 'momentum of economic growth'
came out strongly in PPG3 and this is an issue that we investigate further in relation to recent debates in south-east England. Another key concern in this policy
guidance was the need to review housing supply within the life of the plan, and
not to simply stand back after a plan had been adopted, waiting to see what
would happen on the ground. Planning authorities were called on to be more
proactive:

> It is an essential feature of the plan, monitor and manage approach that housing
> requirements and the ways in which they are to be met, should be kept under regular
> review. The planned level of housing provision and its distribution should be based
> on a clear set of policy objectives, linked to measurable indicators of change.
>
> (ibid.: para. 8)

In the context of more recent debates – concerning affordability-led land release – this is an interesting statement. In 2000, regional and local planning bodies were told to engage in a process of continual monitoring and to ensure that the pattern and distribution of supply reflected 'measurable indicators of change'. This change could be economic. If, for example, investment by potentially major regional employers was being held back by the fear of labour shortage, under the rationale of 'plan, monitor and manage', a regional assembly might seek a mid-cycle review of land allocations. In a sense, it would be responding to an 'economic signal'. But such reviews were likely to be the exception rather than the rule. Despite the rhetoric of plan, monitor and manage, planning authorities knew that they were still in the business of planning for housing up-front. During the preparation of development plans, local authorities were told to 'adopt a systematic approach to assessing the development potential of sites, and the redevelopment potential of existing buildings, deciding which are most suitable for housing development and the sequence in which development should take place' (ibid., para. 29). The plan-led approach remained 'systematic' and concerned with incremental and predictable development. The adoption of a 'sequential approach' to housing land allocations (imported from PPG6 on Retail Development) meant that authorities had a responsibility to use land in a systematic way, taking up recycling opportunities in existing built up areas before considering the allocation of undeveloped land. In practice:

> Sufficient sites should be shown on the plan's proposals map to accommodate at least the first five years (or the first two phases) of housing development proposed in the plan. Site allocations should be reviewed and updated as the plan is reviewed and rolled forward at least every five years. Local planning authorities should monitor closely the uptake of both previously-developed and greenfield sites and should be prepared to alter or revise their plan policies in the light of that monitoring.
>
> (ibid., 34)

Authorities were charged to review plan allocations, but in the restrictive context of a plan-led system. A fear remained that too much flexibility might lead planning authorities to 'prioritise development sites in an arbitrary manner' (ibid., 34). We saw earlier that this same fear exists in relation to a proposed 'affordability-led' approach to housing supply. Housing supply unfettered – or less fettered – by a plan-led approach will be less controllable and could result in a 'market bias'. In its evidence to the recent ODPM Select Committee on Affordability and Housing Supply, the Royal Town Planning Institute (RTPI) has suggested that while the planning system will inevitably benefit from a better understanding of housing markets, 'instead of making the planning system responsive to housing markets, we risk making [it] subservient to housing markets' (Planning, 2006a: 8). Over the last decade, government has paid lip-service to the need for greater flexibility in planning for future housing supply, but has been resistant to the notion that PPG3's 'indicators of change' could include some sort of market signal triggering additional land release for house building. However, Kate Barker's Review of Housing Supply has prompted a reappraisal of this position and it is now looking likely that some place for market signals – measuring sub-regional trends in affordability – will be found within the planning system. But this view is not only a product of 'Barker': the move to RSS, with their sub-regional focus and evidence-based policies, suggests a greater future role for local intelligence of all kinds. It is also proving difficult for the regions to agree up-front house building rates as they move from the old RPG documents to the new RSSs. The south-east of England epitomises this difficulty, with the Regional Assembly in Guildford facing an up-hill struggle to reach agreement on target building rates, which, it is feared, will not reflect future market demand. After introducing the idea of an affordability-led approach to housing supply, in the next section, we focus briefly on the situation in the south-east of England where perhaps the last PPG3-style set of regional housing figures are being rolled out, but where there is also growing concern for the potential impacts of switching from a plan-led to an affordability-led approach to housing supply.

Affordability-led housing supply

The Barker Review of Housing Supply begins with the assertion that 'the UK has experienced a long-term upward trend in real house prices. This has created problems of affordability' (Barker, 2004: 11). It is not Barker's assertion, how-ever, that a simple supply response would immediately bring price inflation under control:

> The supply of housing is not the main factor driving house price volatility and indeed some level of volatility is inevitable owing to the inherent time lags involved in new construction. *New housing supply may also have a limited effect on prices in the short term.* Prices tend to be determined by the stock of houses. In any one year new houses only account for 10 per cent of transactions and add 1 per cent to the stock. In the short run, therefore, prices will inevitably be determined chiefly by demand.
>
> (ibid., 18, emphasis added)

However, there is a view that planning has ignored price signals in the past and that this situation has contributed to the underlying problem of affordability.

Therefore, great emphasis is placed on the need to achieve 'a better balance between planning and the market' (ibid., 31) with planning not simply trying to 'make the market' but actually listening to 'market signals'. The view expressed by Barker was that:

- Regions should establish market affordability targets.
- Regional and local planning should be more responsive to market signals. Planning authorities should allocate a buffer of land for development to allow flexibility to meet market conditions. Land should be released for development in response to defined indicators of housing market disequilibrium.

On the face of it, the idea that 'planning authorities should allocate a buffer of land' is not that new. We saw in the last section that local authorities sometimes allocate 'reserve housing land', to be released for building if the principal land allocation proves to be inadequate during the life of a local plan. But such reserves are only opened up in exceptional circumstances. There needs to be strong evidence of shifting conditions for initial allocations to be changed – this is also true at the regional level where housing targets (target building rates) are fixed and not easily amended. Barker points out that 'a framework that determines housing targets with little regard to demand, and where adjustment of the projected targets is an infrequent and lengthy process, is unlikely to be inherently responsive' (Barker, 2004: 33). The reserve housing land designated within local plans is a fall back: Barker's view was that Regional Planning should integrate market information with housing numbers (the projections considered in Chapters 4 and 6) and earmark sub-regional buffers that would need to be acknowledged in local plans. Rather than local authorities designating their own reserves – without any wider market intelligence – regional planning bodies should be allowed to make strategic decisions, on the basis of price signals, which local planning would be required to respond to. This approach might, to some extent, be seen as an attack on the parochialism of local decision-making which is 'less transparent than might be desirable' and serves 'negative local attitudes to development' (ibid., 33). Arming regional planning bodies with evidence of market signals would give them a stronger hand in dealing with local NIMBY interests, so the first of Barker's key recommendations with regards to housing supply was to create a 'market affordability target' aimed at dealing with imbalances between supply and demand, both in those regions enduring a degree of oversupply, and those facing potential undersupply. This would be a long-term target, with land releases for new housing pushing the region along the right trajectory, and towards a better balance of supply and demand in the longer term.

Regions would aim to establish a market affordability target by producing a base-line assessment of regional and sub-regional housing markets (ibid., 37) and consequently, make an assessment of how much housing would be needed to achieve the target over a given time period. Critically, Barker highlights a need to establish independent Regional Planning Executives (RPEs) whose task it would be to allocate new housing targets to local authorities based on achieving the affordability target.

Developing an approach in which price signals feed into target building rates might not seem excessively radical. Regional figures already reflect the underlying demographics of growth, which are one component of market change (see Meen, 2005). But Barker's proposals were seen by many as a rebalancing of planning and the market, essentially giving the market the upper hand, allowing it to dictate the scale and distribution of future housing supply. Planning must jump when the market says jump: market signals would become an overarching rather than an underlying concern. Hence, the battleground for many is the level at which land is actually allocated – in the context of the local plan.

In the opening section of this chapter, we introduced the idea that the 'status quo' of housing land allocation is plan-led, and that there is a fear that an 'affordability-led' approach would weaken existing local plans. Barker attempts to address this concern arguing that:

> Releasing more land by revisiting the whole plan-making process from scratch would not [. . .] result in timely outcomes. Instead, local plans should be more realistic in their initial allocation of land, and more flexible in bringing forward additional land for development.
>
> (Barker, 2004: 41)

The point here is that price signals – a sudden peak in local housing demand – will not cause an immediate appraisal of plan allocations: rather, the initial allocations should anticipate change. In the last section, we noted that authorities often undersupply housing land in anticipation of unpredictable land 'windfalls'. Barker notes that 'few local authorities operate the reverse policy of over-allocating land to correct for the proportion of sites that prove un-developable. As a consequence of this asymmetry, shortfalls occur' (ibid., 41). Barker's view is that existing planning mechanisms are biased towards undersupply, both because they fail to anticipate physical constraint, and because they fail to understand the market. A 'plan-led' approach – the 'status quo' examined earlier and a product of the 1991 Act – is thought to be one in which *sufficient land* to meet projections of housing requirements is allocated at the beginning of the planning cycle. It closely accords with the view that supply generates its own demand and should therefore be strictly regulated. The sub-text is that the market needs to be controlled: planning is the gatekeeper, there to keep a lid on demand.

But a lack of responsiveness may result in market disequilibrium. The answer, according to Barker, is to create buffers of additional land in areas of high demand, 'managing' this demand and bringing land forward for development. There would be no certainty that this land would be opened up for housing, but it would be there if needed and if its release were 'triggered' by price signals. Barker and her supporters argue that the system would remain 'plan-led' but critics contend that the notion of a 'plan-led' system is washed away if allocations are inherently uncertain. It might still be claimed that land is 'allocated' but this is, in fact, a meaningless statement. Indeed:

> The local plan should not distinguish between this buffer of land and the land that would be allocated ordinarily under the current system. Developers should be able to submit applications for any site identified in the plan, subject to the conditions of the revised sequential test being met. Once sufficient land is being developed to meet an authority's housing target, then an authority could, as now, refuse planning permission for further applications. However, if predefined indicators of local housing market disequilibrium were triggered, then authorities would not be able to refuse planning permission for additional applications on the grounds that their target had been met. This would make the planning system more responsive to market signals.
>
> (Barker, 2004: 41)

Essentially, land would be allocated as before and house building would be permitted to occur in line with an authority's target (its share of regional growth), but – and this is a huge but for the critics of affordability-led planning for housing – additional building would have to be permitted if market signals were triggered, e.g. if house prices were continuing to rise steeply. For Barker, house building would still be accordance with the plan; but for many, the plan would have been superseded by a market imperative.

There are many uncertainties surrounding this affordability-led approach, and many questions that are not answered in Barker's Review of Housing Supply. Recent trends in household formation (especially the 2006 projections that post-date Barker), in house building, in house prices, and in the market disequilibrium observed in the north and south of England suggest that something, in general terms, is wrong with housing supply and with the planning system. There is some desire to improve the system, but there is general disagreement over how this improvement should be brought about. For Barker, supply triggers should be written into the system, based on worsening housing affordability, local house price increases relative to regional averages, an 'increasing premium in land prices for residential use over other uses', employment growth outstripping housing growth, and rising numbers of housing transactions (Barker, 2004: 42). The general form of triggers is suggested, but many questions are left open:

- How would such a system operate in practice? What would it mean for planning authorities and what form might the 'trigger mechanism' take?
- What would be the impact on affordability? Would an affordability-led approach to housing supply reduce market disequilibrium?
- And what are the likely implications of paying greater attention to market signals? Might a potential weakening of land-use control result in less desirable environmental and social outcomes?

The consultation draft of PPS3 (ODPM, 2005a) took some initial steps towards answering the first question. The content of government's latest statement on the role of planning in delivering new housing was briefly described in Chapter 1: the new statement places a strong emphasis on regional planning, and on sub-regional markets and affordability, asserting that future determination of housing provision and distribution should reflect 'government's overall ambition for affordability' (ibid., 10). PPS3 was shaped by the results of two consultations running consecutively in 2005: the first examined 'Planning for Mixed Communities (ODPM, 2005b) and the second 'Planning for Housing Provision' (ODPM, 2005c). The latter consultation was principally concerned with attitudes towards Barker's market-informed planning. Government expressed a need to establish a better balance between supply and demand, achieving long-term affordability, as integral to its commitment to sustainable development (ibid., 9). In the context of 'worsening affordability' – attributed to falling construction rates since the 1960s – government argued that the Barker Review reinforced the need for a step-change in housing supply and 'greater responsiveness' to the market (ibid., 11). Failure to bring about a partnership between planning and the market will, it was suggested, worsen wealth inequalities; prevent first-time buyers from entering the market; suppress household formation and result in overcrowding; result in additional homelessness and force people into temporary accommodation; and constrain economic growth. The case for greater levels of housing supply was set out in the following terms:

> The supply of housing is one of the factors leading to rising house prices and affordability. There are also factors influencing the demand for housing. These include interest rate changes, rising incomes and the return on alternative assets. Notwithstanding demand side effects, there is evidence that an increase in housing supply over the longer-term will have a positive impact on affordability.
>
> (ODPM, 2005c: 12)

The consultation offered strong endorsement to Barker's emphasis on market signals, arriving at a potential way forward. Future housing provision would be framed within 'market areas' with regional planning bodies deciding 'whether sub-regional housing markets should be designated for high levels of new homes (for example, the Thames Gateway), for managed growth, for low levels of new homes, or for managed reductions in housing' (ibid., 18). The RSS should then 'allocate housing numbers to sub-regional housing market areas and to local authorities within them'. At the local level, the plan horizon would be extended to 15 years; local authorities were called upon to rely less on windfalls (in line with Barker's recommendation in this respect) and to maintain a 'rolling supply of developable land' (ibid., 16). In practice, this would mean that the 15-year land supply comprised the 5-year allocation alongside a floating buffer. In the light of changing market conditions – indicated by price signals at the sub-regional level – planning authorities *could* be required to allow developers to dip into the buffer so as to maintain target levels of affordability (in the context of a partial RSS review – see below): 'Providing an increase in land supply should ensure developers have the flexibility to better respond to changes in market conditions' (ibid., 16).

This is, in essence, the system proposed by Barker in her Review of Housing Supply (though government has not gone with the detail of all of Barker's recommendations). The key changes from the status quo to this affordability-led approach are summarized in Table 7.1. It is an affordability-led approach in the sense that allocations to local planning would be made within the framework of regional sub-markets, and sub-market assessment. In 2005, Government proposed a 'market-responsive approach' rather than a triggered approach at the local level. Market responsiveness will possibly be realized at the regional/ sub-regional level, with the focus at the local level on the avoidance of an 'implementation gap'. This occurs where land proves to be un-developable, and therefore supply is restricted and affordability is threatened. This gap is bridged in the proposed system because authorities are required to engage in constant monitoring of land supply, and are required – if necessary – 'to bring forward land from their 10 year supply to ensure supply of developable land is maintained' (ibid., 17). In relation to Barker, this perhaps represents a halfway house: 'At the regional level, plans should use market information, in particular prices, in determining the level and distribution of housing provision within the region. Sustainability Appraisal should be used to reconcile economic, social and environmental objectives and evidence in considering options for housing provision' (ibid., 21). But similar assessments will not *directly* inform or trigger land release at the local level. That said, it is possible – and even likely – that additional 'buffer land' at the local level could be opened up as a result of sub-regional market

Table 7.1 Proposed changes to the framework for planning for housing

	Present policy and practice	*Proposed changes*
Planning for housing market areas	Regions distribute housing provision to local authorities and must take account of household projections, capacity and other constraints.	Regions continue to distribute housing provision but use sub-regional housing markets as a basis for allocating housing numbers as well as other factors and tailoring the approach to delivery to the circumstances of different markets
Identifying land	LAs plan for 10 years of housing supply, 5 years of which is allocated but some or all of this may not be available for development. Windfalls are expected to ensure delivery of housing.	Plan horizon extended to 15 years. The first 5 years is allocated and developable with less reliance on windfall in areas where it is possible to allocate land
Plan, monitor and manage	LAs encouraged to phase land for housing development but many LAs not actively managing their supply, particularly where land in the first phase proves difficult to deliver.	5-year supply rolled forward as land is developed, in line with plans. LAs required to bring forward land from their 10-year supply to ensure supply of developable land is maintained

Source: ODPM, 2005c: 17

re-assessment. The Consultation Paper asserts that housing provision in the sub-regions could 'when appropriate' be 'reviewed through a partial review of the RSS' (ibid.: 23), and this review may be prompted by local authorities experiencing faster than expected land take-up or rising house prices; changes in the regional economy brought about by business relocation; or infrastructure decisions (e.g. new roads bringing new market pressures). So, in a round-about way, review of housing provision at the sub-regional level (undertaken in part by local authorities) may trigger a partial review of the RSS, which may have a knock-on effect for local housing supply. Pressure will be brought to bear on local authorities: to maintain an appropriate land supply through permitting land releases from its additional 10-year supply that accord with reviewed targets within the regional spatial strategy.

One way or another, government seems likely to give greater credence to market signals in future planning for housing. But it is difficult to answer our first question. Official thinking on the exact role of price signals in land allocation and future housing supply remains unclear. This is illustrated in the following statement:

> it would not make sense to provide more land for development on the grounds that the take up of allocated sites was rapid if, on the other hand, house prices were falling. Equally, it would not make sense to hold back land from later phases of development on the grounds that take up of allocated sites was slow (because of downstream hold ups including delays in development control or in obtaining other consents), if on the other hand, there was evidence to suggest house prices were rising rapidly.
>
> (ODPM, 2005c: 30)

Different types of 'signal' can be contradictory. For this reason, at the end of its consultation on housing provision, government remained open to persuasion on the form that market signals should take and the exact role they might play: in fact, the consultation ended with a question to consultees. What value did they consider that market information could add to the judgements of local authorities? Responses to the consultation were published late in 2005 (on the same day as the consultation draft of PPS3):

> It was strongly argued that a 'market-led system' would not address affordable housing needs or bring house prices down. Another concern linked to the role of the market was potential for the 'plan-led' system to be undermined by a 'market-led' approach which would lead to less community involvement in the planning process.
>
> (ODPM, 2005d: 9)

At the same time, 'respondents highlighted the need to "balance" the role of the market and ensure that the apparent emphasis on economic factors did not compromise sustainable development objectives and landscape values' (ibid., 9). Generally, it was thought that too much was being conceded to the market, with the rationale of planning – balancing the economic, social and environment consequences of developing – being relegated behind a dubious market response to affordability. On the one hand, it is accepted that the 'implementation gap' is problematic, especially where completion rates fall some way behind planned provision. But making planning the slave of the market will not reduce house prices – rather it will simply fuel additional demand and not necessarily satisfy local need. In areas of exceptionally high demand, sub-regional analysis may 'trigger' more rapid local land release, but this release may not bring the local market into equilibrium where there appears to be insatiable external demand for homes, perhaps from retiring households, commuters or buyers seeking second homes. This begs a simple question: how much additional housing might be required in order for affordability to be increased and apparent equilibrium to be restored. The ODPM published their own study of affordability targets and the implications for housing supply in 2005. This was undertaken by a team from Reading University (led by Geoff Meen) and concluded that:

> large increases in construction do have significant effects on affordability, measured in terms of the ratio of lower quartile house prices to incomes. But the increases in construction have to be *large*.
>
> (ODPM, 2005e: 48, emphasis added)

The word 'large' is emphasized in the above statement: but how large? This is an almost impossible question to answer. Much depends on local circumstances. Where affordability barriers are marginal, smaller increases in housing supply may have a significant impact. But where there is a large affordability gap, a weak local economy and strong external demand, it may take a considerable level of new supply to produce a more favourable ratio of house prices to incomes. Because of the inherent complexity of affordability, it is also extremely difficult to predict when an affordability target will be achieved. The Reading team considered whether target affordability levels could be achieved by 2016 given a range of additional building levels in different regional and local contexts. They concluded that 'affordability is simply too volatile over the cycle for this to be a reliable target. Supply-side policies, linked to the planning system, cannot be used to offset the short-run cycle' (ODPM, 2005e: 49). This is because observed levels of affordability are not merely a product of wages and housing supply. One question left unanswered earlier was the form that 'price signals' should take. The Reading team demonstrated that simple signals are not appropriate: rather, affordability targets need to be grounded in an understanding of the interactions of different factors, including demography, local housing stock profiles, mortgage and central interest rates (and other financial indicators), regional employment and occupational profile, together with a range of other factors including second-homeownership. Modelling affordability is a complex business. The relative impact of new housing supply on measures of affordability is a regional, sub-regional and local matter. Indeed, the inherent complexity of this issue may lead government to back away from – or attempt to simplify – its commitment to affordability-led housing supply once a final version of PPS3 is issued. That said, the Barker Review set out the broad aim of bringing the rate of house price growth in England down from its current 2.7 per cent to 1.1 per cent (closer to European trends: Barker, 2004: 20–21) as a much broader 'affordability target' over the longer term. It acknowledged 'elasticities' (the price elasticity of supply: i.e. prices responding to supply changes inexactly, as a *function* of supply), but calculated that house price growth could be reduced to this target if supply were increased by 120,000 units per annum (nationally) above currently planned provision (ibid., 11). Meen (2005: 967) has argued that this figure could be lower if prices were less elastic (i.e. if they responded to supply in a simpler way), but because supply has an *indirect* effect on prices and 'and only works indirectly through the housing stock' (as the stock of dwellings builds up, prices slowly respond) the magnitude of provision needed to achieve Barker's target real-price growth is likely to be high, perhaps far in excess of 120,000 units (ibid., 968). As Meen's work provided a platform for much of the Barker analysis, his views on the workability and complexity of price signals, and the ease or difficulty with which national or sub-regional affordability targets might be achieved should be given considerable weight.

Finally, before moving to our case study: what are the likely implications, in terms of environmental and social impacts, of an 'affordability-led' approach to housing supply, and to the higher rates of house building suggested by Barker and Meen? This concern was the subject of a follow-up study to Barker: a 'sustainability study' (ODPM, 2005f) was commissioned by the ODPM in tandem with the 'affordability study' undertaken by the team from Reading. Given different price elasticities (see above), an assumption was made that different additional levels of housing supply would be required to meet general affordability targets. These would clearly impact on land take (for housing and associated infrastructure), on CO_2 emissions and 'waste arising', on water and transport, and on regional economies and communities (ibid., 12–19). But all impacts are dependent on the level of additional supply, and the distribution of this supply between different regions. Housing has an impact, both on the environment and on those communities where it is, or is not, provided. Again, some of these issues are now revisited in the context of the south-east.

Housing supply and planning in south-east England

The level of housing demand, consequential supply, and the potential impacts of additional house building have provoked considerable debate in south-east England. A draft version of the region's 'spatial strategy', published by the RA in 2005 (SEERA, 2005a) has been at the centre of debate over planned housing growth levels between 2006 and 2026 (the life of the plan). The draft of the strategy initially offered three levels of growth and two 'spatial options'. Annual growth levels – 25,500, 28,000 or 32,000 additional homes – represented a continuation of recent building rates, the target rate set out in existing RPG, and a higher rate respectively. The spatial options comprised a 'continuation of existing policy' rolled forward from RPG, or a 'sharper focus' with a bigger proportion of growth accommodated in areas deemed to have greater economic potential or to require regeneration. In Table 7.2, the annual growth figures (proposed) are shown next to the growth areas (top of the table) and the rest of the counties (bottom of the table). The growth shown in the top half of the table is likely to comprise infill and regeneration on larger brownfield sites

Table 7.2 Final adopted spatial options summary

Area	Continuation of existing policy			Sharper focus		
	Spatial option 1			Spatial option 2		
	25,500	28,000	32,000	25,500	28,000	32,000
Kent Thames Gateway	2,900	2,900	2,900	2,900	2,900	2,900
Milton Keynes and Aylesbury Vale	3,300	3,300	3,300	3,300	3,300	3,300
East Kent and Ashford	2,400	2,500	2,800	2,600	2,800	3,100
Central Oxfordshire	1,300	1,500	1,700	1,400	1,600	1,900
Gatwick Area	900	1,100	1,300	1,300	1,500	1,800
London Fringe	1,500	1,700	2,100	2,000	2,300	2,800
South Hampshire	2,800	3,200	3,800	2,900	3,300	4,000
Sussex Coast	2,700	3,000	3,600	2,300	2,600	3,100
Western Corridor and Blackwater Valley	3,500	4,000	4,800	4,300	4,900	5,900
Sub total	**21,300**	**23,200**	**26,300**	**23,000**	**25,200**	**28,800**
Rest of Berkshire	100	100	100	100	100	100
Rest of Buckinghamshire	200	200	300	200	300	300
Rest of East Sussex	300	400	500	400	400	500
Rest of Hampshire	1,200	1,400	1,600	700	800	1,000
Rest of Kent	700	800	1000	200	200	200
Rest of Oxfordshire	700	800	900	300	300	400
Rest of Surrey	200	200	300	200	200	200
Rest of West Sussex	400	400	500	100	100	100
Isle of Wight	400	500	600	400	400	500
Sub total	**4,200**	**4,800**	**5,700**	**2,500**	**2,800**	**3,200**
GRAND TOTAL	**25,500**	**28,000**	**32,000**	**25,500**	**28,000**	**32,000**

Note: Figures are rounded to the nearest 100, and hence may not sum

Source: Technical Note 2, Spatial Options (SEERA, 2005b: Table 8)

(e.g. the Kent Thames Gateway), or urban extensions onto some areas of green-field land (e.g. in the Gatwick Area or onto the London Fringe). The growth shown in the lower half of the table may comprise market town infill, smaller extensions or some small developments onto greenfields. The idea is that these regional figures will trickle down to local planning and become the up-front, plan-led, allocations discussed in the first part of this chapter.

A sustainability appraisal of these different options undertaken by the consultants Environmental Resources Management (ERM) in 2005 concluded that:

> The *higher growth options* (i.e. those which propose a housing growth rate of 32,000/year) are more likely to meet housing demands (and therefore ease problems of affordability) and provide for higher rates of economic growth, but will place more pressure on environmental resources, in particular transport infrastructure, water resources, land-use, waste arising, climate change etc; and.
>
> The *lower growth options* (i.e. based on a housing growth rate of 25,500/year), conversely, would have lower environmental impacts, but would not address existing housing supply problems or support as much economic growth.
>
> (ibid., para. 4.2.3)

Debate in the south-east has inevitably focused on the apparent incompatibility between the environmental capacity agenda, represented by the lowest rate, and a housing supply (and economic development) agenda thought to be best served by, at the very least, an annual growth level of 32,000 units. The lowest figures have been championed by the CPRE, and given more cautious support by Labour's political opponents. Higher figures have been supported by housing charities – especially Shelter – and by a powerful economic lobby. The consultants Deloitte (2005) have argued that 'despite achieving maximum possible improvements in productivity and economic activity, the south-east needs around 35,000 dwellings per annum to sustain an annual GVA [Gross Value Added] growth of 3 per cent to 2026' (ibid., 4). It is believed that only this level of future housing supply in the region will satisfy labour demand and ensure that economic growth does not stall. Debate in this part of England has been both emotional and technical. Essentially, the lower growth levels set out in the Draft South East Plan (below 32,000) represent a business-as-usual philosophy: the 25,500 growth figure is the continuation of an old five-year completions average (1999/00 to 2003/04) that represented a failure to deliver on the old RPG9 target; the 28,000 figure is the RPG9 target (achieved for the first time in 2003/04). Neither seeks to reflect Barker's thinking on market signals or housing affordability, and neither is concerned with the migration patterns that are a key driver of the south-east's housing market. The higher level of 32,000 units, however, is concerned with reflecting the long-term migration trends underpinning regional housing demand. SEERA explains that:

> If long-term trends in migration were to continue over the period 2001 to 2026, the south-east would see the number of households increase by 723,800 (or 22 per cent). This is equivalent to an average 29,000 households per annum. The total number of net additional homes implied by such growth would be 746,200, equivalent to an annual average of 29,800. The twenty year period 2006 to 2026 would see a higher rate of growth, equivalent to an annual average of 31,300 homes per annum.
>
> (SEERA, Technical Note 5, 2005c: 4)

However, more recent trends in migration suggest a different pattern of demographic growth:

> If short-term trends in migration were to continue over the period 2002 to 2027, the south-east would see the number of households increase by 847,300 (or 26 per cent). This is equivalent to an average 33,900 households per annum. The total number of net additional homes implied by such growth would be 874,300, equivalent to an annual average of 35,000. The twenty year period 2006 to 2026 would see a higher rate of growth, equivalent to an annual average of 35,500 homes per annum.
>
> (ibid., 4)

These migration trends suggest a potential future demand for housing that cannot be satisfied by planned provision set out in the draft of the South East Plan. Furthermore, there appears to a risk of exacerbating existing labour-supply shortfalls in the region without acceptance of a higher building rate (Gallent and Tewdwr-Jones, 2005: 34). A recent study for the RA concluded that:

- The planned housing growth levels for the south-east region will be associated with labour supply shortfalls throughout the period of the South East Plan.
- These shortfalls will be greatest in the north (Central Oxfordshire, Milton Keynes and the northern section of the Western Corridor) and in the central area (London Fringe, Gatwick area and Sussex Coast).
- Elsewhere (i.e. in the east and the south) shortfalls will be smaller, but still apparent.

But it added that:

- Higher levels of planned housing growth will fuel further economic growth, and may not be able to keep pace with labour demand. There is no simple formula for ensuring that labour demand is satisfied within the region simply by building more homes.

• The region will continue to rely on external labour supplies, and its reliance on external labour is likely to growth during the life of the SE Plan.

On 'labour supply grounds', the case for additional house building is suspect: while it is true that serious undersupply may erect a barrier to economic growth, higher rates of house building could result in an 'overheating' economy with housing supply unable to keep pace with labour demand. This is clearly a 'theoretical' concern, but the problems of undersupply versus the difficulties of oversupply suggests the need for some median level of growth that balances the needs of the economy with other concerns, including housing affordability and environmental capacity. Perhaps nowhere else at the present time is the environmental perspective on growth more at odds with this housing supply/economic growth agenda. The CPRE, in its recent report *Building on Barker* argues that 'there is not a long-term undersupply of market homes' (2005: 4) and any move to raise house building levels will result in oversupply with severe environmental consequences. The CPRE has taken particular exception with Barker's view – discussed in detail in the previous part of this chapter – that demand, reflected in house prices, should play a greater role in dictating future housing supply: 'we strongly disagree with the Barker Review recommendation that house prices should play a leading role in the planning of new homes, with more land being released when prices are high' (ibid., 6). The CPRE is not alone in its view that supply frequently generates additional demand, and new supply often results in further migration with new housing consumed by affluent migrants rather than those local households barred from the market because of high prices. A resistance to 'demand' and a more limited focus on the measures of need is the standard environmental perspective response to the 'threat' of house building, especially house building outside built-up areas. The arguments are all very simple: demand is generated by house building, and without house building, there is no new demand; towns and villages can therefore remain as they are, with planning simply meeting local need (through planning agreements with landowners) when this need arises.

But fears surrounding the environmental impacts of new housing are matched by concerns over the switch from a plan-led to an affordability-led approach to housing supply. Additional land release should, according to Barker (again, see last section), be triggered by market signals and one such signal is house price inflation (set against wage levels: Meen, 2005: 970). But the south-east is a region of significant contrasts in terms of such market signals. Work by WSP Consultants (2005) for the RA has revealed that in 2001, the south-east region was a 'net exporter of 175,000 commuters – 5 per cent of its resident labour force' (ibid., ii). An exodus of home-buyers from London into the south-east – with subsequent return commuting – is a key feature of the region's housing market. Some villages and towns within easy reach of rail links have become housing demand hotspots with prices rising well beyond the reach of local buyers. What the CPRE does not want is house price rises in these settlements to be used as a trigger for further house building, which it believes will only fuel additional commuter in migration; rather, the only reasonable course of action in such situations is to focus on local need through a provision of affordable homes. This view is echoed in DEFRA's recent affordable rural housing commission report (DEFRA, 2006), though the 'Barker agenda' is seen as having a role in rural areas where too many villages have been 'frozen in aspic' (ibid., 6).

But on occasions, a reliance on market signals might well cause an intensification of demand. The question, therefore is how might planning reconcile the regional and sub-regional view of market efficiency (emphasised in the new PPS3) with the local demand pressures that might result in a concentration of development in and around some rural hotspots? Planning's switch to a more strategic outlook (with greater emphasis on the regional framework) and to a market rationale suggests an erosion of local power; but this is contradicted by a coupling of development planning – in the form of local development frameworks – with community strategies (a product of the Local Government Act 2000). There is now increased danger of Barker's market philosophy finding itself at loggerheads with local interests. It is not at all clear how the new system will work in practice, but the type of conflict witnessed at Stevenage West – see Chapter 6 – is likely to become more commonplace as local authorities use a requirement/market argument to support new house building in the context of government's CP (see Chapter 8). Clearly, there is a need for a great deal of local-market intelligence to be fed into any sub-regional analysis and it is important to ensure that pressure is not exerted on local authorities to release land for house building in overheating markets (as Barker and her supporters point out). Price signals can be read as a need to refuse as well as permit new land allocations; they can provide a case for additional low-cost housing rather than market development. But the concern of the environmental lobby is that a strategic view will take precedence and run contrary to local interests: this is the age-old fear – that planning, and especially a market-motivated brand of planning, will be locally unresponsive. Therefore, such planning agendas – whether market-driven or not – tend to be opposed. The creation of a more 'strategic system' with an elevation of power from the counties to the regions promises to be no more or less controversial than the old system.

The reality is that there is a market for housing that generates both demands and needs: planners can try to work with or resist this market. Migration is also a reality, and the economic growth agenda is important, as is the need to satisfy labour demand. But there is also an important environmental capacity argument: in the south-east, as elsewhere, there is a need to use land wisely, to match development to capacity, and to push back the barriers of constraint where necessary. There are also serious concerns over the resource implications of growth. As well as its general dislike of the market-driven approach, the CPRE emphasises the cost associated with all and any housing, particularly on green-field sites:

> With greenfield housing come new roads and, once hundreds or thousands of new homes have arrived at a new location, several other types of development – power lines, shops, schools and health centres. The Barker Review points out that a decade of accelerated house building would, in itself, cover a small percentage of England's total land surface. However, this truism underplays the non-housing development which follows in the wake of greenfield housing and the way in which development of all kinds is fragmenting the countryside, undermining the qualities of tranquillity, openness and immersion in greenery which most people value about it.
>
> (CPRE, 2005: 33–34)

In terms of physical development, it is conceded that investment in water and waste infrastructure, additional energy generation, more roads, and more basic services will form an important part of the CP (next chapter). Additional development will consume greenfield land in the region, at the fringe and beyond. The Institute of Public Policy Research has noted that an increase in single-person households in the south-east will cause a rise in water demand over the next two decades (IPPR, 2005: 3) that will be accentuated by higher rates of house building: water companies will need to invest in the upgrading of existing infrastructure, and build additional storage facilities. If more than 30,000 homes are built in the region annually, then an additional 44,000 tonnes of solid municipal waste will be generated each year. By 2025, there will need to be 15 large new landfill sites in the region, and 74 smaller sites. There will also need to be more than a thousand newly built recycling facilities and around 300 composting and other recovery/diversion sites. Energy demand will continue to outstrip generation and the RA's own wind, biomass and solar energy target (SEERA, 2005b), linking to the Regional Economic Strategy (SEEDA, 2005), will encourage planning authorities to permit more green-energy production facilities within the region. A spatial option of greater concentration in Growth Areas (see Table 7.2) might alleviate pressure on roads and on infrastructure, but would still require upwards of £20 billion of infrastructure investment during the life of the South East Plan. Given the environmental lobby's concern over land take – and the potential use of Previously Developed Land (PDL) versus green-field sites – the critical question, is how much housing growth (and associated development) can be accommodated 'within urban areas'. Roger Tym & Partners (2005) have made some preliminary calculations for the RA. Not surprisingly, the higher the rate of growth, the greater the need to spill over onto greenfields at the edge of settlements and within the rural–urban fringe. If the South East Plan – due to be put to government in mid-2006 – opted for the lowest growth option, then 73 per cent of development could be within urban areas, leaving 138,000 plus associated infrastructure (out of a total 510,000 homes) to be provided on greenfields. With the highest growth level, just 59 per cent of homes could be 'brownfield', leaving 262,000 (of 640,000) in 'non-urban areas'. Urban capacity is higher in the north of the region (around Milton Keynes) but much lower in the centre and south (e.g. the Hampshire Coast) where more develop-ment would need to utilise greenfield sites. Because there is a finite urban capacity (though the supply of PDL is unpredictable over time), additional growth – over and above the lowest building rates – is likely to be on greenfields. It is little wonder that the environmental lobby appears intransigent and refuses to coun-tenance a market perspective or a house building rate that reflects demographic growth. There appears to be little room for compromise between the environ-mental and the housing requirement perspectives. Even if local action is successful in fending off some development, the mathematics of housing growth and urban capacity, alongside the problem of worsening affordability cited by Barker and others, suggests that additional housing supply above planned provi-sion is inevitable. The only way to resist, as CPRE have realised, is to challenge the national and regional case for house building: to focus not on any particular place, but on the demographics (and, increasingly, the economics) and social changes that are underpinning the housing supply debate in England and beyond.

Conclusions

We have presented this discussion of housing supply in England at a time of considerable debate and uncertainty. On the back of the Barker Review, govern-ment has committed itself to fundamentally rethinking the way the planning system deals with future housing provision. A number of analyses have suggested that the current system is unresponsive and inflexible: it should listen and respond to the market, though how it should do this remains unclear given the inherent complexity of the relationship between local house prices, general price growth and housing supply. But the pro affordability-led camp seems committed to a bigger role for the market, irrespective of these complexities. On the other side of the fence, there are those who believe that planning should lead rather than follow. There are a number of 'good reasons' why planning should retain the upper hand: first, a market-led approach to housing supply may not fully reflect and cost the externalities of development (i.e. the impacts on the environment and on communities) and this is surely a key role of the planning system. Second, the market has an insatiable desire for new housing, especially in those areas popular with investors and second-home buyers. Therefore, too much housing would be needed to create the market equilibriums lauded by the supporters of Barker given the price inelasticity of supply. The exponents of an affordability-led approach might respond with the argument that the stock of dwellings in England is too small: it needs to be expanded now to bring price growth under control in the longer run. Housing supply is a key battleground, divided between the developmental and environmental agendas that characterise so much housing debate in England (Murdoch and Abram, 2002). The question of market signals might be seen as a complicating factor in this context: just another sticking point. But in reality, the affordability-led approach and its inclusion in the latest planning policy guidance on housing, marks a fundamental departure from past practice. It seeks a re-balance between planning and the market and could represent the biggest shift in planning's role in housing provision in recent times.

Chapter 8

Delivering housing in sustainable communities

> This is a programme of action to tackle pressing problems in our communities in England: homes are unaffordable in some areas, but are being abandoned in others. We need decent homes and a good quality local environment in all regions [. . .] This document marks a step change in our approach; a strengthened determination by government to reverse, over the next 15–20 years, some damaging, deep-seated trends [. . .] It is part of the Government's wider drive to raise the quality of life in our communities through increasing prosperity, reducing inequalities, more employment, better public services, better health and education, tackling crime and anti-social behaviour, and much more.
>
> (ODPM, 2003a: 5)

Introduction

This chapter is concerned with 'sustainable communities' and government's plan to deliver future housing within the framework of its Communities Plan (CP) (ODPM, 2003a). In the last chapter, we saw that there is growing pressure to respond more proactively to the current shortfall in housing supply in England, probably through the introduction of a new system of planning for housing that is in some way more responsive to house price signals and the market. But no government can afford to be seen to play to the demands of the market, without acknowledging the need to achieve sustainable development. And more importantly, planning that fails to deal with the externalities of development or concern itself with the quality of outcomes will find little support among its users or within society at large. Coupled with the issue of supply is the need to deliver the right planning outcomes, which promote sustainable development and meet with broader social and economic aspirations. In this chapter, we examine the various facets of government's CP, and the notion of 'sustainable communities'. We address a number of broad questions:

- What is meant by a 'sustainable community' and can it be achieved, at least in theory?

- What is the Communities Plan, and what is its relationship with the housing supply issues identified in the last chapter?
- What is the role of planning in delivering sustainable communities, and how does this role link back to the broader role of planning for housing, which, as we saw in the last chapter, appears to be on the brink of a fundamental change.

Sustainable communities

Sustainable communities are a global phenomenon: they are a policy manifestation of spatial development's orthodoxy in achieving sustainable development supported by social, economic and environmental resources in the interests of the long term and of future generations (Chatterton, 2002; Gibbs, 2002). In a statement that echoes the sentiments expressed when the foundations of the modern planning system were laid more than a century ago, the Communities Plan states that:

> Investing in housing alone, paying no attention to the other needs of communities, risks wasting money – as past experience has shown. A wider vision of strong and sustainable communities is needed to underpin this plan [creating] places where people want to live and will continue to want to live.
>
> (ODPM, 2003a: 5)

This apparent 'reawakening' of a broader vision for places is interesting, partly because of the link back to the purpose of town planning in the early twentieth century, but also because it has now been re-packaged as a distinctly twenty-first century objective: to enhance the sustainable economic competitiveness of cities and regions, as drivers of economic growth in the global economy (Raco, 2005; 2006). In contemporary parlance, 'creation' (of sustainable communities) sometimes appears to substitute the need for 'planning', although a central role for planning – as we will see later – is critical if government is to come even close to the goal of creating sustainable communities. But our initial concern must be with the nature of such communities. Allmendinger and Tiesdell (2004) argue that 'the more a community can meet its own needs, the more likely it is to be sustainable' (ibid., 314). This general definition – which is also reflected in the official 'requirements' of a sustainable community (see Box 8.1) – begs two basic questions. What do the terms 'sustainability' and 'community' mean? And what are the main factors contributing to community sustainability? (Long, 2000: 3). We have dealt with the 'sustainability' component of the first question at various points in this book, though it is perhaps worth revisiting sustainability in the context of the CP. A study by Long (2000) iden-tifies seven distinct approaches to defining sustainability: an environmental approach focusing on the consumption of resources; an environmental approach that concerns itself with human resources and participative outcomes; an eco-logical approach that sees communities as living organisms; a self-sufficiency approach that often has a strong economic focus; an endurance approach that prioritises lasting benefits; a demand based approach that is concerned with solu-tions that deliver what people want in the long term; and approaches that are generally unspecified, but which are concerned with broad goals such as 'success', 'viability' and 'stability' (Long, 2000: 4). Looking through the list of 'require-ments' in Box 8.1, it appears that government thinking mixes a number of

---

Box 8.1 The requirements of sustainable communities

- a flourishing local economy to provide jobs and wealth;
- strong leadership to respond positively to change;
- effective engagement and participation by local people, groups and busi-nesses, especially in the planning, design and long-term stewardship of their community, and an active voluntary and community sector;
- a safe and healthy local environment with well-designed public and green space;
- sufficient size, scale and density, and the right layout to support basic amenities in the neighbourhood and minimise use of resources (including land);
- good public transport and other transport infrastructure both within the community and linking it to urban, rural and regional centres;
- buildings – both individually and collectively – that can meet different needs over time, and that minimise the use of resources;
- a well-integrated mix of decent homes of different types and tenures to support a range of household sizes, ages and incomes;
- good quality local public services, including education and training oppor-tunities, health care and community facilities, especially for leisure;
- a diverse, vibrant and creative local culture, encouraging pride in the community and cohesion within it;
- a 'sense of place';
- the right links with the wider regional, national and international community.

Source: ODPM, 2003a: 5

approaches to sustainability. There is an economic focus, suggesting self-sufficiency; clear resource and participatory concerns pointing to all forms of environmental sustainability; a concern for endurance and cohesion over the longer term; an active and living community that appears organic and able to develop in the future; a demand-led approach, contributing to the creation of vibrant places and cultures; and finally, a broad general element leaning towards cohesion, stability and 'place making'. There is no clear definition of sustainability, but there are a range of ideas expressed in the Plan.

Government might have been expected to clarify its thinking on this concept in the context of Planning Policy Statement 1 (ODPM, 2005h). The statement begins with the assertion that 'sustainable development is the core principle underpinning planning. At the heart of sustainable development is the simple idea of ensuring a better quality of life for everyone, now and for future generations' (ibid.: para. 3). Clearly, this is a statement that fits with Long's (2000) 'broadly unspecified' approach to defining sustainability, though PPS1 goes on to reference the Brundtland report (1987) with its environmental/human resource leanings. The statement also refers back to a 1999 document *A Better Quality of Life* (DETR, 1999a) in which four 'sustainability principles' are established: that development should promote social progress; offer effective protection of the environment; use natural resources prudently; and maintain high levels of stable economic growth. Planning is handed a central role in taking forward these principles, by:

- making suitable land available for development in line with economic, social and environmental objectives to improve people's quality of life;
- contributing to sustainable economic development;
- protecting and enhancing the natural and historic environment, the quality and character of the countryside, and existing communities;
- ensuring high quality development through good and inclusive design, and the efficient use of resources;
- ensuring that development supports existing communities and contributes to the creation of safe, sustainable, liveable and mixed communities with good access to jobs and key services for all members of the community.

(ODPM, 2005h: para. 5)

It is claimed that the principles of sustainable development, and the role for planning set out above, are already part of *Building for the Future* (ODPM, 2003a): 'planning has a key role to play in the creation of sustainable communities: communities that will stand the test of time, where people want to live, and which will enable people to meet their aspirations and potential' (ODPM, 2005h:

para. 6). This is government's core definition of a 'sustainable community', and it bares great resemblance to the general view expressed by Allmendinger and Tiesdell (2004) noted earlier: the more a community can meet its own needs, the more it will be considered sustainable. We would not be the first to suggest that sustainability means all things to all people: but it is sometimes useful to steer clear of focused approaches (e.g. focused on the environment, on the economy or on social capital) and employ a general and unspecified aim for long-term policy – to create stability, enhance cohesion or bring about greater efficiencies. It is useful in the sense that governments are not subsequently tied to specific targets; but it is also useful because these broader aims can cut across the familiar dimensions of economy, environment and society. At this level, we can say that government is pursuing a development model that is guided by the goal of sustainability.

But tying down the concept of 'community' and establishing that 'community' is the right framework in which to pursue sustainable development – is a more fraught exercise. Long contemplates the fuzziness between the concepts of community and neighbourhood. Government policy has tended to see 'community' as a discrete social unit of a particular size: 'a grouping of up to several thousand households, whose occupants share common experiences and bonds derived from living in the same locality' according to Long (2000: 6). Government (and local planning) has preferred to see 'neighbourhood' as something smaller and more manageable, perhaps the local focus of some planned intervention or initiative. These views of communities and neighbourhoods are goal-orientated: what programmes are required and what can be achieved through planning or other policy at different scales (of delivery). They reflect a concern for action rather than people or place. Similarly, they are unconcerned with more conceptual thinking on the notion of 'community'. Pahl (1966, republished 1975) has long been at the forefront of thinking on the social configuration of communities and the social consequences of shared experience and networking. His work has frequently been motivated by a policy imperative, aiming to understand how communities are being re-configured (mixed in terms of social class) and hence how their needs and their economies are being reshaped, while the communities themselves either lose or gain cohesion and stability. In more recent work on 'personal communities', Pahl and Spencer (2004) have challenged the postmodernist thesis which claims that people are increasingly isolated and individualised (ibid.: 199). They develop a typology of personal communities differentiated by the changing balance between friend and family ties, and by the balance between obligation – to conform with 'traditional arrangements' – and choice – to implicitly reject orthodoxy, and perhaps to identify with professional, work-place, relationships to a greater extent than kinship ties (ibid.: 217).

In a sense, this more conceptual thinking gives weight to the belief that sustainability goals might be pursued at the level of the community. In the 1980s, Margaret Thatcher espoused the view that communities had disintegrated (if they ever really existed) and that there is 'no such thing as society [only] individual men and women' (Thatcher, 1987), and hence no rationale for community planning. Despite a move away from 'traditional communities' (based on common experience, need and background), work by Pahl and others seems to confirm that the idea of community retains relevance. But are we talking about a 'place' community? Long contends, that if a community is defined by experience and bonding, then it is concerned, fundamentally, with *people*. Neighbourhood, on the other hand – an area or district with people living in it – is concerned with *place* (Long, 2000: 7). Accepting this division means that achieving sustainability at the 'community' level is about influencing attitudes and behaviour; achieving sustainability in the context of 'place' shares this concern, but is also about physical change and stable, cohesive and integrated place-making. Seen in the restrictive context of policy debate, this division might appear unimportant – communities can be whatever government and policy makers want them to be. However, there needs to be clarity in, and broad acceptance of, what government is trying to achieve, and what role planning is being called upon to perform. The current lack of clarity, and confusion over what constitutes a 'sustainable community' is a theme picked up in work by Allmendinger and Tiesdell (2004):

> The Government's notion of 'sustainable communities' is unclear – particularly in regard to regeneration – and the Government provides little indication of how planners and others should use the concept in everyday practice.
>
> (ibid.: 313)

In reality, the fuzziness of the concept means that planning 'is – or should be – about creating sustainable *places*' (ibid.). Like Long, Allmendinger and Tiesdell associate communities with *people* arguing that 'we are cautious of using the term communities, because it is people – not planners, designers or other professionals – that create communities' (ibid.). At the same time, community has an 'intuitive meaning' that cannot easily be tied down, and 'both the notion of what is "sustainable" and what constitutes a "community" are open to interpretation' (ibid.: 314).

If we are concerned with the *role of planning*, then that role is about the future sustainability of *places*. Planning is concerned with the 'mediation of space' and the 'making of place' according to the UK professional institute, the RTPI. The creation of sustainable 'communities' is a far broader task and is about influencing how people live and how they want to live in the future: it is about creating an entirely different society. Regulation, through planning, has a role to play in creating this new society and place-making – building the places in which people can *choose* to live differently – is important. But at a practical level, planning is directly concerned with *place* though it has an indirect role in influencing *people*. The neighbourhood focus of many local planning initiatives concedes the truth of this statement, and it is also the conclusion reached by Allmendinger and Tiesdell (2004) who suggest four roles for planning in making sustainable places:

1   **Place-making:** giving places identity, ensuring that they 'provide an anchor of shared experiences between people' (ibid., 314), perhaps using urban design to create 'charm' and places that people care about, and will continue to care about in the long term. We might add that planning needs to promote 'collective dwelling' within urban space (expressed through exchange, social intercourse and interaction), and public dwelling, which generates a stable 'agreed' culture (Norberg-Schulz, 1985: 13; King, 2004: 23).

2   **Integrating the social, economic, and physical dimensions of place:** planning provides a pivotal focus for integrated policy solutions and achieving 'multi-functionality' within place. Many of the key functions are set out in Building for the Future and were listed in Box 8.1. Jobs, schools, housing, healthcare, green space, affordable and safe transport might be viewed as key dimensions, alongside cohesion, identity and 'accountable government' (Allmendinger and Tiesdell, 2004: 314).

3   **Linking 'people' and 'place' orientations:** Linking the social with the physical, the community with the place. A tension between movable 'global capital' and immovable 'local community', between mobility and embeddedness (of community) seem problematic (ibid., 314). But the tension can be eased by creating an adaptive labour force, by nurturing local commitment to a place and by building social capital. This is, in part, about giving people ownership in a place (perhaps through participatory planning) and a stake in its future, creating cohesion rather than disconnection, the latter being manifest in a belief that place is unimportant and can be quickly abandoned.

4   **Self-sufficiency and temporal dynamism:** creating places that are self-sufficient with a capacity to respond to change, giving them an adaptable asset base. It requires that planning and regeneration initiatives 'develop places that have the flexibility and dynamism to adapt to changing social and economic conditions' (ibid., 316).

Government has set itself the goal of creating 'sustainable communities' and in both *Delivering Through Planning* (ODPM, 2002b) and *Building for the Future* (ODPM, 2003a), it has handed planning a central role in achieving this goal. Planning is fundamentally concerned with place: through its role in place-making, it is able to influence how people live, thereby contributing to the creation of communities that have a greater chance of enduring over the longer term. Long (2000) has developed a 'hierarchy' of factors that contribute to the sustainability of a community. This is a simple hierarchy, set out in Figure 8.1, in which the direct and indirect influence of planning can be identified. Long suggests that the factors on the first row 'will generally have a greater impact on sustainability than those on the second row' (ibid., 9), while the closer they are to the left, the greater their significance. Interestingly, the demand for housing is considered the most significant factor contributing to sustainability, linking forward to reputation and image, environmental quality, housing quality, crime, social cohesion and exclusion, community mix and accessibility. Whether or not housing really is top of the pile is of course debatable. But housing occupies a central position in government thinking on sustainable communities, and places: it has triggered political concern largely because of worsening affordability in many parts of the UK and the impact this is seen to have on social exclusion and cohesion. To recap some of the concerns picked up in earlier chapters, and analysed at length in Chapter 7, in the south of England for example a vast proportion of the population no longer has access to decent affordable housing and those homes that are available are unaffordable for people on moderate incomes, including many key workers in the public services. In 2005, property prices in London were ten times the average salary. But despite the pressure for additional cheaper housing, new house building has been in decline for decades. Even with the increase in owner occupation and the sell-off of social housing from the early 1980s (see Chapter 3), the private house building industry has not responded (or has been unable to respond) to the increased demand for homeownership. Planning and housing are key areas of concern for the CP, with some commentators viewing the plan itself as merely a tactical distraction from the real task ahead – to bring about a seismic shift in future housing provision, shrouded behind a cloak of 'sustainability'.

But it has to be remembered, that additional housing supply is not the goal of the CP everywhere. The plan is, in fact, concerned with the sustainability of demand. It posits that market equilibrium (a major concern in the last chapter) is the cornerstone of a sustainable community. Some communities and places in the UK do not face the challenge of substantial increases in housing demand, but the difficulties associated with market collapse, resulting in some homes and even entire neighbourhoods being blighted by low demand (DETR, 1999). A

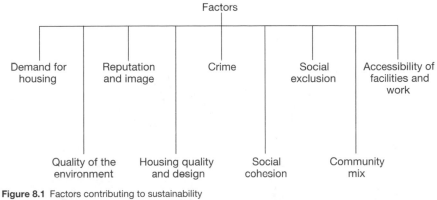

Figure 8.1 Factors contributing to sustainability
Source: Long, 2000: 8

'doughnut' effect has been observed in some northern and midland towns and cities with inter- and intra-regional migration causing a hollowing-out of old urban cores. Given this predicament, it is easy to see why many commentators place housing demand at the heart of community change and stability. In the next part of this chapter, we outline government's Communities Plan in greater detail before looking at the way in which the Plan has become a template for future planning, and particularly planning for housing.

The Communities Plan

The first instalment of government's Communities Plan arrived in 2002 (ODPM, 2002b): 'sustainable communities' were to be delivered, primarily, through a culture change in planning. An authoritarian, public-sector-led approach, was to be replaced by a consensual, partnership-driven model that would work for business *and* empower communities. The thinking set out in *Delivering Through Planning* was an extension of ideas expressed in the previous year's planning Green Paper (2001), but now tied more explicitly to residential development and the persistent challenges of delivering sufficient homes, especially in southern England, and responding to apparent market weaknesses in the midlands and in the northern regions. The second instalment was published within 12 months of the first, with government committing itself to *Building for the Future* (ODPM, 2003a). The Plan, as set out in 2003, offered a broad statement on the housing and planning challenge facing England: essentially an overheating market in the south and a steadily weakening market further north (notwithstanding local market peculiarities). Arguably, it represented New Labour's first coherent response to the challenge that it inherited from the Conservatives in

Plate 16 Victorian terraces with recent street improvements and new apartments in the background (Manchester, 2003)

1997, with John Prescott pointing to the economic and demographic changes driving housing demand and abandonment.

The 2003 document set out a long-term programme of action for delivering sustainable communities in both urban and rural areas, by aiming to tackle housing supply issues in the south-east, low demand in other parts of the country, and the quality of public spaces (addressing what has since been labelled the 'liveability' agenda – see p. 209 onwards). Realisation of the Plan was thought to be dependant on a 'step change' in planning, enabling the creation of 'places where people want to live and work' (ODPM, 2003a: 1). The initial value of the programme was £22 billion, with funding to be used to encourage the design of more sustainable forms of social, economic and environmental development through the management and distribution of economic growth, with an emphasis on mixed use, cohesive communities, sustainable living and higher quality design. There are invariably tensions within the programme, not least between the strategic requirement to sustain the economic position of London and the south-east while trying to sharpen the competitiveness edge of other regions, for example by tackling low demand and poor quality housing in the north. In the spirit of spatial planning and coordination, part of the effort of the programme was also to focus attention and coordinate the efforts of all levels of government and stakeholders in bringing about development to meet the economic, social and environmental needs of future generations. National policies were brought together but also given a regional dimension. More controversially, the Plan recognised the need for stock reduction and rationalization – through demolition in some instances – in the north of England as means of re-establishing required market equilibriums. In this respect, the CP of 2002/2003 sought to build on government's earlier *New Deal for Communities* (NDC) initiative (announced in 1998 and extended in 1999) which focused on, among other things, 'housing and the physical environment' (www.neighbourhood.gov.uk). The idea of 'Pathfinders' – areas where focused support for dealing with neighbourhood decline and low housing demand was to be provided – has now been taken forward in the Communities Plan (2003), which identifies nine Pathfinder areas, all with their own strategic plans that:

> entail radical and sustained action to replace obsolete housing with modern sustainable accommodation, through demolition and new building or refurbishment. This will mean a better mix of homes, and sometimes fewer homes. There will be no blueprint. The problems differ in the nine pathfinder areas; the solutions will too (ODPM, 2003a: 24)

Again, the Pathfinders are concerned with establishing new efficiencies and balances in the housing market, putting the restoration of demand at the forefront of sustainable communities. Other aspects of sustainability are extensions of this primary aim. The Pathfinders:

> will ensure the other essential requirements of sustainable communities, especially good quality, customer-focused public services, pride in the community and cohesion within it are addressed [. . .] They will also ensure clean, safe, healthy and attractive environments in which people can take pride. (ibid.: 24)

Housing is at the forefront of the CP, as we noted at the end of the last section. But often the requirement to address housing undersupply by accelerating the provision of new housing in southern England seems to overshadow the issue of low demand in the north. For some commentators, this fact is held up as evidence of a south-east bias in government policy: it is seen as a bad thing. For others, painting the northern regions as 'failing' and blighted by low housing demand is an over-simplification. While there are serious housing problems in some areas, across the market as a whole (especially in the north-west) there are as many neighbourhoods experiencing high demand as there are low demand.

Plate 17 Boarded-up housing and vacant shop units in East Manchester (Manchester, 2002)

Therefore, giving too much credence to the CP agenda might, it is suggested, result in a biased view of the north. The conclusion is that it is probably best that people focus on the southern growth agenda as the Communities Plan adds little to policy debate north of Watford.

Specifically regarding this southern growth agenda, the CP predates the Barker Review of Housing Supply (published in 2004 and considered in the last chapter) but it seems certain that future revisions to planning guidance, grounded in Barker's analysis, will be retrofitted to the Plan. At the present time (early in 2006), however, emphasis has been placed on ensuring that planned provision in southern England is achieved, largely by stepping up the rate of provision in four 'growth areas' (Thames Gateway, London–Stansted–Cambridge corridor, Ashford, and Milton Keynes–South Midlands), and by ensuring that the construction industry has the right skills – and hence capacity – to deliver. An acknowledgement in the Plan that affordable housing must be provided in a more systematic way, through direct development and through planning gain mechanisms, has since been overshadowed by the Barker Review. However, the initial commitment – to key workers, to reducing homelessness and to reducing reliance on temporary accommodation – remains an important feature of government thinking (now set out in *Sustainable Communities: Homes for All*, ODPM, 2005j). Housing, in general terms, occupies a key position in the Plan with market balance viewed as central to achieving the goal of sustainability. Stabilising demand – as Long (2000) has already pointed out – is a critical first step. Efforts in the north – in the context of the Pathfinders and a Housing Market Renewal Initiative (HMRI) – include selective demolition and stock modification (new build, conversion, enlargement, etc.) which attempt to create equilibrium (or scarcity) where there is oversupply, or change the nature of the current housing stock where it does not appear to meet local needs or aspirations. It is, as with the affordability-led approach to land release discussed in the last chapter, an attempt to listen to the market and re-establish balance. These are the first two principal objectives of the CP.

But while housing demand issues are of principal concern – creating the 'anchor' for place making referred to by Allmendinger and Tiesdell – parallel concerns such as quality, reputation, crime, cohesion and stability (particularly that stability and cohesion which produces 'community') is sewn together in a 'liveability' agenda. This might be seen as the Plan's third principal objective. 'Liveability' – dealing with cross-cutting 'place' concerns – can be viewed as the linkage between the 'people and place orientations' noted above. Indeed, it is 'about creating places where people *choose* to live and work' according to the government's Improvement and Development Agency (IDeA: see www. idea-knowledge.gov.uk). Liveability is viewed as integral to the 'sustainable communities' agenda, with government establishing a 'liveability fund' that is intended to support 'significant local authority projects to improve parks and public spaces' (www.odpm.gov.uk). This fund (£89 million over three years – to March 2006) was part of a bigger package (of £201 million) aimed at improving 'liveability and quality' in local environments. The agenda was, and remains, very much about environmental quality and how to encourage local authorities to prioritise the needs of the local environment for the sake of liveability. It seeks to:

- encourage local authorities to adopt strategic planning and good practice in sustainable management and maintenance of the local environment;
- develop performance management systems for improving service delivery relating to the local environment, based on the application of Best Value, Comprehensive Performance Assessment (CPA) and Beacon Council principles;
- encourage better use of funding available to local authorities for local environment management through closer integration with complementary programmes and initiatives, such as housing, education and sport, health, regeneration and renewal programmes, Lottery, and local partnerships;

- build effective networks for local authorities to learn and share lessons for raising the quality of services and for tackling local liveability issues.

Significantly, the liveability agenda can be thought of as an extension of local authorities' traditional role in land-use control: it is a 'housing-plus' agenda with authorities asked to consider whether places (i.e. sustainable communities) are:

- 'Fit for purpose' – Do they permit the act of 'living', i.e. is a place 'functional'?
- 'Worth living in' – Do they fit with aspirations/desires, not only meeting requirements, but achieving something 'higher' (for individuals/communities), i.e. is a place 'aspirational'?
- 'Easy to live with' – Do they make living as easy as possible given environmental constraints (e.g. possible distance barriers), i.e. is a place made in such a way as to 'facilitate' ease in peoples' everyday lives?

Housing market equilibrium and liveability are the core components of 'sustainable communities'. It is clear that the liveability agenda is, roughly, concerned with the four elements of sustainable places identified by Allmendinger and Tiesdell (2004) and with many of Long's factors contributing to sustainability. Next to the core focus on houses themselves, liveability is concerned with what goes on between homes, with the local environment and wider context. The 'housing-plus' nature of the Plan is key: housing remains central, but a concern for the quantity and quality of homes is extended into a broader liveability agenda. In a sense, the Plan seeks to broaden 'dwelling' into a wider environment of which the home itself is only one component, and hence planning assumes a similarly broad role. Unintentionally, the thinking in the plan is reminiscent of Norberg-Schulz's (1985: 13) 'modes of dwelling' where those who dwell do so across natural, collective, public and private dimensions. A concern for liveability can be viewed as a concern for 'dwelling' with houses providing a pivotal point in peoples' lives, collective dwelling occurring within a wider 'urban space' that fosters social intercourse and interaction (and of course, economic viability), and natural dwelling involving a domestication of nature, providing a 'liveable' environment. Planning for housing has become subsumed within this broader vision: a 'housing-liveability' agenda. We examine planning's role in carrying forward this agenda in the next part of this chapter, but first we look briefly at one final key issue in relation to sustainable communities – investment in and the delivery of support infrastructure associated with new housing.

Yet another instalment of government's communities plan appeared at the beginning of 2005: despite dropping the word 'decent' from the title, *Homes for All* (ODPM, 2005j) cited the importance of delivering 'decent homes' (and getting rid of, or improving 'non-decent' homes) a total of 59 times in its 80 or so pages. *Homes for All* did not offer anything new, but was concerned with taking stock of past 'achievements' (ibid., 2) and looking to the future. It outlined how government would continue to promote growth in southern England while, very loosely, addressing the key question of infrastructure provision; it talked about the environment (emphasising the need to 'save land' rather than liveability, in response to concerns over land take expressed following the publication of the Barker Review) and market renewal in northern England. These were the key themes of *Homes for All*. Also of concern were what might be viewed as ancillary goals: helping first-time buyers, expanding RTB opportunities (now re-branded 'Home Buy'. see Chapter 3), expanding the rental market, and looking at the role local authorities should play in taking the plan forward over the next five years (ibid., 3). Government's general goals were re-iterated, as were the challenges that are faced. Interestingly, it was argued that 'Kate Barker's analysis reinforces our strategy for more growth where it is needed and builds on the approach adopted in the Sustainable Communities Plan' (ibid., 23). The Barker Review – and its emphasis on affordability-led planning – was for the first time seen as part of the Communities Plan, being used to justify additional provision while providing a means of ensuring that homes are provided in the right places (dictated, to a greater extent, by the market). But the three big issues in *Homes for All* – infrastructure, the environment and market renewal – perhaps receive less attention than might have been expected. Before looking more closely at the role of planning, we end this review of the Communities Plan by looking at the question of infrastructure. This has often been a tail-end concern in policy debate, though critics of government's housing plans contend that it should, in reality, take pole-position.

These same critics are more broadly concerned with a lack of detail: specifically in relation to infrastructure provision, environmental quality and how to manage decline in less buoyant markets. While the latter two concerns are addressed directly in *Homes for All* (in chapters dealing with market and community revival and environmental enhancement), details regarding infrastructure provision remain sketchy. Government commits itself to £1.1 billion of additional investment during the following three years within its Growth Areas (ibid., 8), but this might be viewed as rather short-term. In the south-east region alone, it has been estimated that the cost of providing infrastructure during the life of the South East Plan (2006 to 2026) will range from approximately £19 billion to up to £25 billion, depending on the exact level of housing growth promoted. Government's £1.1 million is for London *and* the south-east, but these estimates *exclude* London's infrastructure needs; they also exclude water supply. Assuming a median level of annual housing growth in the South East Plan (which currently seems likely), the cost of providing infrastructure in the south-east will be in excess of £21 billion based on calculations undertaken by Roger Tym & Partners (2004). This study suggests that each 1,000 extra homes will require £38.26 million (see Table 8.1) of infrastructure investment: this estimate is considerably lower than an earlier Kent County Council figure of £96 million that factored in the cost of 'national infrastructure, private sector costs, economic development, town centres and rural development' (Roger Tym & Partners, 2004: ii).

Assuming an annual building rate of 28,000 (the middle way in the South East Plan published by SEERA in 2005), then *annual* infrastructure costs will come to almost exactly £1.1 billion. In other words, the south-east alone would consume government's investment within 12 months. A House of Commons Environmental Audit Committee suggested early in 2006 that 'the ODPM is

Table 8.1 Infrastructure costs associated with new housing

£million per 1,000 dwellings	
Affordable housing (newly arising)	5.85
Community Centres	0.44
Leisure Centres	0.70
Outdoor sports	0.41
Open spaces	0.40
Play areas	0.02
Recycling (waste)	0.38
Libraries	0.17
Cemeteries	0.00
Secondary schools	3.80
Primary schools	2.61
Nurseries	0.16
Fire	0.28
Police	0.24
Ambulances	0.05
Hospitals	1.34
Transport	21.40
TOTAL	**38.26**

Source: Roger Tym & Partners, 2004: ii

determined to build homes first and worry about infrastructure later, if at all' (Planning 1663, 2006b: 4). Of course, the infrastructure costs will not be met by direct government funding alone. A study by Gallent and Tewdwr-Jones (2005) makes the point that 'higher levels of [housing] growth will support higher levels of GVA productivity and generate the revenue to meet infrastructure and service investment costs' (ibid., 92). The real question then is not how much government will invest, but how it will capture some of the development profit for re-investment back into essential infrastructure. Existing planning gain mechanisms will play a part, and so too might government's Planning Gain Supplement (PGS). The latter emerged as a proposal from the Barker Review and government commenced a consultation on the form of a possible PGS in December 2005 (HM Treasury, 2005) arguing that the delivery of sustainable communities might not be possible 'without additional dedicated revenue to support growth' (ibid., 5). Barker's suggestion was that 'government should impose a Planning-gain Supplement on the granting of planning permission so that landowner development gains form a larger part of the benefits of development' (ibid., 6). Government has responded by arguing that in order to 'support growth' – of the type planned in southern England – a PGS should be levied on the uplift value of land on which development permission is granted. In England, a hectare of mixed agricultural land has an average value of just over £9000; a hectare of land for residential use has a value close to £2.5 million. Industrial and warehousing land has a value in excess of £600,000 per hectare, and land allocated for business (B1 uses) is valued at £750,000 (ibid., 7, 2005: figures from the Valuation Office Agency). The basic idea is that the 'uplift' (the difference between pre-development permission value (i.e. current use value or CUV) and full development permission value (i.e. planning value or PV)) can be taxed with revenues received 'dedicated to local communities to manage the impacts of growth, and to funding the local and strategic infrastructure necessary to support and stimulate new development and contribute to long-term sustainability' (ibid., 7). Planning obligations (under Section 106) would be scaled back to make room for the PGS approach, which would not be used in all instances, but which could – it is argued – make for a more transparent system of taxing development than the current Section 106 approach. But critics have rounded on the complexities of the proposed system, and the inequalities that it could generate. The RTPI, for example, have claimed that infrastructure investment will be polarized in southern England where the lion's share of PGS will be generated: good news, perhaps, for the development of sustainable communities in the south, but not such good news for the north (RTPI, 2005: 1). And echoing the sentiments of the Environmental Audit Committee, it adds that developers will only need to make a PGS payment (on the basis of self-assessment) once development commences.

This means that 'government is putting the cart before the horse by insisting that money for infrastructure can only be taken once development actually begins' (ibid., 2).

Some of the technical complexities of PGS have been set out by Ricketts, who argues that 'assessing a current use value can be complicated by issues such as mixed site ownership, mixed uses and factors such as restrictive covenants' (Ricketts, 2006: 2). Valuation is a complex business: in particular, large sites:

> might entail a number of full and outline consents making the relevant date for PGS assessment complex – e.g. where a developer divides a large site into different parts and obtains full permission for each either at the same time or consecutively, what effect will this have on Planning Value?
>
> (ibid., 3)

Moving on from the initial valuation (to arrive at the CUV – see p. 213), it is not yet clear who will pay the PGS – the landowner or the developer – once a Development Start Notice (DSN) is served. And some development is known to commence (illegally) before the DSN is served. This could mean that CUV is calculated at a later stage when some uplift has already been generated and so the final uplift element (PV-CUV) might be reduced. Rickett's argues that HM Revenue and Customs would need to police the self-assessment, becoming involved in initial valuation, the estimation of uplift and the calculation of PGS. It might subsequently have to pursue developers if a shortfall were identified. But in the meantime, what happens to the provision of infrastructure to support sustainable communities? A lack of ring-fencing of PGS means that it might not even be earmarked for infrastructure and ultimately, it might add to the bureaucracy of planning, which government has committed itself to removing.

So the question of infrastructure, and how it is paid for, remains. Sustainable Communities should be built on 'robust infrastructure' (ODPM, 2005j: 10) with poor infrastructure making 'it hard for communities to thrive in the long term' (ibid.: 12). *Homes for All* pointed to the input of additional government resources and also to the future role of gain mechanisms and the potential of PGS (ibid., 25). It also highlighted funding for individual schemes in particular places (ibid., 30), but the general question of infrastructure – the gap between direct funding and estimated costs – still looms large. Individual projects are attracting investment as government seeks to demonstrate its commitment to building sustainable communities. Hence, money will be provided for a Thames Gateway Bridge and for town-centre improvements in Medway, Barking and Southend. But if the estimate of £38.2 million per 1,000 homes is anywhere near correct, then developing the Thames Gateway alone will cost more than £7.6 billion.

We now turn to the role of local planning in taking forward what we have described as a 'housing-liveability' agenda, established in the CP. *Homes for All* talked of the need for local authorities to take a lead, in the context of the new planning system, but it is thin on detail. Clearer messages emerged in another government consultation launched in December 2005, this time looking at 'Local Strategic Partnerships' (ODPM, 2005i) and their capacity to deliver 'sustainable community strategies'. Here, there was the same acknowledgement that housing must be fixed within a broader community and liveability agenda at the local level, and hence 'planning for housing' must be seen as one element of a broader strategy. On the one hand, planning is viewed as just one tool for delivering this agenda and hence its status seems diminished. But on the other hand, closer examination of planning's role reveals that it remains pivotal to delivering the housing, in the right quantity and of the right type and fixed within a framework of liveability, that the country seems to need.

Planning for a housing-liveability agenda

The CP might be viewed not only as a framework for housing and community development, but also as a template for future planning. A bolder concern for housing design, faster planning, additional affordable housing (and improvements in the planning gain approach), the efficient use of land and brownfield recycling, the promotion of Growth Areas and a bigger role for the regions were initially considered to be the practical challenges for planning in relation to the CP (Chartered Institute of Housing/Royal Town Planning Institute, 2003). These concerns retain currency, but the Plan seems to suggest a far broader role for planning – or rather, for *spatial* planning (see Chapter 9) – in the context of the reform agenda, which was already being rolled out when *Building for the Future* appeared in 2003. Essentially, planning is called upon to:

- move to a new level of housing provision, and to tackle the challenges of undersupply;
- coordinate and integrate land-uses in a more 'multi-functional' way;
- integrate with other frameworks (economic, social and environmental) to facilitate and coordinate broader outcomes;
- work in partnership with other agencies and sectors, and re-engage with communities to ensure greater ownership in and sustainability of outcomes;
- engage with a liveability agenda, with place making, and with wider environmental concerns often directly linked to the designated Growth Areas.

In the remainder of this chapter, we examine each of these challenges in turn. Our aim is to set out some of the broad issues to be tackled by planning – and local planning in particular – though detail of how planning might adapt and evolve in the future is contained elsewhere in this book. We have, for example, already considered housing provision at some length in the last chapter. Coordination, integration and partnership working are issues examined in the context of planning reform in the next chapter. So here, we confine our comments to issues of general principle rather than detail, linking these principles to the CP.

Housing provision

Housing demand and market equilibrium are central planks of the Communities Plan. In the last chapter, we examined the issue of housing supply and how a different approach to housing land allocations – guided by a central concern for affordability – might be used to achieve market equilibrium and steer new homes to areas of greatest need. But this strategy, as we saw, is not without its risks or its opponents. To recap, Barker (2004) argued that government should become more concerned with 'improved market affordability', setting affordability targets, establishing regional planning executives to advise on the scale and distribution of housing needed to meet these targets, and introducing greater flexibility with extra land releases within local development frameworks triggered by 'market signals'. These market signals will be read within a sub-regional context with data collection orchestrated by regional planning in partnership with local planning teams. The aim will be to ensure that Sustainable Communities are built, first and foremost, on stable housing demand.

After consulting on Barker's recommendations – and commissioning independent studies into environmental sustainability and affordability (ODPM, 2005f; 2005e) – government published a response in which it signaled its intention to feed some of her recommendations into new planning advice. Clearly, a broader view of affordability is taking root with planning being called upon to think about affordability in a 'macro-economic' sense: this may mean less emphasis on the 'procurement' of affordable social housing through planning (a strategy of 'muddling through' according to Hoggart and Henderson, 2005: 194), and more attention being paid to controlling house prices through general supply.

At present, the practicalities for local planning are uncertain. An ODPM-sponsored study into 'supporting the reform of local planning' (ODPM, 2006a) revealed that during the transition from old-style development plans to new (post-2004) Local Development Strategies, many authorities are using local Area Action Plans (AAPs) as a vehicle for carrying forward additional housing growth proposals (ibid., 32) and are waiting for greater clarity in the policy framework (e.g. regarding the role of market assessment and the final treatment of Barker's proposals) before thinking through the long-term impacts of planning reform on housing allocations, and how these should be dealt with in core strategies. So, at the time of writing, we are in a period of transition. Government has not yet responded to its PPS3 consultation. This means that for many authorities, it is either business as usual in terms of land allocations for housing, or anticipatory plans – reflecting a need for additional housing – are being put in place that will only be galvanised once greater certainty is established. Interestingly, the ODPM study into local planning and how it should respond to the reform agenda makes only a handful of references to housing and avoids any mention of market signals, demonstrating perhaps the uncertainties that remain.

Of course, local planning cannot deal with the growth agenda without reference to other agencies. The role of regional planning in establishing the market context for housing has already been noted, but English Partnerships (the government's regeneration agency) will also have a key role. It will take a lead in land assembly and focus on strategic housing development; it will also work more closely with the Regional Development Agencies, particularly in furthering the objective of land recycling. The funding allocated to both the Agency and to Regional Assemblies will increase and they will engage directly in the remediation of brownfield land: but exactly how local planning will change remains unclear. In Chapter 7, we noted some broad shifts in principle:

- Regions will continue to distribute housing provision but use sub-regional housing markets as a basis for allocating housing numbers as well as other factors and tailoring the approach to delivery to the circumstances of different markets.
- The local plan horizon will be extended to 15 years. The first 5 years is allocated and developable with less reliance on windfall in areas where it is possible to allocate land.
- A 5-year supply will be rolled forward as land is developed, in line with plans, and Local Authorities will be required to bring forward land from their 10-year supply to ensure that the supply of developable land is maintained.

The emphasis will be on market responsiveness and continuity in land supply: this is viewed as a key step toward achieving Sustainable Communities.

Multi-functionality in planning

Inherent in the concept of sustainability, and the objective of building sustainable communities, is the idea that places must perform a number of functions. This finds expression in the idea of a 'housing-plus' or 'housing-liveability' agenda. There are two important points to raise here. The *first* is that the CP calls on planning – implicitly – to play a bigger part in place making: essentially to move outside its traditional land-use focus and to embrace a wider remit that includes socio-cultural and economic concerns. It must deal centrally with housing and with place, but also pay greater attention to community and to people. This is the rhetoric: the reality is that government's Planning and Compulsory Purchase Act 2004 has tried to push planning towards a broader 'spatial' model; planning that embraces the ideas of collaborative, community-centred, and communicative action (Healey, 2003: 120; Abram and Cowell, 2004: 210) and a different style of governance. According to Albrechts (2004: 747), planning should provide 'an active force in enabling change'. It should also become an integrating force, bringing together different agendas, reconciling interests and creating visions that these interests can buy into (Friedmann, 2004: 52). There is a wide literature on the evolution of planning and the departure from a land-use model towards a spatial agenda, which is as much about governance and place-management as the control of land. The 2004 Act does not stand on any theoretical pinnacle, but it reflects an undercurrent of change. The move to a more strategic brand of spatial planning is reflected in the replacement of RPG, which merely set out the targets of central government, with RSSs, which seek to develop regional and sub-regional evidence-based agendas for future development. These strategies provide a framework in which to coordinate local development planning, which is now undertaken in the context of local development documents, incorporating development frameworks, AAPs and community strategies (see Chapter 9). Planning professionals are supposed to *facilitate* the process of planning, working with communities to build visions around which different groups can unite.

The *second* point relates to the focus of this spatial planning and how it takes an integrated and 'multi-functional' view of the components of place and of community. Sustainability demands that places function, in a balanced way, on several fronts. Arguably, past land-use planning has led to the dominance of single functions in particular places and has not paid sufficient attention to the links between space-using activities or the way places 'work'. In research examining landscape and landscape planning, Brandt *et al.* (2000) have argued that spaces perform basic functions – economic, ecological, communitarian and aesthetic; and that they have historical association. They add that 'it is a task of spatial planning to assign function and future forms of function and use to land' (ibid., 26). We noted government's assertion that sustainable communities have key requirements or ingredients at the beginning of this chapter. Planning has a role in dealing with these requirements and ensuring that places function across a number of dimensions. A broad literature on 'multi-functionality' – which began life in the natural sciences before shifting towards landscape science – is now influencing thinking on spatial planning (Priemus *et al.*, 2004; Rodenburg and Nijkamp, 2004) and offers some insights into why multi-functionality is important and how it can be achieved. Brandt *et al.* elaborate upon their basic functions suggesting the following meanings for the components of multi-functional landscapes/places:

- 'ecological functionality', meaning that places are 'areas for living' for both human and non human life;
- 'economic functionality', with places providing 'an area for production';
- 'socio-cultural functionality', or 'an area for recreation and identification' with socio cultural attributes;
- 'historical functionality', or 'an area for settlement and identity' which offers a sense of socio-cultural continuity;
- 'aesthetic functionality', with places providing 'an area for experiences'.

The idea of multi-functionality – which sits well with both sustainability and with the housing-liveability agenda outlined earlier – seems to provide loose framework for both spatial planning and for the delivery of sustainable communities. Or at least it is a way of thinking about these concepts, providing some goals for local planning and underscoring the need for planning to think beyond any single issue.

Integration across frameworks

Clearly, integration across frameworks is an important prerequisite to achieving 'multi-functional' places. The ODPM's 2005 Consultation on Local Strategic Partnerships (LSPs), introduced earlier, set out some of government's thinking on how local partnerships might ensure that hitherto disjointed or fragmented local or regional-local strategies might be integrated. It was concerned with the way in which LSPs coordinate the design and the delivery of programmes and strategies within the Sustainable Communities framework (this issue is examined below); a move to develop what are called 'Sustainable Community Strategies'; regional and sub-regional (including local) linkages; and the overarching aims of Local Development Frameworks (in bringing together an array of objectives: ODPM, 2005i: 13).

LSPs (a product of the Local Government Act 2000) have a responsibility to 'set out the vision of an area and coordinate and drive the delivery of local services leading to improved outcomes for citizens that go beyond the remit of any one partner' (ibid., 13), and are called upon to develop 'Sustainable Community Strategies' (SCSs). The production of an integrated Community Strategy has been the prime role of LSPs since 2000, but in 2005 it was decided that the objectives of these strategies should (a) be evolved to reflect the previous five-years experience of developing strategies, and (b) be brought into line with the CP and, in a sense, be re-branded as a sustainable communities delivery framework. The Egan Review (2004) emphasised the need for 'local leaders to take a more cross-disciplinary and integrated approach to social, economic and environmental issues' (ODPM, 2005i: 17) and this was to be reflected in the new SCSs. Some of the means by which greater integration might be achieved are set out in the 2005 Consultation:

- There should be some form of baseline assessment of the different components of a local community (employment, services, housing, the environment and so forth) so the SCS and individual frameworks (planning, housing, transport, etc.) begin from a shared evidence-base.
- This assessment should map trends establishing the interplay between issues and therefore show where common and overlapping interests exist.
- It should make forecasts and bring together data-sets; this forecasting should build on the priorities established in 'other local and regional partnerships' plans and strategies (ibid., 18).
- Any analysis of local conditions should be shared between the SCS and the LDF for the area; integration is dependent on ensuring that partnerships recognise the same challenges from the outset. Indeed, 'planning relating to neighbourhood renewal, culture & biodiversity should be subsumed within Sustainable Community Strategies at this stage' (18).
- The integration and complementarities of strategies should be clearly established in 'Local Area Agreements' (LAA), with Action Plans built on the SCS and Delivery Plans based on the LAA becoming a single strategy.
- Overlaps between frameworks should be identified and duplication avoided; accountability should be established within a SCS/LAA Action Plan and in the long term 'future iterations of theme, area or service-based plans should take into account the overall Sustainable Community Strategy and vice versa' (18).

Integration of frameworks begins with the development of a shared evidence base; it is evolved through a partnership approach; and it is maintained through fixed agreements and protocols designed to eradicate duplication and contradiction. It sounds fairly straightforward, but Carmona *et al.* (2003) have shown that integration across frameworks is often dependent on peoples' willingness, commitment and desire to work together (ibid., 233). In particular, it is important to have:

- agreed authority-wide corporate objectives based on a strategic vision (and this vision, often politically motivated, has to be shared);
- a willingness to share information and resources (avoiding a 'bunker mentality');
- commitment to joint working at the highest level (with heads of departments or different organizations avoiding the temptation to forge ahead alone, even if they feel other partners are intolerably slow);
- a desire to seek collaborative shared solutions to problems.

There is a 'human factor' that can stand in the way of greater integration. This may prove particularly important within planning departments in the years ahead. Reform of the system suggests that professional planners should assume the role of facilitators and avoid what many consider to be a natural tendency towards paternalistic control. Local planning needs to find a way of working more effectively within the context of multi-authored SCS.

Re-engagement with other agencies and with communities

Local collaboration, alongside effective working with regional planning, is essential if planning is to play a full part in carrying forward government's housing-liveability aspirations. There is a broad literature and a number of studies on the nature of effective 'partnering' (see, for example, Hambleton *et al.*, 1996; Taylor, 1997; Newchurch & Co., 2000) and much has been written on community engagement, beginning with Arnstein and her 'ladder of citizen participation' in 1969. Generally, engagement between stakeholders – 'lay' and 'professional' – is critical in relation to sustainable communities because although planning may have a direct hand in place-making, it is people who make communities (Allmendinger and Tiesdell, 2004: 313). Therefore planning needs to work with people to ensure that places provide a context for communities: that these places are liveable and provide an arena for the processes – social interaction, the sharing of values, the development of identity – that generate community. Working with people – in the widest sense – may be seen as an important step towards achieving government's objectives as surely as working against people – and against communities – will ensure failure. Carmona *et al.* (2003: 168) point out that this type of engagement will help:

- develop and refine designs and policies and fully explore alternatives;
- ensure that the gap between professional and lay perceptions is minimised and build trust between the different parties;
- build consensus about appropriate levels of intervention and prescription;
- give extra weight to policies and guidance in an area that is frequently challenged;
- ensure that amenity interests and design professionals are working towards mutually agreed goals;
- develop a sense of local ownership for policy, guidance and development solutions;
- build community capacity and enthusiasm to ensure that the community has an ongoing influence in their area;
- spread knowledge and awareness of professional and planning objectives;
- tap into local sources of knowledge and expertise;
- speed-up post-participation decision-making.

The Planning Green Paper of 2001 and the subsequent Planning and Compulsory Purchase Act 2004 reflect the same desire to foster engagement, particularly up-front in the planning process, and subsequently speed-up later stages by forestalling opposition to development proposals (by ensuring wider ownership in these proposals). But this engagement becomes even more critical in relation to sustainable communities, with planning seeking to create places – in partnership with other interest groups – that ultimately prove to be stable and cohesive. These objectives – stability and cohesion – are unlikely to be achieved if planning contributes to the production of places where people feel alienated, perhaps because they primarily serve business interests or car users, or do not meet the needs of the elderly, of young people or the disabled. The 'enthusiasm' for place noted by Carmona *et al.* is central to ensuring durability. In line with the view expressed by Allmendinger and Tiesdall (2004: 314), engagement is about linking 'people and place orientations', creating cohesion as opposed to disconnection, and creating places that people value and are less likely to abandon. Planning has a key role in facilitating this process and in creating the places in which new housing is situated.

Engaging with liveability

We reached the conclusion earlier that the CP has significantly broadened the remit of planning in relation to housing: it has established a 'housing-liveability' agenda. We also noted that the architects of the early planning system never intended that planning should focus on singular 'regulatory' issues such as housing supply without thinking about how places function or developing visions for future place-making. In this sense, the CP might be seen as part of a re-awakening, reflecting planning's primary and original mission. Integration across frameworks and facilitating engagement are means by which planning can realise the liveable places, and ultimately the communities, in which new housing is developed. But there are also practical steps to be taken: neighbourhood initiatives that frequently deal with the detail of place-making. On the back of government's funding package for environmental improvement – the 'liveability fund' introduced earlier – planning departments have appointed liveability or cultural coordinators:

- In Sheffield, the 'City Council is working with communities across [a] Liveability Programme area to develop neighbourhood identities and embark on environmental improvements that will enhance residents' quality of life and sense of belonging'. The aim is to foster local place-identity through revisions to streetscapes.
- In Leicester, the city is 'currently going through a phase of intense, mostly physical, regeneration, under a number of separate initiatives, all at different stages of planning and implementation and the need for effective co-ordination is crucial for the success of these projects. A collaborative positive relationship between all the different groups, including all sections of the community, is key to keeping people on board and to effective resource management'. The aim is to foster a sense of ownership in the processes of place-making.
- In Blackburn and Darwen, 'half the borough's housing stock is terraced, often in poor condition and with limited living space. Many communities also suffer from poor health and high levels of juvenile nuisance, so the creation of more recreation space serves a number of objectives. [A] Neighbourhood greens project aims to create eight new or improved local recreation areas in densely populated and deprived neighbourhoods. The eight sites are all council-owned; two are local Victorian parks in need of investment, two serve "community campus" facilities (a community centre, access point, health centre and schools), and four are rundown and largely disused recreation areas'. The aim is to enable communities to take charge of green spaces.
- In Mansfield, night-time revellers 'can now get home more easily and are less likely to get caught up in alcohol-induced violence, thanks to the intro-duction of an integrated night time transport initiative'. The aim, in this instance, is to create a place where people feel safe.

Plate 18 Brooklyn Street, Bolton – low-demand housing subject to market renewal initiatives and street improvement aimed at recreating liveability (Bolton, 2003)

This short list of initiatives – four of 27 case studies reviewed on government's IDeA website – share the goal of improving the way in which people connect with place. Liveability is concerned with the processes that create communities (as in the Leicester example) and with place-making, perhaps designed to re-create the 'charm' (Allmendinger and Tiesdell, 2004) that is lost because of anti-social behaviour, poor design or bad planning. The agenda is certainly important in the north of England as government, through its Pathfinder initiatives, attempts to stabilise communities. But it is also a goal of all new strategic development, and central to sustainability: ensuring that places are 'fit for purpose', 'worth living in' and 'easy to live with'. In the Thames Gateway, a strategy was put in place in 2005 with the objectives of 'greening the gateway', arguing that 'a network of varied and well-managed greenspace should be the setting for new and existing residential and commercial areas' (ODPM, 2005g: 5). This space should be seen as 'functional', functioning with and as part of the sustainable communities that government aims to develop in southern England. Through partnership working, and through positive engagement, planning is charged with taking forward a housing-liveability agenda.

Conclusions

For some critics of government's housing policies, the idea of sustainable com-munities is merely a smoke-screen behind which to conceal an unprecedented programme of residential development, possibly justified by a switch to an afford-ability-led rationale underpinning future planning for housing (see Chapter 7). For others, the phrase itself has been robbed of any meaning: it has come to represent the antidote to everything that is wrong with the planning system and its outcomes since the Second World War. Planning has delivered disjointed answers to development dilemmas; sustainable communities will offer coherent answers: planning has resulted in low-quality housing in ugly developments: sustainable communities will be attractive and well designed: planning has been slow and bureaucratic: sustainable communities will be borne of a visionary process and will be representative of real 'place making'. The concept itself is often associated with the government's 'Growth Areas', and the pairing of the CP with the need for growth suggests that new housing is likely to be accom-modated within urban extensions onto the rural–urban fringe, and might in some cases eat into London's Green Belt. It appears to be an urbanising agenda, extending into the countryside around towns and prompting the current wave of anti-sprawl sentiment sweeping through southern England. But the Plan has also become a branding for all forms of development activity. It is about more than 200,000 homes in the Thames Gateway: it can perhaps be seen as New Labour's attempt to break the development stalemate.

It can also be seen as a broader agenda for the planning system: one that is not new but which the system lost as it sank into a regulatory and narrower focus in the years after 1947. In the stampede to 'create' sustainable commun-ities, planning's status at first appears to be diminished: it becomes a facilitator rather than a doer. But it occupies a pivotal position in government's aspirations for future housing provision set within more durable communities. Some power will gravitate upwards to the regions, especially if a market-led approach to housing land allocations is allowed to take root. But local planning is central to the realisation of broader aspirations: to carry forward strategic housing objec-tives within the context of liveable places, which ultimately become sustainable communities as planning influences the way people live.

Chapter 9

Reframing planning
Spatial strategies and community development

Introduction

The central aim of this book has been to review planning's role in housing provision and to question whether planning has and can in the future make a positive contribution towards delivering decent homes for all. Many of the previous chapters have examined how planning as a process has directed housing development and governed the release of land (Chapters 4 and 7), grappled with strategic and local pressures (Chapter 6), or been used to harness development value for social benefit including the provision of 'affordable homes' (Chapter 5). The two previous chapters, 7 and 8, have reflected on current changes to planning's role in housing provision in the context of affordability-led land allocations and the Sustainable Communities Plan. At various points we have touched upon planning's 'shifting sands': that is, the way the planning system is changing and how this change might affect planning for housing. This current chapter aims to focus in on the planning process itself and whether a new ethos is required to plan for homes and communities. Within the chapter, we look at how planners and housing developers, through culture change, could create and utilise a planning process towards the common goal of delivering housing in the various contexts examined in previous chapters.

By examining this relationship, we are also able to identify why planning's current role in housing development is not always a positive one and how the planning system may have to change (fundamentally and through local implementation practices), in order to facilitate the production of 'better quality places' and government's sustainable communities. Overall, the purpose of the chapter is to demonstrate how planning can play a more positive role in housing development, creating better urban and rural environments.

The shifting sands of planning, politics and government

Planning is changing across Europe at the present time (Tewdwr-Jones and Williams, 2001). And it is changing within the context of a changing state,

as part of a more fundamental reform of territorial management that aims to
– inter alia – improve integration of different forms of spatial development
activity including residential and non-residential development (Tewdwr-Jones
and Allmendinger, 2006): the 'functions' considered in the last chapter. This, of
course, bodes well for housing development, which needs to be integrated with
a host of related concerns. At one level, devolution and decentralisation of the
state and its implications for spatial planning must be analysed in respect of other
aspects of a push towards regionalism and localism. At another level, the current
reforms which privilege regional-scale policy interventions will inevitably require
changes in the divisions of powers and responsibilities at local and national levels.
The political and institutional process of devolution and decentralisation involves
a major rescaling of both spatial planning and development, which is unfolding
rapidly and unevenly across Britain. Much of this rescaling is occurring within
terms and boundaries set by the state, since these new activities are sponsored
or supported by various tiers of government. But other recent activities within
spatial development are choreographed by non-state actors and are frequently
organised territorially and culturally.

Planning, conceptually, is subject to significant reform as a statutory
process, through the provisions of the Planning and Compulsory Purchase Act
2004, and as a tool of political institutionalism as it becomes increasingly
stretched, tugged, expanded and loaded, with increasing expectations of it delivering at various spatial scales, within and outside existing territories, that suggest
both forces of continuity with and radical breaks from the past (i.e. continuity
with its original mission, but a break from the regulatory mindset that has taken
root in the last 60 years). The biggest change currently being enacted in practice
is the extension of planning from its narrow regulatory base within various territories and various scales simultaneously, to a broader integrating and spatial
governing activity, particularly at regional and sub-regional levels (Tewdwr-Jones,
2004; Allmendinger and Haughton, 2006), with particular implications for the
strategic delivery of new housing (see Chapters 6 and 7), which is becoming a
key sub-regional (the level at which future market assessment will be undertaken)
concern, and will no longer in the future be framed within 'structure planning'.
This is being rolled out with trepidation politically, and uncertainty professionally, but within existing political and socio-geographical territories to ensure
legal authority. For many planners, it is a vastly different type of planning from
the certain, legal and political activity they have been used to. For housing developers and other private interests, it can seem equally bewildering.

The second phase of the planning overhaul is to transcend those existing
geographical, territorial and institutional boundaries, if planning is to serve a
more forward-looking purpose in the decades ahead. There is general acceptance

that historical boundaries, administrative delineations, and professional silos will not deliver the type of effective planning (for housing and more broadly) and governance in the future that is, politically and economically, being expected. Many of these boundaries are being broken down in the context of regional planning, highlighted by the move to a statutory spatial planning framework, in which there is a broadening of concern for the linkages between policy areas and between sub-regions. This is an issue we return to in the final chapter. The more difficult part of reform, which could benefit the social and environmental as a counterpoint to the economic and political, is to encourage strategy makers to 'think outside the box' of their own pre-determined territory. Change is in the air professionally and managerially, and politically there is little option but to go with the grain of this change.

There are bound to be difficulties with planning (some of the practical uncertainties were noted in Chapter 7), and with the delivery of housing development, within all territories in the next decade. Spatial strategy making is expected to become a collaborative tool of public services and policy development, alongside planning's traditional role as a land-use regulatory activity, while being stretched across several tiers of government and owned across state and non-state agents of governance. There are broader issues that fall from this discussion, which individual territories – in their contention over spatial governance – having to contend with:

* ownership, and the rights and responsibilities of elected government versus stakeholder interests at the sub-national scale, raising the spectre of too many competing voices in the way we plan for future housing supply;
* legitimacy, and the rights of a professional elite in this day and age to make supposedly-still rational decisions for the public benefit;
* control, and the attempts of the central state to retain responsibility for broader development, economic and infrastructure issues while ideologically proposing more neighbourhood, local, sub-regional and regional policy making processes, both within established territorial boundaries, and transcending them.

We are entering one of the most turbulent periods for spatial strategy making in the UK that finds form in three ways – legislative, devolved and coordinative. The legislative and policy framework of planning has undergone yet another period of reform, intended to modernise planning as a public service for the twenty-first century (Allmendinger *et al.*, 2003). In contrast to the legislative reforms to planning during the Thatcher and Major years, when planning was reduced to nothing more than a 'regulatory rump' (Thornley, 1993;

Allmendinger and Tewdwr-Jones, 1997), reforms under the Blair government have – perhaps somewhat surprisingly – potentially reinvigorated planning into a proactive coordinating activity, intended to assist in delivering development as part of continued economic growth (this is clearly a key agenda in regional planning as we see in the next chapter). The Planning and Compulsory Purchase Act 2004 completely reforms the planning policy and strategy-making function at national, regional, sub-regional, local and community levels: as we noted in earlier chapters, Regional Planning Guidance Notes are replaced with 'Regional Spatial Strategies'; 'Sub-Regional Strategies' are introduced for the first time; and Structure Plans, Local Plans and Unitary Development Plans are replaced with 'Local Development Documents', 'Action Area Plans' and 'Supplementary Planning Guidance'. The frameworks in which new housing is provided and communities are 'shaped' are undergoing a fundamental change; it is also the case that communities are being given a bigger say in the direction of this change.

Under the provision of Part I of the Local Government Act 2000, 'Community Strategies' (and now Sustainable Community Strategies: see Chapter 8) are to find implementation at neighbourhood level within Local Development Frameworks. The key objective is to enhance the quality of life for local communities while contributing to the achievement of sustainable development. It must provide a long-term vision for the area, an action plan, a shared commitment to implementation, and arrangements for monitoring. A key element is the involvement of local people. In Chapter 6, we looked at the example of the proposed Stevenage West development in Hertfordshire. The history of Stevenage West – which began with a strategic allocation of new housing in the Hertfordshire Structure Plan in 1998 – is one of intractable controversy and local opposition. Arguably, a system of suddenly closer community involvement would not smooth the frictions that have been apparent in Stevenage; but a different planning system may have delivered a different type of development more attuned to the aspirations of local groups. Whether or not this would have happened in practice is difficult to say, but this is at least the hope of the architects of the current round of planning reform. In revising the new planning process to take account of the Community Strategy agenda, the government has stated categorically that closer collaboration between planners and those who produce these strategies can help improve the quality of life in communities across the country; those subject to new house building (as in Stevenage), and those subject to housing and community-based regeneration strategies. The then Planning Minister, Keith Hill, stated in November 2003 that:

> The planning system can really boost the quality of life in our communities, delivering homes, jobs and regeneration [. . .] The Government is committed to making

the planning system faster, fairer and more responsive to the needs of the community and business. The old system didn't always take account of the views of local people. We are changing this to make sure people can play a part in the planning decisions which shape their communities.

(Planning Minister Keith Hill, 12 November 2003,
ODPM, 2003g, Press Release)

Government's focus is on the faster delivery of development on the one hand, and front-loading the policy and strategy process on the other: the hope is that by building consensus around strategy and policy, it can avoid further rounds of conflict and delay in the development process. The use of such tools at 'pre-application discussions' regarding new housing and 'development control forums' involving community groups is examined at some length by Carmona *et al.* (2003), who conclude that these are useful means of involving local people earlier in the planning process, but they hold no absolute guarantee of a less fraught process. Development might well proceed more smoothly once agreement is reached in its form; but there is still the matter of form to contend with upfront. That said, the mere fact that people feel able to influence the direction of development, rather than simply having to respond to a limited number of options at a later stage is likely to prove to be a step in the right direction. In the case of Stevenage, the community was left reeling at the prospect of a large strategic allocation of new housing, parachuted down from above, being bolted onto an existing settlement. This prompted an immediate and negative response, largely because it reduced local confidence in the planning process and left people feeling alienated from a system that appeared autocratic and distant. The new Sustainable Community Strategies (ODPM, 2005i) will take some time to implement, and they may not be welcomed by all stakeholders; however, they are likely to lead to noticeable change over the longer term.

Another aspect of the reform agenda – and one that challenges the idea of a uniform planning system – concerns scale and uniqueness. For far too long, the UK government expected planning to be devised and implemented uniformly across all parts of Britain: one country, one system. But such an ethos lies counter to the process of regionalisation. It also contributed to the notion that planning was failing to deliver housing development in the right locations, to cater for the desires and expectations of local and regional actors (see Chapter 6), and produced standardised plans and policies that did not always deliver tailored solutions. Certainly, the standardisation of new housing forms in the 1980s contributed greatly to the negative perceptions of development that still shape reactions to new housing proposals (see Leishman and Warren, 2006). The intention is now for planning to become increasingly differentiated in different

parts of the UK as a consequence of devolution, decentralization and regionalisation (Tewdwr-Jones, 2002; Haughton and Counsell, 2004), and is being
facilitated – albeit nervously – by a central state that realizes that a national planning process (originally devised in the aftermath of the 1939–1945 war years) is
incompatible with government policies intended to foster either economic competitiveness or housing solutions appropriate for different regional contexts
(Tewdwr-Jones, 1999). Hence, there is now greater differentiation of housing
strategies at the regional level, which are designed to respond to different structural and local challenges. 'Spatial strategies' provide frameworks for evidence-
based policies, with special emphasis given to understanding local housing market processes (Chapter 7), and the linkages between housing, local economics
and environmental concerns. Many regional assemblies have commissioned independent studies into housing, transport, demography and infrastructure and are
developing sub-regional plans that aim to bridge the gap left by the abolition
of Structure Plans. The emphasis is on understanding context within a framework of broad principles being set out in the new Planning Policy Statements
(including the final version of PPS3) and in the government's 'Communities
Plan', which is centrally concerned with context and with creating communities that are defined by a 'multi-functionality' that brings together jobs, homes
and other opportunities in more self-sustaining spaces. The same is true in the
home nations. Scotland, Wales and Northern Ireland are developing their own
spatial strategies separate to those being developed in English regions with a
desire for differentiation (Berry et al., 2001; Allmendinger, 2002; Harris et al.,
2002). Of course these processes are nevertheless occurring within the confines
of pre-established boundaries; but the ethos marks a distinct break away from past
practices.

The final aspect of reform concerns integration and the new role for
spatial strategy-making in achieving coordination between disparate actors and
strategies. New forms of planning are being explored as tools to help resolve
community, sub-regional and regional problems (Counsell, et al., 2003), alongside a renaissance for planning as the means of achieving policy integration and
coordination and the promotion of sustainable development (Tewdwr-Jones,
2004). The emphasis here is to look at planning not as a delivery process per se,
in the style of planning under the welfare state, but rather as a strategic capacity
and political integration mechanism intended to cement the increasingly fragmented agents of the state, all of whom possess their own agendas, political
objectives, strategies and resources, but who need to cooperate in order to deliver
projects and developments. Planning is being looked at to ensure compatible
working and strategic coordination when desired. This process extends the
remit of planning beyond mere land-use development and the 1980s-1990s

'regulatory rump' into a coordinative process where professional planners' duties concern management of agency integration (Healey, 1997; Lloyd and Illsley, 1999). Because many agencies and groups have a concern for new housing and related development – especially support infrastructure – a broadening of the role of planning seems like a natural step in the right direction: broadening of institutional capacity (to deal with a wider range of issues) seems to be essential at a time when it is generally accepted that housing is more than bricks and mortar. As we saw in the last chapter, housing as a field of concern encapsulates physical, social, aesthetic and environmental considerations, and therefore housing development cannot be steered by those whose expertise extends only as far as the proper use of land. An extension of responsibility is essential in order to legitimise and build confidence in planning. Such a responsibility has already formed a significant element to new government policy on the role of and expectations on planning post-2004 (ODPM, 2004a), and influenced the professional planning body's agenda on the role it expects its members to perform in the twenty-first century (RTPI, 2003). These three drivers of change within spatial plan-making are transforming the activity and scope of planning, across scales and across territories in varied ways and at varied times.

Four initiatives set the hallmark of the changed ethos of planning – and its links to housing provision – in the years ahead: local government modernisation and the focus on community and neighbourhood; the planning reforms of the Planning and Compulsory Purchase Act 2004; the relationship between community and local development; and the introduction of spatial planning alongside the traditional land-use regulatory planning framework. Each represents an important driver of change in relation to housing development and the function of planning in relation to that development. The next section sets the immediate context and expectations for the reform agenda, by reviewing each of the four initiatives.

Local government modernisation and community

Following the general election in 1997, the government signalled an intention to 'Modernise Government' (Cabinet Office, 1999). For local government, the first priority was to improve performance, which was thought to be the main cause of reduced public confidence in local authorities (DETR, 1998a). This was to be achieved first through the introduction of the Best Value regime of local performance indicators that was followed by the introduction of CPA in 2002 (Martin, 1999). Following devolution, the four administrations in England, Scotland, Wales and Northern Ireland also signalled a strong desire to involve the public in decision-making and setting service standards (Local Government

Act, 2000). In terms of more general decision-making, the Government published guidance that indicated a more thorough and systematic approach to taking account of and using citizen views within decision-making (DETR, 1998a).

One of the principal themes developed by the Labour government after 1997 as part of its modernising agenda was ensuring greater public accountability of local government. There were also concerns in the new government about democratic engagement, with lower participation rates in elections and particularly low involvement from young people. But problems of non- participation at an electoral level were paralleled by the problem of conflict locally. Haughton and Counsell (2004: 137) have drawn attention to the local 'dramas' that often accompany planning decisions, especially those concerned with house building. Arguably, a past lack of any systematic approach to 'taking account of views' resulted in the ad hoc development of a consultative approach in which local communities have been consulted upon development 'options' but have not always been given an opportunity, by land-use planning, to shape those options from the start. The Labour government, especially in relation to housing and planning, has been concerned with exactly when communities participate and their capacity to be involved in policy design rather than simply being a sounding-board for planning decisions that have already been taken.

Within this context, the establishment of Community Strategies in 2000 (see above) illustrates the enhancing of neighbourhood partnerships and development of community voices in local government policy and decision-making (particularly in relation to housing development) at a time when the traditional approach and reliance on local government alone has been questioned (Tewdwr-Jones *et al.*, 2006). Community Strategies – and the evolving SCS – are intended to provide a more robust assessment of the social and economic problems facing individual communities, and to provide a means of bringing people into the process of policy design. In addition, two other common themes have been developed. The first, is the encouragement of local authorities to move to establish LSPs in England and Local Economic Forums (LEFs) and Community Planning Partnerships (CPPs) in Scotland, to act as overall partnerships for their areas. These are to be the arena in which house builders, voluntary groups, police representatives and community groups come together and start to work through local policy aspirations from the bottom up. These are to coordinate much of the work of local thematic partnerships, such as those for crime and disorder, and further develop the partnership ethos from economic governance to broader governmental sectors. The second, non-statutory initiative was the implementation of the Prime Minister's target for the achievement of e-government (electronic access to local government services) by December 2005.

In terms of the planning process, this major programme of local government reform has had a series of direct implications for the operation of the planning system that can be understood in three key ways. First, the new decision-making processes separated the 'executive' from the ability to make planning application decisions for the first time. It also required that the full council (rather than the planning committee and planning department) adopt the Development Plan. Second, a series of new operational frameworks were introduced that have considerable influence on the way in which councils undertake the planning task. Of particular significance here are LSPs as cross sectional and multi-agency partnerships. Each council now has a duty to prepare a Community Strategy that involves engaging the commitment and participation of local partners. The LSPs provide an obvious means of providing this partnership for the process of preparing the Community Strategy, which may be used to take forward community aspirations in relation to new housing or housing renewal (see Chapter 10). The last element of the new operational framework is the power of well-being. This power, enshrined in statute, is expected to be used as a first resort and to be a strong framework for a variety of new ways of working.

Thus, since 1997, there have been significant reforms in both local government and planning that have important implications. For planning, local authorities have been required primarily to be focused on performance in this period, although there have been important changes in the decision making processes set out in the new constitutions. For local government, it now has to meet a more joined-up approach to delivery, with one-stop shops, customer tracking of their planning and licensing applications, a performance-dominated culture, and increasing pressure to ensure full citizen engagement in decision making. On too many housing developments, the only 'customer focus' has been provided by the speculative house builder, whose only real concern has been for prospective home buyers who are attracted by the prospect of acquiring a new home with a 10-year National House Building Council (NHBC) warranty at a reasonable price. There has been little concern shown for the customers of the local authority who have come to view planning not as a 'service' but as something that is inflicted upon local communities, and which serves the needs of business. Despite accusations that the reformed planning system remains committed to serving business interests, there is some hope that a completely new way of dealing with communities as customers of the planning service will help promote a sense of community well-being as opposed to alienation. Notwithstanding the fact that some of the supporters of CASE (see Chapter 6) reside some distance from the Stevenage development, it is evident that in Stevenage and elsewhere, many communities feel frustrated and alienated by planning decisions over new housing. Development forms reflect an official public-sector led view of what is right, often aiming to create new bolt-on communities, rather than seeking to extend and add vibrancy to existing communities. Of course, this is not the case in all instances. But a model that devises 'options' and then seeks endorsement for these options is unlikely to reflect community aspirations; it is more likely to anger and frustrate. Therefore, modernisation is likely to make some contribution to a mode of planning for housing that re-engages with people.

Planning reform

Community Strategies have – and will, in their revised structure (see Chapter 8) – form an important feature of the new structure of local government, and hold out the promise of more effective planning for housing. Their preparation is a duty for the whole council of the local authority that now has more specific and defined roles than in the past. Community Strategies are meant to be the 'plan of plans' or overarching policy statements for each council; and this arguably gives housing a more central place within community development (linking it to wider concerns: to the environment and liveability; to crime and safety; to the economy and personal well-being; and to health). The purpose of the plan is to provide a coordinated approach to the social, economic and environmental well-being of the authority area, again dealing fundamentally with the linkages between housing and the raft of other concerns that are central to community well-being. As such, they provide an opportunity for a programmed approach and one where public sector and external funding – such as that from RDA or the EU – can be targeted. The plan also helps ensure that sub-authority issues across the public, private and voluntary sectors are tackled in an integrated way. Community Strategies potentially provide a more effective means of understanding the community infrastructure – public open space, leisure, child-care and so forth – that needs to accompany new housing development, though it does not answer the critical question of how this infrastructure should be paid for. This is a concern that we considered in Chapters 7 and 8, and return to in Chapter 10.

Community Strategies are also seen as a key component in the commitment towards the reduction in the requirement on local authorities to submit so many plans to government as part of the 'audit culture'. In their role as the 'plan of plans', Community Strategies may also be seen to take precedence over all of the other policies and strategies produced by a council. The relationship between reformulated SCS and other required plans – including LDFs – is currently being worked through. Nevertheless, some local authorities that meet high levels of service standards will be released from all requirements to submit plans to central government, but with two main exceptions: a Community Strategy and a Best Value performance plan (again, re-enforcing the central importance of these documents). A third requirement relates to the submission of their development plan if this falls within the period of exemption from plan submission.

Since the implementation of the Local Government Act 2000, a high percentage of local authorities have now prepared or are preparing their Community Strategies. This represents very rapid implementation if compared with the proposed changes in the planning system that were first discussed in late 2001, introduced within the Planning and Compulsory Purchase Bill in 2002, and became law when the Bill received Royal Assent in May 2004. The speed of implementation of the Community Strategy preparation at the local level is in stark contract with these reforms of albeit complex and established systems. Nevertheless, it is an inevitable consideration that once the new LDFs (the new Development Plan system to be implemented by the Planning Act of 2004) are implemented, this will create an entirely changed plan-context at the local level. In England, the new relationship between the Community Strategy and the revised development plan process is radical, and again this has implications for planning for housing.

A Community Strategy can have a spatial expression, although at present the relationship between a Strategy and the development plan remains vague (ODPM, 2003a; ODPM, 2003d). The 2004 planning legislation talks of LDF becoming the spatial expression of Community Strategies (and therefore an expression of aspiration, including aspiration in relation to community well-being and housing). The Local Government White Paper of 2001 concentrated primarily on the delivery agenda: performance, leadership, finance, e-government, local public service agreements and working together with central government around the citizen. Little in the White Paper was said about the development of the role of the Community Strategy from the 2000 Act and subsequent guidance refers both to working in partnership through the LSP and involving the local community and individuals more clearly in decision-making.

By contrast, although the guidance on Community Strategies had indicated that Community Strategies would have a spatial expression and a clear link with development plans, the planning Green Paper of 2001 described the arrangements for preparation of local plans as 'being overtaken' by new local authority policies and programmes, including the Community Strategy (DTLR, 2001a: paragraph 4.7). More significantly, the planning Green Paper set out the relationship between the Community Strategy and local planning by advocating a major role for this new relationship:

> Community strategies will play a key role in informing the preparation of Local Development Frameworks. In turn, the Framework must assist in delivering the policies in the Community Strategy.
>
> (ibid., para 4.7)

Traditional development plans have tended to focus on land-use policies, narrowly defined, but the form of the new Community Strategy document is innovative and groundbreaking; it is essentially a vision and action plan for improvements in the district that local people need and want. It is not restricted to land-use planning, or 'just housing' or 'just environment'; it can cover any topic. Responsibility for the preparation of the Strategy, will not rest with professional planners alone but with the LSP, which has been seen as 'the key to our strategy to deliver better towns and cities' (DTLR, 2001c: 34) by bringing together the public and voluntary organisations to identify and take action on local priorities. This view is reinforced in a 2005 review of LSPs (ODPM, 2005i). Extending the enterprise-led urban regeneration process, the Community Strategy is a more comprehensive and strategic multi-agency scheme. LPAs, as the service providers in the local authority and as one partner within the LSP, are to cooperate and contribute to the preparation and implementation of the Strategy. Within the Communities Plan, the planning system and strategic partnerships have a vital role in shaping the strategy and in:

> Supporting communities that: are economically prosperous; have decent homes at affordable prices; safeguard the countryside; enjoy a well designed, accessible and pleasant living and working environment; and are effectively and fairly governed with a strong sense of community.
>
> (ODPM, Planning Division, 2004b)

Therefore, although the local authority retains ownership, the Strategy is to be prepared in conjunction with the LSP where one exists. Thus, the LSP's partnership working will provide a considerable input from other public agencies, the voluntary sector and the business community. The Community Strategy should not only be developed in conjunction with the LSP, it should also focus and shape the activity of local organisations including those in the public sector, of which the council's actions should be part.

In the reformed planning system, communities will – in theory – be given a more prominent role in shaping the local policy agenda, as will other stakeholders who will come together in the context of LSP. Communities will be viewed as communities of customers with whom the local authority shares a reflexive relationship; they will no longer be communities of consumers who are rarely given the opportunity to shape the products they are asked to consume. This shift in planning's central rationale – from relative insularity and paternalism to a new openness – suggests a fundamental shift in the way planning will need to deal with new house building. But how far can it really deviate from the current status quo? Most regions are now engaged in the development of new Spatial Strategies, and they have inherited housing allocations (see Chapter 6) from RPG. The core strategies of the RPGs contain policy-based housing figures, and many regions – especially in southern England – are being asked to revise these figures in light of government's Communities Plan, which seeks to concentrate growth within designated 'Growth Areas'. Despite the inevitable controversy surrounding planned growth, especially in relation to official inter-ventions at the level of regional planning to ensure compliance with the strategy set out in the CP, government has recently extended the number of Growth Areas and is insisting on concentration at strategic sites. Growth targets now find their way into sub-regional strategies and from a 'spatial planning' perspective, strategic growth looks like the best way of meeting housing demand: new communities over a certain size have a greater chance of being self-sustaining (i.e. with a preferential homes–jobs balance) and can be more easily provided with support infrastructure. But does this mean that communities – despite talk of a more open and inclusive planning system – are likely to be presented with the same limited number of development options? If the government wants to see strategic housing allocations as part of its growth agenda and the south-east needs in excess of 650,000 new homes over the next 20 years, how will these developments be demonstrably different from those coming on stream in the early years of this decade? If Community Strategies fail to reach consensus over the need for housing, where will this leave local planning? And will the new plan-ning system simply create a new impasse in planning for housing? Answers to some of these questions have not yet surfaced, though they are revisited towards the end of this chapter and in Chapter 10.

Communities and local development (strategies and LDFs)

The implementation of the new planning framework after 2004, alongside the emerging process of local governance and LSPs, and the preparation of Com-munity Strategies, will yield more distinct differences. The Sustainable Commun-ity Strategy (S)CS is to be produced in a shorter timescale than a traditional development plan or even the new LDF, to go through a shorter period of adop-tion and to be clearly focused on outcomes. No specific processes for approval or external validation of the Community Strategy has been given in the guidance apart from its ownership that will rest with the community as a whole. In order to consider the relationship between the Community Strategy and the emergent LDFs, the ODPM commissioned research from Entec, published in 2003 (ENTEC, 2003). This research considered some of the key issues about the emergent relationship between the two documents. The project team acknowledged that a range of approaches to Community Strategies have already emerged, although they reported that 'common themes are emerging in terms of their coverage, increasing *local distinctiveness* and a more structured approach as their focus changes from vision to implementation and delivery' (ibid., iv, emphasis added).

Community Strategies are seen to range from those with much detailed content to those that are more vision statements. The research identified some good practice principles for the future relationship between LDFs and the Community Strategies, including policy and process linkages. The study also identified some key issues that are already emerging, with evidence that Community Strategies have a high amount of spatial content but are not necessarily linked to development planning processes. Second, the Community Strategy pulls together the many other plans prepared at the local level such as those for neighbourhood renewal and other area-based initiatives, which only increases their spatial content further. The local distinctiveness promoted by Community Strategies is critical, investing communities with the potential to deliver tailored solutions that are crucially important in relation to new housing schemes, which are too frequently viewed as 'one-size-fits-all'.

But a key political problem relates to the tension between broadly owned Strategies and 'official' Development Frameworks. Strategies may well be viewed as a cultural threat to planning within an authority that has always seen planning as a strategic duty, and not something to be negotiated. The potential for conflict and tension – or possible synergy – between Community Strategies and LDFs, as identified within a number of key themes and issues that we go on to review below, could be high and will need to be actively managed. They provide a range of issues to be both managed and marshalled in order for any local authority to gain the most from both processes. These issues are perhaps further compounded by the lack of discussion about these tensions and how best they can be resolved to the community's advantage.

All this suggests the development of elements of integration and submergence within planning. As a policy mechanism firmly embedded within the local government institutional context, local planning is being affected demonstrably by the Modernisation process and public-orientation agenda. Three significant themes stand out:

1   the increased emphasis upon performance, monitoring and targets;
2   the role of Community Strategies in subsuming and broadening the role
      of development plans;
3   the role of LSPs in embedding planning within frameworks of local stake-
      holders.

Much of what has been said here links back to the discussion of 'sustainable communities' presented in Chapter 8. Broader ownership of the planning
process means broader interest in local housing solutions that meet community
objectives. Empowerment, through this strategy, is a route to delivering the
housing-liveability agenda emerging in government's Sustainable Communities
Plan.

Spatial planning

Spatial planning – which has been referenced throughout this book – has been
defined as critical thinking about space and place as a basis for action or intervention (RTPI, 2003). The origin of the term stems from European spatial
planning practices, particularly the exercise for the preparation of the European
Spatial Development Perspective (ESDP) in 1999, and was used for that exercise
to emphasise a process of planning that was something more than the land-use
regulatory and zoning practices of individual Member States (CEC, 1999). The
implementation, or rather translation, of the principles of the ESDP into Member
States' national and regional planning policies has been chequered across the EU,
and Britain stands out as one of the best examples of where the form of the
ESDP has been applied to emerging national and regional spatial plan-making.
This is no disadvantage to Britain; as the reform of the Structural Funds will
occur post-2006, the European Commission is starting to signal a desire to
couple Structural Fund resource and allocation plans to clear spatial programmes.
      Within England and Wales, the Planning and Compulsory Purchase Act has
provided a new opportunity for the development of spatial planning. Planning
has the purpose of contributing to the delivery of sustainable development and
the new legislative planning framework is intended to create a robust system for
the future of planning. The renewed emphasis on a purpose for planning through
legislative change provides motivation to professionals, developers and planning
users. It is important to consider how visionary planning can be developed to
meet the needs of a range of stakeholders, to ensure the delivery of sustainable
development and sustainable communities, and to shape places that people feel
proud of. Again, these themes were introduced in the last chapter.

The key here is to think beyond the confines of the present. Planning, for far too long, has centred on procedures and strategies. There is, one may say, nothing inherently successful about producing a strategy or plan unless that strategy or plan can be implemented or leads to the shaping of better places. In line with government ideology, attention is starting to focus on the users of the planning system: how can planning be utilised as a framework to enable development to occur, or for communities, individual and business users to express a voice within development decisions?

The introduction of statutory Regional Spatial Strategies and sub-regional strategies, the replacement of development plans with LDF, Action Plans and master planning schemes, and the enhanced links between Local Development Documents and Community Strategies through enhanced participatory measures, creates a very new context, institutional framework, and purpose for planning. This degree of change has not been witnessed within the planning framework for over 30 years. Within Wales, Scotland and Northern Ireland, the changes towards spatial planning are already underway. The Welsh Assembly Government (2003) produced a consultation version of its Cabinet-backed Wales Spatial Plan in September 2003 and Northern Ireland already possesses a RDS (Department for Regional Development NI, 2003). The Scottish Executive is working on the preparation of a National Spatial Planning Framework. Even London possesses its own form of spatial plan, the Mayor's London Plan (Mayor of London, 2002). The broader role for spatial planning in addressing European finance or global investment issues has certainly been recognised in these areas.

Planning practitioners sometimes balk at the reforms, suggesting that they are nothing more than another set of changes to planning, and we have certainly had many of those over the last three decades. But these reforms are the first changes to planning that are genuinely positive; they place planning at the heart of coordinating change and bringing about more successful places. Within these reforms are heightened expectations on what planning aims to achieve. The politicians are vesting the planning framework with a great deal of importance. This suggests that processes will need to change and the changes will affect not only the institutional framework of planning, the tools of the trade, but also the ethos within planning activities, such as planners' attitudes towards public consultation, and the mindsets and cultural attitudes of practitioners towards their work, and towards working across boundaries. This is particularly important, as we saw in the last chapter, if interests are to come together to deliver new housing in Sustainable Communities.

In order to capitalise on this new motivation within planning, the term spatial planning is useful in both expressing a shift beyond a traditional idea of land-use planning and describing many aspects of planning practice that provide proactive possibilities for the management of change, including policy-making, policy integration, community participation, agency stake-holding and development management. Spatial planning is not merely about the use and development of land; it suggests coordination between various actors in planning and their desires, it concerns the management of development rather than the receipt and issuing of planning permissions; and it places the meaning of places, particularly to potential users of places, at the heart of its concerns. When compared to traditional land-use planning, one immediately recognises that we are entering uncharted territory with spatial planning. And that is exactly why the successful implementation of spatial planning is going to require commitment from practitioners, planning lawyers and politicians. By raising the stakes of planning to embrace more users, and by giving an enhanced voice to various groups in society, the audience for planning at the local and regional levels will widen expectations and optimism will be raised about what planning is there to do and who it serves.

A key aspect of how spatial planning may be different from existing planning process relates to delivery; spatial planning involves key objectives relating to sustainable development, policy and strategy integration; and participation and inclusiveness. Spatial planning is value-driven and is intended to recognise and mediate between conflicting sets of values. It is also action-orientated and is intended to mediate between retaining existing spaces and creating new opportunities for both development and place making.

Spatial planning is a positive force to guide change. The partners involved in spatial policy-making recognise that better quality and more informed planning can be achieved with public, private and voluntary sectors working together both to develop new planning policy and to coordinate action to achieve sustainable development. The principles of spatial planning, and the links to housing provision – including many of the principles noted in earlier chapters – are listed in Table 9.1.

Spatial planning will become a core component in the delivery of sustainable residential development. It is the process concerned with the coordination of strategy and policy, with the active involvement of planning users, and with land-use and physical development in the public interest. But we should not believe that spatial planning will only occur on a site-by-site basis. Spatial planning can occur at any governmental level, from European, to national, to regional, strategic and local; it may be a strategic exercise, a local partnership process, or a community-centred activity. Successful planning is not one where a planning application is decided within eight weeks or where a development plan is adopted within four years of preparation. A successful spatial planning framework is one that is layered, integrated and dynamic. Spatial planning is more

Table 9.1 Spatial planning and housing

Spatial planning	Housing
Broad-ranging, concerning the assessment of the spatial dimensions of various activities and sectors, and interactions between them.	Delivering a housing-liveability agenda; concern for the linkages between homes and jobs, and between housing provision and infrastructure.
Visionary, by opening up planning to a range of participants, and by relating processes of planning policy-making to notions of place.	A concern for place-making and for design, creating places and communities that people value and which will anchor communities.
Integrating, through the bringing together of both spatial issues relating to the development and use of land, and the users of planning.	Creating places that are functional on a number of levels; delivering the liveability agenda described in Chapter 8.
Deliverable, applying strategy to programmes for action, through proactive processes, involving coordination and choreography between different over-lapping sectors and resources.	Planning that can deliver the ambitious programmes that are now in place; planning that can move beyond the slow bureaucratic processes of the past and deliver decent homes in sustainable communities.
Participative, where planning is a facilitator and dependent on new forms of partnership and engagement with a range of bodies, stakeholders, businesses and communities.	Creating communities of choice in which people feel a sense of ownership and do not feel alienated; instil a belief that new homes are a positive form of future development; that they are people orientated.

multi-dimensional, linking development to place, time and the agents of change, and an important principle of spatial planning is that it avoids narrow, exclusive and disjointed practices: rather, it is integrated and multi-functional (see Chapter 8). It is outcome-focused, but also programme-based. Spatial planning relates the implications of potential development on particular locations with explanation and prediction. It will be a challenge, particularly because the current practices of planning do not always perform successfully in a joined-up way. And it will take time to operationalise, with new planning practices, relationships and coordination only emerging through good practice and experience.

Planning in the future will perform a role in making sense of the processes of change, rather than seeking ways to dominate. For LPA planners, this will mean developing new skills in educating planning users, mediating between conflicting interests, marrying-up resource and infrastructure requirements to development schemes, and taking into account issues that, previously, planners would have considered beyond their remit. Spatial coordination requires an assessment of the socio-economic and environmental issues that require attention within a given area. It will consider demographic changes, migration, housing needs, social problems such as crime and drug dependency, technological changes within a spatial scale, the spatial implications of increased globalisation, and a reflection of the unique cultural issues that can exist in places. Spatial planning involves the management of these changes in the most effective and fair ways through integration, participation and openness. This transformation of planning's role clearly has important implications for the way housing is delivered, with housing viewed not as an allocation on a development plan, but as a response to and part of socio-economic change.

Assessing the spatial implications of change means looking to other sectors, such as trade and industry, health, education, the police and justice system, to consider new ways in which problems can be solved and new opportunities created; it means the involvement of professionals and policy-makers from these sectors in partnership with planners. A key question that planners should consider is how can development make a difference to overcome the range of problems facing areas? Spatial planning means constant policy development, monitoring, and rethinking places in new ways. It means developing both short- and long-term trajectories for the future prosperity of areas, and attempting to achieve consensus on time differences. And it means looking at the broader picture, beyond the boundaries of particular development sites, to identify whether broader social, economic and environmental objectives can be achieved for communities by the active involvement of more partners in helping the shaping of places. Spatial planning is an ongoing, enduring process of managing change, by a range of actors, in the interests of sustainable development.

Arguably, land-use planning – the pre-2004 status quo – has retrenched into a non-threatening, visionless activity, dominated by a greater importance attached to plan-making and league tables rather than with the creation and shaping of places and the inclusion of people who use planning's end-products. In relation to housing, it has focused on land allocation and housing numbers. The 2004 Planning Act, together with the CP, calls on planning to rethink its role in relation to housing. Housing should not be viewed as a space-using activity – as a simple 'land-use' – but as a component within a sustainable place, and ultimately a sustainable community. Land-use planning tended to treat housing in isolation: spatial planning should seek to understand linkages, creating multi-functional places and delivering the housing-liveability agenda set out in Chapter 8.

Spatial planning frameworks must also address resource allocation and the financing of development. The new planning framework should attempt to address this problem, through the use of Action Plans and master planning techniques, but it will require local planning officers to be better skilled in financial and business matters. Developers will require relevant and targeted spatial policies; plans must meet the needs of the private sector and develop the confidence of businesses to invest in places (perhaps delivering this investment through PGS – see Chapter 8). The frameworks must be translated into the planning system from a negotiated outcome achieved from active involvement of stakeholders and community representatives. Planning currently benefits those who are able to 'speak the language' and, clearly, that potentially discriminates against large sections of society. The outcomes of spatial planning frameworks must be easily understood by all those who have participated in policy-making and those who use and rely on planning to shape spaces and places.

Spatial planning processes should be open, fair and transparent; they must inspire communities and businesses; and they should deliver quality and speedy decisions, having achieved integration with other plans, strategies and policies. Planning must be considered as a positive device in delivering economic and social change, in the shaping of our communities, and in ensuring that a range of interest groups are given a voice within policy and development decisions. In this area, past planning for housing has fallen short of the expectations of the architects of the planning system: in this sense, spatial planning is not a new approach; rather, it is the belated fulfilment of anticipated potential.

Positive planning – a key prerequisite to the delivery of sustainable communities – requires the rethinking of the local political support for policy- and strategy-making. Politicians must provide strong leadership in generating a clear vision for their areas and to encourage wide participation in discussion over the development of appropriate strategies to meet the vision. The strategies and plans of the future must be a product of participation, consensus (where possible), and particular needs. It will be the planning policy- and spatial strategy-making process, rather than development control decisions, where positive planning could yield the most benefit. Strong, relevant and up-to-date strategies and plans that are the product of participatory processes, will prove to be of immense value to development management. In the future, there may well be scope for plans and strategies to become much more orientated toward action and programmes. One essential requirement of these new spatial planning practices is enhanced links and much closer cooperation between planners within different sections of local planning authorities. Those responsible for development control must be involved in policy development at an early stage of strategy preparation.

Conclusions

The Planning and Compulsory Purchase Act 2004, the new frameworks emerging at the regional level, devolution to Wales, Scotland and Northern Ireland, the duty of well-being that was handed to local government in the Local Government Act 2000, and the desire for LDFs to become the spatial expression of SCSs, all provide the opportunity for the onset of spatial planning. Spatial planning is a chance for planning to centre itself in the heart of debates about places and changes to places, and not sidelined as an irrelevant and annoying regulatory activity.

Throughout the book we have argued that planning's role in housing provision has been problematic at the level of implementation: too often it responds negatively to development interest and pressure and some of the procedures in place may constrain housing supply, or at least slow the process of providing new homes, at a time when there is urgent need to accelerate delivery. Carmona at et (2003) have unearthed a handful of examples of planning authorities, together with house builders and RSLs, employing a range of initiatives aimed at overcoming barriers and thereby delivering better (i.e. better designed) housing with greater speed and efficiency.

However, government believes that there are too few examples of authorities and house builders working together effectively, and has argued that the planning system, along with some planning policy and procedures, is holding back development. Hence *Planning Policy Statement 12: Local Development Frameworks* (ODPM, 2004c) calls for a 'step change' in the system itself (particularly its culture of 'blocking development') which should become a focus of all sorts of physical and community development.

In recognition of the importance of up-to-date development plans, the government has advocated a move to LDFs, which will be simpler, leaner and kept under constant review. A belief in the importance of 'place making' (Chapter 8) at a site level has resulted in the introduction of Action Plans of various types, giving authorities the means to establish site aspirations and set out clear design and density directives. In order to make the entire process more inclusive, government will require authorities to set out their strategies for engaging local communities within a Community Statement attached to the LDF.

It is the Community Strategies – and perhaps SCSs – that may well have the biggest impact on housing development; they may provide a framework in which to reach compromise over housing schemes, ending the problem of public-sector-led planning simply parachuting-in new development and thus alienating itself from communities. Alternatively, these Strategies may simply create an arena for new tensions in the planning process, prolonging debate over the form of new housing development, and frustrating efforts to deliver decent homes for all. The key questions posed earlier in this chapter reveal where there is uncertainty about the take-up, influence and delivery of these new mechanisms within the context of planning for housing. They reveal apparent contradictions within government ideology and policy towards planning more generally. The 'new localism' ethos that promotes widening participation within local policy-making may be at-odds with the necessity for strategic direction to ensure development is provided and that economic growth occurs. Enhancing community involvement, and raising the expectations of public participation within policy processes more generally, suggests a transfer of discretion from local authorities to a larger body of organisations and people. If this occurs for the allocation of additional land for housebuilding, for example, the degree of contention surrounding where to allocate such additional sites may prove to be problematic, particularly if they are in the very regions that are under severe pressure and where market signals appear to be out-of-step with community aspirations. Against this transfer in policy-making debate from local authority to the public, there is a necessity at national, regional and sub-regional levels for housing figures to be provided at levels that may be outside the comfort zone for members of communities. It is, in essence, a perfect example of the clash between bottom-up forms of policy- and decision-making, with the top down strategic direction required for new development: who ultimately has the final say, and at what cost? This dilemma is not new; it was exactly the same issue that plagued the Conservatives in the late 1980s in their quest to release more greenfield housing land for major housing developments. The result at that time was the focus on local choice, where local people and local authorities were suddenly awarded far greater say in the planning system to determine policies and decisions for new development proposals, thus neatly allowing central government to pass the buck to the local level.

In the future, we may see the introduction of central government incentives or 'sweeteners' – in the form of additional block grant – awarded to those local authorities allocating additional housing land within their LDFs. If this happens, it may represent an admission on the part of the government that its own new localism and spatial planning approaches have tipped the balance of power away from LPAs. It also suggests that uncertainty over the acceptability of such development persists. The question to examine in this context will be whether local authorities will be prepared to accept such incentives and, as a consequence, face the potential for serious local political backlash from members of their own communities (assuming that members of these communities cannot be persuaded of the necessity for such development). This may also lead to much greater tensions between the regional, sub-regional and local government tiers in the amount and location of new housing land to be released, and paradoxically undermine both sustainability and community objectives. Perhaps one route out of this dilemma will involve strengthening strategic planning at the regional and sub-regional levels for new site selections that, in turn, will limit the discretion of local communities to determine site location themselves. Local communities, for their part, might be handed greater influence over issues of design, density and landscaping (the form of development); in other words, there would need to be a clear separation between issues of principle and issues of delivery. If these dilemmas are not considered thoroughly enough at this point in time, there is every danger that the amount of housing required will not be met on the one hand, and that the planning system will – yet again – be cursed by the development industry and by the government for failing to deliver. Overt attention has been paid to-date in the housing debate to issues of land supply; very little has been stated about resolving the political and governmental difficulties in ensuring project delivery on the ground, which have stemmed – in part – from the very institutional processes of which planning and local governance are a part.

Chapter 10
Conclusions

Introduction

In each of the chapters of this book, we have examined one or more aspects of the evolving role of the planning system in providing new homes. An account of 'historical development' in Chapter 2 revealed how land-use planning evolved as a broad regulatory framework for development in all its forms: the system was given a practical framework through the creation of a local government structure towards the end of the nineteenth century. The detail of how the system should and could operate emerged gradually during the first 50 years of the twentieth century, often demonstrating its strengths and weaknesses as it responded to a variety of challenges immediately prior to the First World War and then in the inter-war years. Planning became the delivery mechanism for a society that wished to decentralise, enjoy the twin benefits of developing towns and protecting the country (where necessary), and achieve greater housing quality. After the Second World War, a desire to consolidate these achievements, embark on a programme of land reform, and establish a clear social agenda led to the creation of what is now thought of as the modern planning system, or at least a system that remained largely unchanged until very recently.

In the post-war era, planning's role in housing development continued its gradual evolution, embracing systems-based approaches to built form and the wider tenets of modernist thinking. But during this period, developments in housing policy and social welfare were to have an equally profound effect on planning's changing role. A move away from state housing provision, marked initially by the growing importance of the housing association movement and eventually by the privatisation of municipal housing after 1980 (and then the part-privatisation of further social housing funding after 1988 – see Chapter 3), marked a climatic shift in planning's wider environment. Much of planning's early legacy was based on a relatively comfortable relationship within local authorities, with planning simply laying the foundations for state housing provision. Under these circumstances, planning's role was inevitably limited and there was little need to concern itself with issues of design, location, or cost, all of which were

Plate 19 System-built low-rise social housing (Welshpool, 1993)

Plate 20 1960s pre-fabricated system-built housing being incrementally replaced with traditional family houses in the 1990s (Welshpool, 1993)

fixed internally by the state. Yet in the years following 1945, this situation was turned on its head: the majority of future housing provision was to be provided by speculative builders, and it was to be planning's role to ensure that private interest did not undermine or eclipse a wider social agenda. Hence, there has been a need to widen the role of the planning system. It has become the key vehicle through which the state seeks to influence housing provision, as its direct control over this provision has waned. The challenge for planning in recent years has been how to effectively influence the design standards achieved through speculative development, how to ensure that new development is directed to the right locations, and latterly, how to guarantee that the new homes provided through private investment fit the needs of society in terms of cost, which determines affordability and allows wider access (further diminishing the need for direct state involvement in new housing provision): in other words, how planning intervenes   issues examined in Chapters 4, 5 and 6. In recent years, this widening role for the planning system has been rationalised under the auspices of sustainability: achieving development in the right locations (and balancing developmental and environmental agendas – see Chapter 1), ensuring quality in design (which, coupled with the right densities can reduce energy consumption) and guaranteeing access, all result in patterns of development which are inherently more sustainable. The 'rationale' of sustainability is gauged in a variety of ways: the right quantity of homes ensures economic sustainability through a healthy market in which the provision of houses is not constrained and there is less risk of under-supply, excessive price inflation, and potential collapse. It also suggests wider economic sustainability by avoiding restrictions on the free movement of labour and capital. Sustainability is also judged against social goals, and the desire to see balanced communities in which wealth and wisdom can be shared across generational, social and ethnic groups. But the ultimate prize of sustainability remains environmental (a prize that often supersedes all others and is viewed as the real 'rationale' of sustainable development) and ecological quality, the design and location of new homes must contribute to reductions in energy consumption, and limitations on future land-take should result in protection of land resources for successive generations. In the previous three chapters, we have sought to show how planning's role in housing provision has evolved in the first six years of the new millennium. All the aforementioned issues retain currency, but government seems to be seeking a fundamental change, promoting a focus on spatial planning and community involvement, situating housing within a broader governance agenda, and rethinking the relationship between planning and the market.

This final chapter has the aim of completing our discussion of the future role of planning in housing provision: what planning should and could achieve relative to the responsibilities of the state, for example, in creating better places, a sense of community, and quality neighbourhoods. But this future and evolving role needs to be examined in the context of recent problems that have yet to be resolved. Planning may be moving on, but many of the housing challenges identified in this book remain. Here we have two aims: first to conclude the narrative of housing debate in the UK, highlighting the continuing challenge for planning, and second to consider the wider role and purpose of planning – in relation to this challenge – and the shifting balance between public and private responsibility in the twenty-first century.

The challenge for planning

Balancing environmental and development agendas in the context of market-led planning

In the opening chapter we offered an overview of some of the broad themes shaping current housing debate in the United Kingdom: these fell under two headings – the sustainability of new development and the affordability of new homes. Each of these headings represents a competing 'rationale' for planning. Affordability is a rationale concerned with ensuring the 'right balance' between supply and demand, avoiding housing scarcity, and with this, the 'rising land values and spiralling house prices and rentals' that put 'pressure particularly on those with low incomes' (Haughton and Counsell, 2004: 107). Underpinning the 'affordability' rationale are those techniques – including the calculation of trend-based household formation figures examined in Chapters 4 and 6 – that aspire towards providing the right number of houses in a given location. The Barker Review of Housing Supply (2004) is closely aligned with this view of planning's role in housing provision. It is concerned with labour demand, with wage inflation pressures and with the connections between the housing market and the wider economy. A major proposal emerging from Barker was that housing supply should take greater notice of 'market signals', with a more responsive planning system ready to release additional land where there is a risk of 'affordability targets' not being met. But the critics of Barker – of which there are many – have argued that Barker's emphasis on housing numbers and supply means that the Review greatly underplays the importance of 'sustainability', and is largely blind to the environmental impacts of new house building, particularly in the congested south-east of England (see Chapter 7).

Government's support for an affordability rationale is tempered by a need to also support a rationale of sustainability (largely an 'environmental' rationale – see above). For this reason, in 2005 it commissioned parallel studies into the practicality of implementing Barker's 'affordability targets', and the consequences of a planning approach that would result in additional periodic land releases (in order to meet regional targets). Many commentators have framed current housing debate within this idea of 'competing rationales' (Haughton and Counsell, 2004: 109; see also Murdoch and Abram, 2002). This is certainly a useful way of conceptualising current debate and understanding the entrenched positions of different groups. But if we are to define a role for planning in relation to housing in the future, surely it must be this: to negotiate a way between the entrenched positions and to achieve the twin goals of affordability and sustainability.

This is the point that has been reached in the narrative of 'planning for housing' in the United Kingdom. The friction between competing rationalities may result in a stalemate in some instances. In Stevenage (see Chapter 6), a development that was given the green light in principle in 1998 had not resulted in even a single additional home being built by 2005. In October, 2005, the Deputy Prime Minister announced that he was 'minded to approve' the development having scrutinised the results of the previous year's Public Inquiry into the proposal – from the West Stevenage Consortium – to deliver 5,000 homes west of the A1(M). But he was only minded to approve 3,600 (the first phase) of this total, a decision that surprised the development consortium (they wanted more) and that angered North Hertfordshire District Council, which remains committed to blocking all housing development on its portion of the Stevenage West site (see Chapter 6), and which immediately indicated its intention to mount a legal challenge. Only Stevenage Borough seemed happy with this intervention by the ODPM, which may at long last (not withstanding further opposition) offer a solution to the stalemate at Stevenage West.

Resolving or avoiding local disputes

Experience at Stevenage is not unique; similar dramas are being played out across the country and there are many 'localised struggles over the location of new housing' (Haughton and Counsell, 2004: 137). In many places, an impasse is reached that is only resolved through some form of central intervention that often leaves local communities frustrated and opens government to the accusation that it favours 'soviet-style' central planning. This has been a key feature of the planning system over recent years: its inability to resolve local disputes over new housing. And in the light of the government's Communities Plan (ODPM, 2003a) – and an announcement in November 2005 that further, albeit smaller, 'Growth Areas' are to be earmarked for development – it seems likely that such disputes will become more commonplace. Government accepts the reality of dual rationalities in planning for housing, but each rationale has a different set of supporters rallying to its cause. This is apparent at a national level, a regional level and more locally. It defines housing debate. Government has sought to broker a compromise (setting new targets for land recycling and for housing density), but a continued need to build on greenfield sites (Barlow et al., 2002) results in conflicts that sometimes appear intractable. This issue was raised in the last chapter: given the power of SCSs – relative to LDFs – how will a compromise be reached between competing interests? Community voices may be louder but the need for additional housing, irrespective of local opposition, will remain. The need to build consensus – through active participation – around housing development issues is critical, at both a national and a local level. But the achievement of this objective still seems to be a long way off.

The housing–jobs balance

Future spatial planning policy – the product of a reformed planning system – will need to be concerned with the linkages between labour and housing, the resource management implications of growth, the question of urban intensification, issues of transport use, how to provide support infrastructure, and how to ensure that planned growth is responsive to the market.

The linkages between planned housing growth and labour demand and supply, is a theme that is high on the agenda in the south-east of England where the regional assembly in partnership with the region's other key stakeholders is in the process of putting together a draft of its RSS (see Chapter 7). Regional planning has always been concerned with the homes–jobs link, but this issue has taken on new importance given the focus of government's Sustainable Communities Plan, which is centrally concerned with the dual rationales set out above, and Barker's view that housing, labour demand and economic growth are intertwined. In this particular region, a study by Deloitte (2005: 1) has recently suggested that proposed housing growth in the region (expressed in the form of three possible annual housing completion rates, ranging from 25,500 to 32,000 units) will not support economic growth and will result in a labour supply shortfall and create jobs–homes imbalances at a sub-regional level (affecting some counties to a greater extent than others). However, such studies seem to suggest that economic growth has an insatiable demand for housing growth, which feed on each other (again, see Chapter 7 and Gallent and Tewdwr-Jones, 2005). It is almost inevitable that economically dynamic regions such as the south-east will need to source a proportion of their labour needs from beyond their own borders and that inter-regional commuting will play a part in serving economic growth. Given the rapidity of economic shifts, it seems unrealistic to think that an exact 'jobs–homes' fit can be achieved through regional planning, or that such an exact fit is desirable given the inevitability of labour-demand shifts. Planning needs to be responsive to labour: this means not only delivering homes for today's market, but also ensuring that the stock profile will meet the needs of future households. Responding only to the here and now is a strategy fraught with risk.

Managing finite resources

The resource implications of growth and how these resources – including water demand and supply, waste processing and energy generation – are managed is another major concern. Again, in the south-east of England, we saw in Chapter 7 that the RA has recently been considering different 'spatial options' for growth, attempting to choose between more dispersed and more concentrated patterns of development. Greater dispersion of new development as opposed to concentration in key 'strategic sites' might reduce the weight of opposition to new development (though the number of local conflicts is likely to be greater), but it is more difficult – and expensive – to provide the necessary infrastructure and resources to serve thinner, more patchy growth. Hence, the Assembly favours a more pronounced concentration of growth (in Government's 'Growth Areas' set out in the CP), making it easier and cheaper to provide electricity, water and waste-processing facilities. As in Stevenage, the case for 'strategic concentration' has won the day. In parts of the Thames Gateway, the re-use of brownfield land is likely to be a popular development option. But in the Western Corridor (the M4), in Ashford (Kent) or in Central Oxfordshire, the need to build on agricultural land will inevitably result in more local struggles, with the competing rationales of affordability and sustainability unable to achieve any easy compromise. The issue of resource consumption has been the subject of a recent study by the Institute for Public Policy Research (IPPR), which has argued that a combination of household growth and a reduction in average household size will result in significantly increased water demand over the next 20 years (IPPR, 2005: 3), with climate change expected to exacerbate 'water stress' (ibid., 12). But again, a concentration of future development will make it easier for water utilities to meet anticipated growth in demand. The same is true in relation to waste management. Housing growth in the south-east of England is expected to generate between 35,000 and 44,000 tonnes of additional 'municipal solid waste' (MSW) each year (the region will need to manage up to 7 million additional tonnes in the period up to 2026, excluding the inevitable construction waste). New facilities will need to be provided for dealing with this waste; facilities that are likely to generate at least as much hostility as new housing itself. The RA (SEERA, 2005d) has projected that the number of large landfill sites in the region will need to double;

there will need to be almost six times as many recycling plants, and eight times the current number of composting facilities. Again, a reliance on centralised, strategic management (reducing the costs associated with the transportation of waste), is likely to become another source of tension. And finally, in relation to energy generation, housing growth will accentuate the current regional deficit in the south-east increasing pressure to produce more electricity within the region (AEA Technology, 2005: 20) possibly at a single site.

Building on brownfields

It is almost inevitable that a concentration of development at strategic sites will result in an accusation that government and regional planning is not making adequate use of existing brownfield development opportunities. SEERA has recently argued that:

> development in urban areas is not necessarily an easy option: factors such as high development costs and land assembly can act as obstacles. The infrastructure and other requirements associated with the cumulative impact of small-scale development in urban areas also need to be taken into account.
>
> (SEERA, 2005a: 71)

However, the intensification of urban land-use remains a key objective of regional and local planning. In the south-east of England, work by Roger Tym & Partners (2005) has suggested that between 59 per cent and 73 per cent of planned housing growth can be accommodated within existing urban areas depending on how much growth Regional Planning wishes to support. As it now looks likely to pursue a middle path – an annual building rate of 28,000 homes – it appears that a regional average in excess of 60 per cent is achievable, though with considerable variation across the region. In reality, some greenfield sites will be earmarked for housing despite the priority placed on urban intensification; particular pressures may be felt in central parts of the south-east prompting new battles in the Surrey countryside (around Gatwick) or on the west Sussex coast.

But perhaps the most persuasive case for strategic development and for a concentration of housing development in designated 'Growth Areas' relates to transport. Strategic Transport Modelling (STM) undertaken by the RA and reported in Gallent and Tewdwr-Jones (2005: 65), demonstrates that a concentration of housing growth within the Growth Areas would reduce average trip times and an additional take-up of 'greener' travel modes as a result of people working closer to home. However, all growth in the region will be conditional on additional investment in transport infrastructure: Roger Tym & Partners

(2005) have estimated that for every 1,000 new homes, there will need to be an additional £21.4 million spent on transport infrastructure (providing new services, improving roads, buying new rolling stock and so forth). Housing growth generates its own transport demand, providing a further challenge for the planning system: and at least part of this challenge is about finance.

The question of infrastructure

The costs of providing the infrastructure needed to service growth has become a central issue in current housing debate. As we noted in Chapter 7, the same study by Roger Tym & Partners calculates that for every 1,000 homes, almost £40 million will need to be spent on transport, hospitals, police, schools, waste management, open space, affordable housing and a whole host of other items necessary to deliver the government's 'sustainable communities'. In the south-east alone, the infrastructure bill will be as high as £25 billion over the life of the new South East Plan. Nationally, it will run into hundreds of billions of pounds. The question of how this will be paid for is high on the political agenda at the current time: Barker has suggested that revenue generated as a result of land-value uplift might be used to pay part of this cost – through a PGS – but the feasibility of this has been questioned in a recent study carried out on behalf of the Royal Institution of Chartered Surveyors (Johnson and Hart, 2005). The authors of this study contend that PGS is unworkable largely because it is 'unjust': the Barker proposal is for a tax not only on the planning gain element, but against market value, making it unpredictable; the tax could place too great a burden on developers; and the idea of a PGS has not attracted wide support (ibid., 2–3). For these reasons, Johnson and Hart are more supportive of a tariff-based approach, and the idea of standard charges and pooled Section 106 contributions (which might be referred to in Spatial Strategies where there is a need to consider the infrastructure demands of strategic Growth Areas) set out in ODPM Circular 05/2005 (ODPM, 2005k: para B29-B35). Whatever the outcome of current debates and consultations, it is inevitable that some system of extracting 'planning gain' coupled with direct treasury expenditure will be called upon to pay for future housing growth. Planning will certainly have a role in generating money for infrastructure, though the exact nature of this role is not yet clear.

Affordability and the market

Addressing affordability through general housing supply and through a planned response to 'market signals' is another key challenge for the new planning system (see Chapter 7). In the south-east of England, policy-based projections of future housing demand and need rely on a model that seeks to constrain migration by limiting dwelling growth. This model has been criticised on economic grounds (Deloitte, 2005: 4); it is certainly not a model that is led by the market, or that seeks to reflect market pressure. Rather, it seeks to squeeze the market in the hope that demand pressures will be transferred elsewhere. Furthermore, we noted in Chapter 7 that planned housing growth in the south-east has totally ignored short-term migration trends (observed in recent years).

It is not yet clear how Barker's Affordability Targets will operate in prac-tice, but given that the south-east is opting for a 28,000-unit building rate, it appears that a 'theoretical' shortfall of 7,500 units per annum may be generated. But this 'theoretical' shortfall may create real affordability pressures in the region reflected in market signals (more rapid house price inflation in some areas, and a widening affordability gap expressed in terms of an income to mean house price ratio). If short-term migration trends do continue in the south-east, then the 7,500 shortfall might be translated into an additional requirement that needs to be met with several new strategic allocations during the life of the South East Plan of the type that are likely to prompt local controversy, and to result once more in retrenchment behind the opposing rationales of affordability versus sustainability.

The growth agenda, market equilibrium and regeneration

The key features of current housing debate are likely to be re-enforced by govern-ment's growth agenda and the need for new strategic housing allocations, especially in southern England. How will the new planning system respond to this challenge? And how will it respond to the very different challenge of housing market failure in the northern regions? Low demand in the north is often viewed as the antithesis of growth pressure in the south, but government sees the chal-lenge here also in the context of delivering more sustainable communities (the debate has shifted from a focus on housing renewal to a broader social agenda in recent years: Cameron, 2006). Despite an apparent need to rationalise housing stock (creating the 'scarcity' that could potentially kick-start the market), pressure exists to build more homes in the north of England. The view that the south is dominated by high demand and the north by low demand is far too simplistic. Despite well-publicised inner-urban problems in parts of Liverpool and Greater Manchester (in the north-west region), the market for new homes in Cheshire remains relatively strong. Likewise, there is also a buoyant market for new-build within highly localized urban areas or on greenfield sites, where the demand is for 'executive' homes that serve a very different market from the inner-city terraces that have been abandoned in parts of East Manchester and elsewhere. Haughton and Counsell (2004: 115) case study the north-east of England where, despite a well-documented pattern of market failure, there has been 'considerable support for the argument from political leaders and planners that there was a need to diversify and up-grade the region's housing stock by looking for higher allocations of new-build housing, specifically to increase the stock of executive-style housing'. As in the north-west, new house building is sometimes viewed as an antidote to outward migration. Such regional aspirations will certainly bring planning into conflict with environmental groups including Friends of the Earth and the CPRE, as has been evident in both the north-west and north-east. But perhaps the biggest problem generated by this population-retention and growth rationale is that it diverts resources and attention from those inner-urban areas blighted by abandonment and decay, and by consequent social tensions. In very general terms (the same terms were applied in our overview of growth pressures above), there is a 'market failure' with which planning must grapple in the north of England and, albeit to a lesser extent, in the English midlands. This challenge is multi-faceted: it is about dealing with empty public and private stock, mixing strategies for re-use with selective demolition as a means of rationalizing dwelling numbers; it is also about the geographical immobility of labour, mirroring the situation in the south but with very different underlying causes. Immobility in southern England is driven by the strength of the housing market. This is also true within micro-markets in the north, but here we also have the problem of people becoming locked into transitional markets, unable to recoup the invested equity from their homes through onward sale. In the worst-case scenarios, homeowners have been forced to abandon their homes in the areas most affected by low demand and market failure. The role of planning in government's HMRI is critical, and it is being called upon to integrate policies into local plans (and new development frameworks) that promote demolition on the back of rigorous community consultation, alongside policies that aim to bring some homes back into effective use through conversion into bigger, or sometimes smaller, units.

But urban decline is inexorably linked to a variety of social pressures. Market collapse will leave many communities feeling isolated and abandoned by political leaders, especially if they see new development occurring on peripheral sites. 'Competitive local planning' (Haughton and Counsell, 2004: 146) can be a particular problem, with some planning authorities 'feeling compelled to provide planning permission for new housing' on edge locations, for 'fear that people would simply move out to adjacent areas and commute back into their jobs'. In many northern towns this has resulted in a 'doughnut' effect: a hollowing out of inner-urban cores and a promotion of peripheral development

Plate 21 Low-demand housing in the north-west – an empty tower block in East Manchester provides an opportunity to publicise the 2002 Commonwealth Games (Manchester, 2003)

centred on major road junctions, fulfilling the aspirations of those who wish to commute by car to jobs located elsewhere. Those remaining in the former core may be characterised by old age, by low-income or by racial grouping. They may become marginalised, forming a residual private-sector group. In this instance, planning must sometimes shoulder a large part of the blame for creating new social and racial divisions, as it attempts to retain the most affluent and well-educated sectors of the local population (and attract newcomers through 'competitive local planning'), but often neglects the needs of those remaining in the core. Given the experiences of some northern towns, it is easy to see why government talks in terms of promoting more sustainable, balanced communities. But it is less easy to see how this will be achieved.

Some planning authorities – in partnership with private landlords, housing departments and RSLs – have undertaken clearly innovative market-renewal initiatives in the north of England. In Bolton, for instance, the local authority led a renewal scheme in the Brooklyn Street area of Halliwell (one of the town's constituent wards). Originally comprising 244 terraced units of low-demand mixed tenure (mainly owner occupation and private renting), a scheme was rolled out by Bolton's housing department and Portico Housing Association – with

Plate 22 Terraced housing in the north of England – Brooklyn Street renewal area (Bolton, 2003)

funding from the Housing Corporation – involving acquisition, demolition and conversion together with individual unit facelifts and a variety of environmental works. The scheme utilised the Housing Corporation's so-called 'New Tools' for dealing with low demand: 'acquisition for demolition', 'acquisition for redevelopment', 'medium life rehabilitation', 'two into one conversion' and 'home improvement package' (Leather, 2003: 21). Leather notes a variety of administrative (compulsory purchase) and cost-related problems with the use of these tools for dealing with low demand, but concluded that they have 'contributed substantially to the successful regeneration' of this area (ibid., 50). They have rid Brooklyn Street of eyesores, resulted in environmental improvement and generated new confidence among residents. Since 2000, entire rows of the pre-1919 terraced housing have been demolished (using the 'acquisition for redevelopment' or AFR tool), and many units have been knocked-through to produce bigger homes (using the 'two into one conversion' or TIOC tool), often for use by ethnic South Asian households who make up the largest minority ethnic group at 35 per cent of local population. By June 2001:

> the worst problems of fly-tipping and litter had been tackled, and unsecured properties had been boarded up. The partners felt that the departure from the area of a small number of private tenants who had been exhibiting anti-social behaviour had been a major factor in sustaining these improvements. Portico Housing Association had also established a local office in the area, and was conducting an environmental audit, with action points followed up by the local authority. Although still showing environmental stress, the appearance of the area had improved greatly.
>
> (Leather, 2003: 57)

A key objective of housing market renewal is to create a new scarcity (and desirability) in the housing stock through rationalisation, which is one outcome of the Housing Corporation's 'New Tools'. In the case of Brooklyn Street, average prices rose from £26,000 in 1995 to £32,000 in 2002: an improvement, but still a third below the average for the borough. However, throughout the period of the Brooklyn Street initiative, Bolton's planning department has continued to grant permissions for new housing development on peripheral greenfield sites (see Karn *et al.*, 1998), potentially undermining efforts to promote regeneration in the inner-urban wards. It is perhaps unrealistic to think that those homebuyers looking for the ubiquitous 'executive style' homes on the outskirts of Bolton could be attracted to areas like Brooklyn Street or Oxford Grove (an adjoining area subject to renewal using the New Tools approach) with their well-publicised social and environmental problems. But it seems obvious that a continuation of new-build in parts of the north-west will inevitably work against efforts to regenerate and bring people back into inner areas. Arguably, Bolton and similar northern towns present a challenge that is very different from that found in larger urban centres including Manchester. Manchester has been successful in promoting new styles of urban living, creating flats in former cotton warehouses that have proven attractive to young singles. There appear to be few opportunities for towns like Bolton to follow suit: they simply do not have the same appeal. But in Manchester too, the granting of new permissions for large numbers of flats in the inner city will impact on efforts to regenerate areas such as East Manchester or Wythenshawe in the south of the city. The problem is this: despite the outward appearance of urban decline in large parts of the north, these regions also have some very vibrant inner city and suburban markets. Competitive authorities and the private sector clearly want to exploit these market opportunities: the challenge for planning is how to balance out the opportunities and threats, delivering a more integrated response to the challenges posed by a highly complex housing market. There is some hope that in the north and in the south, an approach to planning for housing that is less competitive and more integrated can deliver decent homes for all.

More than just housing

Low demand, as Long (2000) has pointed out, is not only indicative of market failure, but also the failure to engage with place-making with the aim of delivering communities that are cohesive, and endure over the long term. The final, but most fundamental, challenge for planning is to look beyond housing and to see the delivery of decent homes as part of a wider agenda: to deliver liveable places that are fit for purpose and worth living in today and in the future. The path to liveability will be punctuated by all the challenges noted above: the need to strike a balance between competing rationales; to avoid disputes where possible, and resolve them where necessary; to make communities sustainable in an economic sense; to deal with the resource implications of growth and strategic planning decisions; to use land efficiently; to make infrastructure a priority and not an afterthought; to ensure affordability and avoid market exclusion; and to build growth on a platform of market stability. In the final part of this chapter, and of this book, we think about the future role of planning in dealing with these complexities.

A future for planning: place, community and meaning

How can planning assist in the twin duties of promoting the development of neighbourhoods and communities – including communities such as Brooklyn

Street in Bolton, Stevenage in Hertfordshire, or Pembrokeshire's smaller, more sensitive villages – and managing the processes of change relating to housing provision, environmental protection, migration, social change and economic development? We do believe that the reformed planning process – discussed in Chapter 9 – does start to provide the conditions for distinctive place-based perspectives on the sorts of problems facing different parts of the country, both rural and urban. And the fact that spatial planning recognises the different conditions existing in different parts of territories, highlighting broad zones where specific problems occur and where broad policies are required, demonstrates in our view that some parts of government have listened to those voices calling for more localised or regional solutions to the distinctive problems that exist. A focus on sustainable communities highlighted within the current ethos of planning illustrates that a variety of solutions may be required at different scales and in different places. But LPAs across the UK should not now sit back and wait for the government to provide the localised prescriptions for the way forward. The responsibility rests on the authorities to be innovative and forward-looking. Local authorities may be handicapped to some extent by their own administrative and geographical boundaries for issues of a more strategic nature, such as large-scale strategic housing development, and therefore we question whether the spirit of spatial planning and creativity in local policy-making can truly be realised within the existing two-level structure of local government; the impending review of local government may be the first step towards initiating a debate concerning the appropriateness of integrated city-regions (ODPM, 2006b), which can meet the strategic and local needs on the one hand and reflect the true current patterns of major economic growth.

Spatial planning undoubtedly provides a broad framework; national and regional planning strategies provide an opportunity for integrated national and regional policy; it is up to local planners to demonstrate what localised solutions are required, and why. It can be assumed that the Government will intervene if it considers that individual authorities are attempting to skew the planning system overly to localised issues without sufficient local evidence or justification (hence, the Welsh Assembly's opposition to Pembrokeshire's local need housing policy – see Chapter 6). But that does not mean that localised solutions will not be permitted.

The existence of the Sustainable Communities Plan (Chapter 8) and the onset of spatial planning (Chapter 9) provide England and Wales with a potentially more territorially-aware planning framework in which to address community problems, but so far few councils, professional planners or developers have taken up the challenge. Nor has the government shown much leadership to date: it has certainly not signalled its intention to redirect the planning system

towards addressing neighbourhood issues despite recent ministerial pronounce-
ments on communities and neighbourhood more broadly. Rather, the whole
planning process is being strangled by the government's desire for local authorities to prepare plans, strategies and performance audits, and ensure a maximum
number of housing completions; we remain trapped in an institutional game of
planning-by-numbers caused by both developers' obsessions with building units,
not homes, and the government's preoccupation with judging planning success
against building rates. That said, the big question that remains unanswered is
how to deliver enough homes locally, regionally and nationally while ensuring
that communities feel that they are partners in the planning process and not
simply alienated bystanders.

It is perhaps time to find new ways of engaging people in planning, on
their terms, not the terms of government alone, of local politicians, or of planners. This is not only to ensure that planning becomes a tool of communities; it
is to ensure that people give confidence back to local governance and to be part
of participatory democracy in the light of deepening cynicism towards politicians
and professionals generally. Planning has to reinvent itself as a framework for
people and for communities. Planning has historically been a step ahead of other
areas of government activity because of the necessity for public participation. It
was the first area of government to have public input (as a consequence of the
Skeffington Report of 1969), but over the years since then, successive governments have diluted the contract between people and planning. New forms of
community engagement and innovative participation techniques can help, and
the production of Community Strategies offers a framework in which to re-
engage with people. But what does this framework mean for actually dealing with
new housing provision? We noted in the last chapter that almost irrespective of
new forms of participation, the housing that is currently being built or is
earmarked to be built in government's 'Growth Areas' will need to be built, even
where there is strong opposition from the general public. Participation will not
miraculously circumvent the need for new house building, or the need for
strategic housing allocations on greenfield sites. It will not make difficult choices
any less difficult. However, it is a means by which people may come to understand why a particular level of housing development is required; why the most
sensible option, in many instances, might be concentration on a single site;
and what the implications might be – economically and socially – if housing
supply is constrained. This is a very different vision of the future from what we
have today: knowledge is a professional resource, passed between planners, developers and other 'key stakeholders'; it is used to develop 'options' – including the
south-east's 'growth level' and 'spatial' options noted in the first part of this
chapter – which, a long way down the line, are presented at an EIP. At this point,

the options – built on highly technical considerations – are fed to the public and a response is gauged. The planners have spent some months anticipating how people might react; their consultants have prepared careful counter-arguments; and they are fully prepared to defend their position. This is planning today: consultation as an afterthought and a half-hearted attempt to gain at least some community 'acceptance'. But this acceptance is gained through bamboozling people with mathematics, with a 'we know best' attitude, and with stern warnings of the implications of rejecting professional advice. The consequences of this approach are well-documented: it has resulted in an impasse at Stevenage West, and at countless other potential development sites up and down the country.

The alternative is to accept a responsibility to work with communities, and to share knowledge and understanding: not to present options or employ scare tactics, but to foster local ownership in any planned strategy for housing development. Government's Growth Areas strategy may be the right one, but its imposition – at a time when government is talking up the importance of community strategies and participation – is certainly the wrong one. Of course, there needs to be some spatial overview – some aspiration that cuts across local boundaries – but government needs to make it clear that the 'ideas' (rather than options) it presents, are for the consideration of local communities, in partnership with local government and with professional planners. This is perhaps the way to avoid the frustration and alienation that often accompanies the latest planning pronouncement. It is perhaps time to assert a new contract between planning, the planning profession, developers and the public. Planners employed within the public sector should have a duty to not only inform the public, but also to educate, to inspire and to give confidence to the public, to allow them a voice in the process of managing change within their own communities. Place matters, not in terms of a strategy, or a ten-year plan, or an administrative boundary. Place matters for people because of the history, memories and rituals a place possesses: it is the essential framework for 'community' (see Chapter 8).

There is more to a place, to a community, than bricks and mortar, and league tables and strategies. And it is about time that the planning system was allowed to reflect that, and that planners themselves began to really engage with communities with a view to developing a shared understanding of the challenges represented by housing growth. Government, local authorities, planners and communities should remove the shackles from planning and – with impetus and enthusiasm – start to address the real problems of delivering housing in sustainable communities in a meaningful way – a way that reflects the desires, needs and ambitions of communities themselves. Hence, the challenge for planning – if it is to be able to cope with the specific challenges relating to housing, affordability, sustainability and community – concern:

- The extent to which planners and other policy-makers are able to engage in a meaningful way with communities, appreciating their particular localized problems, relating to a range of social, community, cultural and economic issues.
- The extent to which local planning authorities are willing to take responsibility themselves, without a desire for detailed approval from the government, on issues relating to community development, housing pressure and affordable housing, and the degree to which planners are willing and able to negotiate with developers and other implementation agents.
- The extent to which the government are willing to loosen their control over the policy- and decision-making of LPAs, where authorities prove that they are responsible, and by encouraging LPAs to produce localised solutions to the particular housing and planning problems afflicting communities.
- Whether local planning authorities are able to develop stronger links between community identity and spatial planning, by establishing innovative public participation techniques and jargon-free interaction.
- The availability of data and other evidence to enable local planning authorities to promote sustainable communities based on the unique social, economic, environmental and cultural attributes of each community within its boundaries.
- The degree to which the 1947 statutory land-use planning system can be transformed into a twenty-first century coordinating and spatial framework that operates outside a narrow legalistic box concerned with physical development alone and to view communities in the whole.

We noted earlier in this chapter that planning's inability to resolve local dispute over new housing development has been its key failing in recent years. But perhaps a more fundamental failing is that planning itself – and not housing development – is the underlying cause of local dispute. It often alienates communities even before any specific housing proposals are brought forward. Its insularity and its technocratic outlook have given it an impassive air, conveying the image of a rigid process that intervenes and imposes, that has an intransigent view of the 'public good' and that acts in the interests of communities without bothering to ask what those interests actually are. This suggests that planning itself is the biggest barrier to delivering decent homes for all. In the long term, it may be able to bulldoze through development proposals: even Stevenage West looks as if, at long last, it will get the go-ahead after the direct intervention of the Deputy Prime Minister. But local communities are likely to feel aggrieved for a long time, and are not likely to forget the way in which this development was imposed on the existing community. It is perhaps the hope of the local council that 5,000 new homes will house 5,000-plus new voters, who will be more appreciative of the Stevenage West building programme than a great many of the existing local electorate.

Planning is as vital today as at the time its foundations were laid more than a hundred years ago. It is about meeting the challenge of our ever-changing urban and regional spaces and of responding to the needs and demands of our societies. And all of us can relate to what those changing demands mean everyday because we live and work with the pressures of urban growth, rural protection and inadequate infrastructure. Cities, towns and villages are more than just concrete, construction and housing numbers. This is a point that needs re-emphasising. The brand of planning that has found itself embroiled in countless local dramas over new housing development is a rigid, paternalistic process: but planning needs to be a fluid process. It has to adapt and change to the conditions within which it is supposed to operate. It is not only about physical development and urban renewal. It is pausing to think about the meaning of places, about how people use and understand places, and how places can capitalise on their own identities and distinctiveness, to deliver development and create better quality places to live and work within. This of course means thinking about aesthetics and about design, issues that were examined in Chapter 5. It is also about participation and how planning works with communities: issues addressed throughout this book. Consensus is perhaps an over-used word in the current nomenclature of planning, but only consensus – around the need for new housing and the form that housing development should take – will give planning the legitimacy and potency it needs in the twenty-first century.

As a professional discipline, there is one undeniable fact: planning has not always been at pains to understand how places are used and viewed by the people who live and work within them. Often, planning has failed to see cities as living places, places of work and of homes, of interactions and communication: hence, it all too often provokes a negative response, with planned intervention viewed as antisocial, prioritising the needs of business over people. Unless we start to change our way of thinking about planning and places, there is an ever-increasing danger that regenerated and rebuilt cities – or the Growth Areas and urban extensions that are currently in the planning pipeline – will become more remote places, where people will not feel comfortable; and where investment and prosperity will become exceptions rather than the rule. Hence planning faces a detailed challenge – relating to housing development and the delivery of decent homes for all – and also a general challenge, which is really about rethinking basic principles and practices that will enable the planning system to respond to all manner of challenges in a way that generates consensus and support rather than conflict. The challenge is for planning to become more deeply embedded in the social process, with planning not understood as 'intervention' for the sake of place-making, but rather as an inexorable part of that place-making.

Opportunities for planning

Today, in an era of globalisation, greater urban diversity, multiculturalism and migration to and from cities, inequalities in standards of living and incomes, and escalating housing costs as the price of improved urban economic performances, merely providing new development and renewing cities through planning is not enough. It is more important to deal with places and communities and with people who make those communities, and who possess or should possess a sense of ownership in their community. In the UK, planning was once a purely state-led activity – but despite the argument that more limited forms of public involvement may expedite the planning process (because democracy takes time), evidence suggests, as in the case of Stevenage West, that this is not always the case. Communities have become more bullish and less prepared to accept the apparent autocracy of government, and so conflict has become commonplace. Many planners point to the growth in NIMBY attitudes among some sections of the public, and a tendency to reject most if not all new housing development proposals. There are, of course, elements which, because of particular vested interests, are ready to oppose development in certain locations; perhaps some of this opposition emanates from a lack of confidence in public and private pensions and a belief that only increases in the value of private property will guarantee an individual's future financial security. But surely this 'self interest' argument cannot explain the weight of opposition to most large-scale planning applications. Planning has to take some responsibility for the emergence of the 'no culture' that often stands in the way of housing development. This is on top of the fact that planning, especially in the 1980s, too eagerly granted planning permission on greenfields for red-brick housing developments of an appalling standard, creating the ubiquitous lower middle-class ghettos common to urban fringes and shire counties. Planning needs to accept its responsibility for generating this 'no culture', perhaps making a plea to society at large to give it a second chance. The difference is that this time round, planning cannot go it alone: it needs to embrace all stakeholders within a completely shared process, and to be sensitive to their needs and desires, if it is to perform any meaningful role in creating quality places. But given the inevitable diversity of views and interests – social, economic and environmental – the possibility of creating an agreed vision for cities or for the countryside (one that rebuilds, renews and enhances, but also deals with those everyday spaces between developments that give places local character and meaning) will be one of the biggest challenges that we all face. It has as much to do with the way people live in the future, as it does to the planning process.

There is also a social and economic case for greater speed and certainty in the planning system: speed is not only in the interests of housing developers, but also in the interests of families and communities lacking the basic housing needed to achieve social well-being. Inclusive and less-insular planning has to ensure that development and renewal in cities and across regions can be enacted quickly, with confidence and certainty, and be responsive to economic and social needs. Planning in the UK has not always responded as quickly as we would have liked to development opportunities and moves are being enacted to do something about this. But it is also a fact that the number of different actors and agencies required to bring about change is increasingly complex and confusing. Landowners, developments, governments, investors, utility companies, all have strategies and plans, even for specific sites, and planning's role in the future must partly take on the role of integrating – coordinating – between these diverse actors. Planning has to facilitate development and assist in the creation of vibrant places. Planning does not necessarily deliver development itself. It is a vital mechanism in the political process, which should aim to remove barriers to new opportunities, but critically, also to allow those who hold views and opinions on the places they live and work to be given a voice in development and masterplanning schemes. Clearly, there is another challenge here for planning: to balance interests that appear, at first glance, to be at odds with each other. Speed is for business and has an economic goal in mind; longer participatory processes are for communities, and result in consensual outcomes. But are the rationales of business and communities really so different and incompatible? Planning debate often suggests that they are, and that it is only speculative builders that benefit from faster planning decisions: community interests are best served by a protracted planning process. This is of course nonsense. There is an urgent need for new housing in the UK, and not only to secure the future of the construction industry. People need homes: in the north of England, efforts are being directed at rationalising housing stock to meet community needs. In the south, economic growth and migration pressures are generating new housing needs at all scales and in all types of community. Neither the needs of business or people will be served by a planning system that is bogged down in bureaucratic debate and unable to deliver.

Positive planning for housing

The new ethos for planning in the UK therefore has to be one of spatial planning – positive planning – to give confidence, to inspire, to coordinate and to enable. The planning system in the UK has been reformed in 2004, with this new ethos, with new types of plans and strategies, new streamlined procedures, and new resources to bring about institutional change in the next five years. This will not lead to a quick fix or change to planning overnight; many of the reforms will take some years to bed down. But the real change is one of implementation and delivery in practice, and to ensure that those within the planning profession are prepared to be part of this ongoing change, and are prepared to adopt the new ethos of positive, inclusive planning. It will require a monumental shift in attitudes, and cultural adaptation on the part of those responsible for mediating change in the built and natural environment: government and business interests need to quickly accept that fact.

Spatial planning – examined in the last chapter – is not a practice: it is an approach, a belief in reinvigorating planning for today and tomorrow. It encapsulates many of the ideas, especially the need to combat insularity, that have been outlined in this chapter. It may operate at any scale, involve development management – not development control – and sets an agenda that engages people. This is essential; planning has to pull people in to the policy process, partly for them to have a clear say in their own future, but also because it is the only effective way to ensure the diversity of voices within cities or within the countryside can be heard. At the same time, spatial planning does not operate in isolation; it provides the spatial expression of policies and strategies of other agencies and organisations. Planning is no longer owned only by members of the planning profession. This is to ensure that economic, environmental and social equity concerns become integrated when polices are formulated. Incomplete consideration of these issues is the root cause of delay and conflict in the planning system and will always stand in the way of development, whether housing or any other form.

There are real challenges ahead. The legislative change enacted in the UK in 2004 is not the end of a process, but the start of a new one. Planning is a fluid process that should mean different things in different places. The biggest challenge is the promotion of positive planning agendas. Planning is not only about controlling what we build. Planning's purpose is to integrate strategies with a clear vision to enable the creation and renewal of places that people enjoy. Local planning therefore has to refocus towards the neighbourhood and the community. It is time for public-sector planning to return to its roots and serve the communities it has responsibility for. This will mean finding new opportunities to create spatial expressions for existing and future problems that might be social, economic or environmental in nature. Spatial planning needs to ensure that a wide ownership of a vision and of strategies occurs, with a focus on the meaning of places rather than the importance of drafting plans. The onus switches clearly to professionals, community leaders, neighbourhoods, and even developers, to expect, promote and use positive planning. A cynic might argue that the planning reforms instituted by the Labour government amount to an abdication of responsibility: planning was having great difficulty in pushing through unpopular development and government was regularly having to intervene to resolve local conflict, especially conflict embroiling the latest housing proposals. With the new system – which offers no guarantee that future planning will be any different – government is able to stand back, claim that it has empowered communities, and wait to see what happens on the ground. New responsibilities have been handed to local groups and to Blair's 'stakeholders': they may fail, and government may once again have to intervene to resolve a local impasse, or to ensure that housing targets are not missed. But the real challenge is for business, communities, and local planners as the facilitators of a *potentially* new way to plan for housing. We say 'potentially' because failure to work together locally is likely to result in a return to old practices, and to an interventionist approach. In the spirit of Nettlefold (1914), planning's function is to create the right living conditions and decent homes for all, and is a necessary duty of a modern state. Performing that function has never been easy or straightforward when it comes to new housing development, but overcoming this difficulty – and managing the pressures and tensions that often accompany issues of housing supply and provision – is a duty that confronts us all.

References

Abram, S. and Cowell, R. (2004) 'Learning policy – the contextual curtain and conceptual barriers', *European Planning Studies*, 12, 2: 209–228.

Adams, D. and Watkins, C. (2002) *Greenfields, Brownfields and Housing Development*, Blackwell Publishing: London.

AEA Technology (2005) *Energy Supply and Long-Term Planning for the South East*, AEA Technology: Place of publication not stated.

Albrechts, L. (2004), 'Strategic Planning Re-examined', *Environment and Planning B: Planning and Design*, 31, 5: 743–758.

Aldridge, T.M. (1980) *The Housing Act 1980: A Practical Guide*, Oyez Publishing Ltd: London.

Allen, C., Camina, M., Casey, R., Coward, S. and Wood, M. (2005) *Mixed Tenure Twenty Years On: Nothing out of the Ordinary*, Chartered Institute of Housing: Coventry.

Allmendinger, P. (2002) 'Planning under a Scottish Parliament: a missed opportunity?', *European Planning Studies*, 10, 6, 793–798.

Allmendinger, P. and Tewdwr-Jones, M. (1997) 'Post-Thatcherite urban planning and politics: a Major change?' *International Journal of Urban and Regional Research*, 21, 1: 106–116.

—— and Tiesdell, S. (2004) 'Making sense of sustainable communities', *Town and Country Planning*, November: 313–316.

—— and Haughton, G. (2006) 'The fluid scales and scope of spatial planning', *Environment and Planning A: Environment and Planning*, 38 (in print).

——, Tewdwr-Jones, M. and Morphet, J. (2003) 'New order: planning and local government reforms', *Town and Country Planning*, 72, 9: 274–277.

Armstrong, H. (1999) 'A New Vision for Housing England', in Brown, T. (ed.) *Stakeholder Housing: A Third Way*, Pluto Press/Labour Housing Group: London.

Arnstein, S. (1969) 'A ladder of citizen participation', *American Institute of Planners Journal*, July: 216–224.

Ashworth, W. (1954) [second edition 1968] *The Genesis of Modern British Planning*, Routledge & Kegan Paul: London.

Baker, M. and Wong, C. (1997) 'Planning for housing land in the English regions: a critique of household projections and regional planning guidance mechanisms', *Environment and Planning C: Government and Policy*, 15: 73–87.

Balchin, P. (1981) *Housing Policy and Housing Needs*, Macmillan: London.

—— and Rhoden, M. (2002) *Housing Policy: An Introduction*, Routledge: London.

Ball, M., Harloe, M. and Martens, M. (1988) *Housing and Social Change in Europe and the USA*, Routledge: London.

Banister, D. (1997) 'Reducing the need to travel', *Environment and Planning B: Planning and Design*, 24, 3: 436–449.

Barker, K. (2004) *Review of Housing Supply – Delivering Stability: Securing Our Future Housing Needs*, HM Treasury: London.

Barlow, J. (1999) 'From craft production to mass customisation: innovation requirements for the UK house building industry', *Housing Studies*, 14, 1: 23–42.

—— and Chambers, D. (1992) *Planning Agreements and Affordable Housing Provision*, Centre for Urban and Regional Research: University of Sussex.

——, Cocks, R. and Parker, M. (1994) *Planning for Affordable Housing*, Department of the Environment: London.

——, Bartlett, K., Hooper, A. and Whitehead, C. (2002) *Land for Housing: Current Practice and Future Options*, Joseph Rowntree Foundation: York.

Bateman, A. (1995) 'Planning in the 1990s – a developer's perspective', *Report*, No.1: February: 26–29.

Baxter, S. (1909) 'The German way of making cities better', *Atlantic Monthly*, 104: 72–95.

Beames, T. (1850) *The Rookeries of London: Past, Present and Perspective*, Thomas Bosworth: London.

Berry, J., Brown, L. and McGreal, S. (2001) 'The planning system in Northern Ireland post-devolution', *European Planning Studies*, 9: 781–791.

Bevan, M., Cameron, S., Coombes, M., Merridew, T. and Raybould, S. (2001) *Social Housing in Rural Areas*, Joseph Rowntree Foundation and the Chartered Institute of Housing: Coventry.

Birchall, J. (ed.) (1992) *Housing Policy in the 1990s*, Routledge: London.

Bishop, K. and Hooper, A. (1991) *Planning for Social Housing*, National Housing Forum: London.

Bohl, C.C. (2000) 'New urbanism and the city: potential applications and implications for distressed inner-city neighbourhoods', *Housing Policy Debate*, 11, 4: 761–801.

Booth, C. (1902) *Life and Labour of the People of London*, Macmillian & Co.: London (17 volumes).

Booth, P. (1996) *Controlling Development: Certainty and Discretion in Europe, the USA and Hong Kong*, UCL Press: London.

Bramley, G. and Watkins, C. (1995) *Circular Projections: Household Growth, Housing Development and the Household Projections*, Campaign for the Protection of Rural England: London.

—— and —— (1996) *New House Building and the Changing Planning System*, Joseph Rowntree Foundation: York.

—— and Karley, N.K. (2005) 'How much extra affordable housing is needed in England?', *Housing Studies*, 20, 5, 685–715.

——, Munro, M. and Lancaster, S. (1997) *The Economic Determinants of Household Formation: a Literature Review*. DETR: London.

Brandt, J., Tress, B. and Tress, G. (eds) (2000) 'Multifunctional Landscapes: Interdisciplinary Approaches to Landscape, Research and Management', Conference material for the international conference on Multifunctional Landscapes, Centre for Landscape Research, University of Roskilde, Denmark, 18–21 October.

Breheny, M. (1999) 'People, households and houses: the basis to the "great housing debate" in England, *Town Planning Review*, 70: 275–293.

—— and Hall, P. (eds) (1996) *The People: Where Will They Go?* Town and Country Planning Association: London.

Brundtland, G.H. (Chair) (1987) 'Our Common Future', Report of the World Commission on Environment and Development, United Nations: New York.

Burdett, R., Travers, T., Czischke, D., Rode, P. and Moser, B. (2005) *Density and Urban Neighbourhoods in London*, London School of Economics: London.

Burton, E. (2000) 'The compact city: just or just compact: a preliminary analysis', *Urban Studies*, 37, 11: 1969–2006.

Cabinet Office (1999) *Modernising Government*, Cabinet Office: London.

Cameron, S. (2006) 'From low demand to rising aspirations: housing market renewal within regional and neighbourhood regeneration policy', *Housing Studies*, 21, 1: 3–16.

Campaign to Protect Rural England (2005) *Building on Barker*, CPRE: London.

—— (2006) 'Huge household projections are a massive environmental challenge', CPRE Press Release, 14 March.

Capstick, M. (1987) *Housing Dilemmas in the Lake District*, Centre for North West Regional Studies: Lancaster University.

Carlyle, T. (1840) *Chartism*, James Fraser: London.

Carmona, M. (2001a) *Housing Design Quality: Through Policy, Guidance and Review*, Spon Press: London.

—— (2001b) 'Sustainable Urban Design – A Possible Agenda', in Layard, A., Davoudi, S. and Batty, S. (eds) *Planning for a Sustainable Future*, Spon Press: London: pp. 165–192.

——, Carmona, S. and Gallent, N. (2001) *Working Together: A Guide for Planners and Housing Providers*, Thomas Telford Publishers: London.

——, —— and —— (2003) *Delivering New Homes: Planning, Processes and Providers*, Spon Press: London.

——, Blum, R., Hammond, L., Stephens, Q., Dann, J., Karski, A., Pittock, C., Rowlands, S. and Stille, K. (2006) *Design Coding in Practice: An Evaluation*, ODPM: London.

Carpenter, M. (1864) *Our Convicts*, Longman, Roberts & Green: London.

Chadwick, E. (1965) [1842] *The Sanitary Conditions of the Labouring Population of Great Britain*, Edinburgh University Press: Edinburgh.

Champion, A.G. (2000) 'Flight from the Cities?' in Bate, R., Best, R. and Holmans, A. (eds) *On the Move: The Housing Consequences of Migration*, York Publishing Services: York: pp. 10–19.

Chartered Institute of Housing/Royal Town Planning Institute (2003) *Planning for Housing – The Potential for Sustainable Communities*, CIH: Coventry.

Chatterton, P. (2002) 'Be realistic: demand the impossible'. Moving towards "strong" sustainable development in an old industrial region? *Regional Studies*, 36, 5: 552–561.

Cherry, G.E. (1972) *Urban Change and Planning*, Alden Press: Oxford.

—— (1974) *The Evolution of British Town Planning*, Leonard Hill Books: Leighton Buzzard.

—— (1979) 'The town planning movement and the late Victorian city', *Transactions of the Institute of British Geographers*, New series, 4, 2: 306–19.

—— (1996) *Town Planning in Britain since 1900*, Blackwell Publisher: Oxford.

Clark, D. (1984) 'Rural Housing and Countryside Planning', in Blacksell, M. and Bowler, I. (eds) *Contemporary Issues in Rural Planning*, in *SW Papers in Geography*, pp. 93–104.

Clark, M. (2000) *Teleworking in the Countryside: Home-based Working in the Information Society*, Ashgate: Aldershot.

Cloke, P. (1979) *Key Settlements in Rural Areas*, Methuen: London.

Commission for Architecture and the Built Environment (2001) *The Value of Urban Design*, Thomas Telford Publishers: London.

—— (2005) *Making Design Policy Work*, CABE: London.

—— and the Department of the Environment, Transport and the Regions (2001a) *The Value of Urban Design*, Thomas Telford Publishers: London.

—— and —— (2001b) *By Design: Better Places to Live*, Thomas Telford Publishers: London.

Commission of the European Communities (1999) *European Spatial Development Perspective*, CEC: Luxembourg.

Commission for Rural Communities (2005) *State of the Countryside 2005*, CRC: Sheffield.

Cooper, S. (1978) *Public Housing and the Private Sector 1970–1984*, Gower Publishing Company: Farnborough.

—— (1985) *Public Housing and Private Property*, Gower: Aldershot.

Cope, H. (1999) *Housing Associations: Policy and Practice*, Macmillan: Basingstoke.

Counsell, D., Haughton, G., Allmendinger, P. and Vigar, G. (2003) 'New directions in UK strategic planning: from development plans to local development strategies', in *Town and Country Planning*, 72, 1: 15–19.

Countryside Commission (1998) *Planning for Countryside Quality*, Countryside Commission: London.

Cronin, A. (1993) 'The elusive quality of certainty' *Planning Week*, 1, 4: 16–17.

Crook, A., Currie, J., Jackson, A., Monk, S., Rowley, S., Smith, K. and Whitehead, C. (2001) *The Provision of Affordable Housing Through the Planning System*, Department of Land Economy, University of Cambridge: Cambridge.

Cullingworth, B. (1996) 'A vision lost', *Town and Country Planning*, 65, 6: 172–174.

—— (1997) 'British land-use planning: a failure to cope with change?', *Urban Studies*, 34, 5 and 6, 945–960.

—— and Nadin, V. (1997) *Town and Country Planning in the United Kingdom*, (12th edn) Routledge: London. (Most recent edition is Cullingworth, B. and Nadin, V. (2006) *Town and Country Planning in the United Kingdom*, (14th edn), Routledge: London.

Deloitte for South East England Development Agency (2005) *Sustaining Success in a Prosperous Region: Economic Implications of the South East Plan*, SEEDA: Guildford.

DEMOS (1999) *Living Together: Community Life on Mixed Tenure Estates*, DEMOS: London.

Department of the Environment (1981) *Proposed Modifications to the Cumbria and Lake District Joint Structure Plan*, DoE: London.

—— (1984) *Circular 15/84: Land for Housing*, DoE: London.

—— (1988) *Planning Policy Guidance Note 3: Land for Housing*, DoE: London.

—— (1989) *Planning Policy Guidance Note 3 (re-draft): Housing*, DoE: London.

—— (1991) *Circular 7/91: Planning and Affordable Housing*, DoE: London.

—— (1992) *Planning Policy Guidance Note 3: Housing*, DoE: London.

—— (1994a) *Quality in Town and Country*, DoE: London.

—— (1994b) *Regional Planning Guidance for the South East*, DoE: London.

—— (1995a) P*rovision for Social Housing – Background Analysis: Households in England, their Housing Tenure and their Housing Stock 1991–2001*, DoE: London.

—— (1995b) *Our Future Homes: Opportunity, Choice, Responsibility*, DoE: London.

—— (1996a) *Circular 13/96: Planning and Affordable Housing*, DoE: London.

—— (1996b) *Household Growth: Where Shall We Live?* DoE: London.

Department for the Environment, Food and Rural Affairs (2006) *Affordable Rural Housing Commission – Final Report*, DEFRA: London.

Department of the Environment, Transport and the Regions (1998a) *Modern Local Government: In Touch With the People*, DETR: London.

—— (1998b) *Circular 6/98: Planning and Affordable Housing*, DETR: London.

—— (1998c) *Planning for Communities of the Future*, DETR: London.

—— (1999a) *A Better Quality of Life: Strategy for Sustainable Development for the United Kingdom*, DETR: London.

—— (1999b) *Projections of Households in England to 2021*, DETR: London.

—— (1999c) *Low Demand and Unpopular Housing* (Policy Action Team 7 Report), DETR: London.

—— (2000a) *Planning Policy Guidance Note 3: Housing*, DETR: London.

—— (2000b) *North West Housing Demand and Need Research*, DETR: London.

—— (2000c) *Quality and Choice: Decent Homes for All*, DETR: London.

—— (2001) *Regional Planning Guidance for the South East* (RPG9), DETR: London.

Department for Regional Development Northern Ireland (2003) *Regional Development Strategy for Northern Ireland*, DRDNI: Belfast.

Department for Transport, Local Government and the Regions (2000) *Our Countryside: The Future – A Fair Deal for Rural England* (Cm 4909) DTLR: London.

—— (2001a) *Council Tax: A Consultation Paper on Proposed Changes for Second Homes and Long Term Empty Homes*, DTLR: London.

—— (2001b) *Planning Obligations: Delivering a Fundamental Change*, DTLR: London.

—— (2001c) *Planning: Delivering a Fundamental Change*, DTLR: London.

Derbyshire, B. (2000) 'Greenwich Millennium Village: A Case Study of Sustainable Housing', in Edwards, B. and Turrent, D. (eds) *Sustainable Housing: Principles and Practice*, Spon Press: London: pp. 88–95.

Dilke, Sir Charles (Chairman) (1885) 'First Report of the Commission on the Housing of the Working Classes [England and Wales] with minutes of evidence and appendix (1884–1885)', Vol. II, in British Parliamentary Papers, Irish University Press Series: Shannon.

East of England Regional Assembly (2004) *Regional Planning Guidance (RPG14) for the East of England Draft Strategy*, EERA: Bury St Edmunds.

Edwards, B. (2000a) 'Design Guidelines for Sustainable Housing', in Edwards, B. and Turrent, D. (eds) *Sustainable Housing: Principles and Practice*, Spon Press: London: pp. 124–141.

—— (2000b) 'Sustainable Housing: Architecture, Society and Professionalism', in Edwards, B. and Turrent, D. (eds) *Sustainable Housing: Principles and Practice*, Spon Press: London: pp. 7–10.

Empty Homes Agency (2002) *England's Empty Homes – Unlocking the Potential*, EHA: London.

Engels, F. (1841) [1969 edition quoted, first published in the UK in 1892] *The Condition of the Working Class in England*, Penguin Books: London.

ENTEC (2003) *The Relationships Between Community Strategies and Local Development Frameworks*, Office of the Deputy Prime Minister, London.

Environmental Resources Management (2005) *Draft Sustainability Appraisal Report on the Consultation Draft of the South East Plan*, ERM: London.

Friedmann, J. (2004) 'Strategic spatial planning and the longer range', with an introduction by Healey, P. and comments by Albrechts, L. *et al.*, *Planning Theory & Practice*, 5, 1: 49–67.

Gallent, N. (1997) 'Planning for affordable rural housing in England and Wales', *Housing Studies*, 12, 1: 127–137.

—— (2000) 'Planning and affordable housing: from old values to new Labour', *Town Planning Review*, 71, 2, pp. 123–147.

—— (2007) 'Household Projections and Strategic Housing Allocations', in Dimitriou, H and Thompson, R. (eds) *Strategic and Regional Planning in the UK*, Routledge: London.

—— and Bell, P. (2000) 'Planning exceptions in rural England – past, present and future', *Planning Practice and Research*, 15, 4, 375–384.

—— and Tewdwr-Jones, M. (2005) *Impacts of Regional Growth in South East England: A Review of the Evidence Base*, South East England Regional Assembly: Guildford.

——, Mace, A. and Tewdwr-Jones, M. (2002) *Policy Advice on Second Homes in Rural Areas*, Countryside Agency: London.

——, Mace, A., and Tewdwr-Jones, M. (2003) 'Dispelling a myth? Second homes in rural Wales', *Area*, 35, 3, 271–284.

Garside, P.L. (2000) 'The impact of philanthropy: housing provision and the Sutton Model Dwellings Trust, 1900–1939', *Economic History Review*, 53, 4: 742–768.

Gentle, C., Dorling, D. and Cornford, J. (1994) 'Negative equity and British housing in the 1990s: cause and effect', *Urban Studies*, 31, 2, 181–199.

George, H. (1880) *Progress and Poverty*, Appleton & Co: San Francisco.

Gibbs, D.C. (2002) *Local Economic Development and the Environment*, Routledge: London.

Giddens, A. (1998) *The Third Way*, Polity: Cambridge.

Gold, J.R. (1997) *The Experience of Modernism*, Spon Press: London.

Goodchild, B. (1996) *Housing and the Urban Environment: A Guide to Housing, Design, Renewal and Urban Planning*, Blackwell Science: Oxford.

Goss, S. and Blackaby, B. (1998) *Designing Local Housing Strategies: A Good Practice Guide*, Chartered Institute of Housing and the Local Government Association: Coventry.

Government Office for the North West (2002a) *Draft Regional Planning Guidance for the North West (RPG13) incorporating the Secretary of State's Proposed Changes*, GONW: Manchester.

—— (2002b) *Draft Regional Planning Guidance for the North West (RPG13) Schedule of the Secretary of State's Proposed Changes and Statement of Reasons for Changes*, GONW: Manchester.

—— (2003) *Regional Planning Guidance for the North West* (RPG13), GONW: Manchester.

Government Office for the South East (2000) *Regional Planning Guidance Note 9: South East*, GOSE: Guildford.

Grant, J. (2005) *Planning the Good Community: New Urbanism in Theory and Practice*, Routledge: London.

Hall, P. (1996) *Cities of Tomorrow* (updated edition), Blackwell Publishers: Oxford.

—— (2001) 'Sustainable Cities or Town Cramming?' in Layard, A., Davoudi, S. and Batty, S. (Eds) *Planning for a Sustainable Future*, Spon Press: London: pp. 101–114.

——, Gracey, H., Drewett, R. and Thomas, R. (1973) *The Containment of Urban England*, Allen & Unwin: London.

Hallett, G. (ed.) (1993) *The New Housing Shortage: Housing Affordability in Europe and the USA*, Routledge: London.

Hambleton, R., Essex, S., Mills, L. and Razzaque, K. (1996) *Findings 44: Inter-agency Working in Practice*, Joseph Rowntree Foundation: York.

Hamnett, C. (2001) 'London's Housing', *Area*, 33, 1: 80–84.

Harris, N., Hooper, A.J. and Bishop. K. (2002), 'Constructing the practice of spatial planning: a national spatial planning framework for Wales', *Environment and Planning C: Government and Policy*, 20, 4: 555–572.

Harrison, J., (1992) *Housing Associations after the 1988 Housing Act*, School for Advanced Urban Studies: Bristol.

Haughton, G. and Counsell, D. (2004) *Regions, Spatial Strategies and Sustainable Development*, Routledge: London.

Healey, P. (1997) *Collaborative Planning: Shaping Places in Fragmented Societies*, Macmillan: Basingstoke.

—— (2003) 'Collaborative planning in perspective', *Planning Theory*, 2, 2: 101–123.

Heap, D. and Ward, A. (1980) 'Planning bargaining – the pros and cons or, how much can the system stand?' *Journal of Environmental and Planning Law*, October: 631–637.

HertsDirect (2003a) 'Hertfordshire under pressure to find space for extra homes', www.hertsdirect.org/environment/plan/extrahousing (accessed 30 March 2004).

—— (2003b) 'Hertfordshire authorities respond to East of England Regional Assembly', www.hertsdirect.org/environment/plan/eoferesponse (accessed 30 March 2004).

Hill, O. (2005) *Letters to Fellow-workers 1872–1911*, Kyrle Books: London.

HM Government (1980) *Housing Act 1980*, HMSO: London.

—— (1988) *Housing Act 1988*, HMSO: London.

—— (1996) *Housing Act 1996*, HMSO: London.

—— (2000) *Local Government Act 2000*, TSO: London.

—— (2004) *Planning and Compulsory Purchase Act 2004*, TSO: London.

HM Treasury (2005) *Planning Gain Supplement – A Consultation*, HM Treasury: London.

Hoggart, K. (2003) 'England', in Gallent, N., Shucksmith, M. and Tewdwr-Jones, M. (eds) *Housing in the European Countryside: Rural Pressure and Policy in Western Europe*, Spon Press: London.

—— and Henderson, S. (2005) 'Excluding exceptions: housing non-affordability and the oppression of environmental sustainability?' *Journal of Rural Studies*, 21: 181–196.

Holmans, A. (1995) *Housing Demand and Need in England 1991–2001*, Joseph Rowntree Foundation: York.

—— (2001) *Housing Demand and Need in England 1996–2016*, Town and Country Planning Association: London.

——, Kleinman, M., Royce Porter, C. and Whitehead, C. (2000) *Technical Report*, Shelter: London.

Holmes, C. (2006) *A New Vision for Housing*, Routledge: London.

Hooper, A. and Nicol, C. (1999) 'The design and planning of residential development: standard house types in the speculative house building industry', *Environment and Planning B: Planning and Design*, 26: 793–805.

Horsfall, T.C. (1904) *The Improvement of the Dwellings and Surroundings of the People: The Example of Germany*, Manchester University Press: Manchester.

House Builders Federation (2002) *Building a Crisis: Housing Under-supply in England*, House Builders Federation: London.

House of Commons (2002a) *Affordable Housing: Memoranda submitted to the Urban Affairs Select Committee: Memoranda by Council for the Protection of Rural England (CPRE) (AFH 68)*, TSO: London.

—— (2002b) *Planning Green Paper: Thirteenth Report of Session 2001–02*, TSO: London.

Housing and Planning Review (1998) 'Planning and Affordable Housing', (editorial), *Housing and Planning Review*, 53, 2: 3.

Howard, E. (1898) *To-morrow: A Peaceful Path to Real Reform*, Swan Sonnenschein: London.

Institute for Public Policy Research (2005) *IPPR Commission on Sustainable Development in the South East: Managing Water Resources and Flood Risk in the South East*, IPPR: London.

Johnson, T. and Hart, C. (2005) *The Barker Review of Housing Supply and Planning Gain Supplement*, Royal Institution of Chartered Surveyors: London.

Jones, C. and Murie, A. (2006) *Right to Buy: Analysis and Evaluation of a Housing Policy*, Blackwell Publishing: London.

Jones, G.S. (1976) *Outcast London: A Study in the Relationship Between Classes in Victorian Society* (2nd edn), Penguin Books: London.

Joseph Rowntree Foundation (1994) *Inquiry into Planning for Housing*, Joseph Rowntree Foundation: York.

—— (2006) *Homes for Rural Communities – Conclusions from the Rural Housing Policy Forum*, JRF: York.

Jowell, J. (1977) 'Bargaining and development control', *Journal of Planning and Environmental Law*: 414–433.

Karn, V., Wong, C., Gallent, N. and Allen, C. (1998) *Bolton Housing Needs Study*, Bolton Metropolitan Borough Council: Bolton.

King, D. (1999) 'Official Household Projections in England: Methodology, Usage and Sensitivity Tests', Joint ECE-EUROSTAT Work Session on Demographic Projections, Working Paper No. 47, Perugia, Italy, 3–7 May .

King, P. (2004) *Private Dwelling: Contemplating the Use of Housing*, Routledge: London.

Lake District Special Planning Board (1977) *Draft National Park Plan*, LDSPB: Kendal.

—— (1978) *26th Annual Report 1977–78*, LDSPB: Kendal.

—— (1980) *Cumbria and Lake District Joint Structure Plan*, written statement, LDSPB: Kendal/Cumbria County Council: Carlisle.

Langstaff, M. (1992) 'Housing Associations: A Move to Centre Stage', in Birchall, J. (ed.) *Housing Policy in the 1990s*, Routledge: London.

Leather, P. (2003) *Evaluation of the Housing Corporation's Pilot New Tools Projects*, Housing Corporation: London.

Leishman, C. and Warren, F. (2006) 'Private housing design customization through house type substitution', *Construction Management and Economics*, 24, 2: 149–158.

Letter from John Reynolds (EERA) to Lord Rooker (2004): www.eelgc.gov.uk/eelgc Docs/Agenda%20item%204%20annex%20B.doc (accessed 30 March 2004).

Letter from Lord Rooker to John Reynolds (EERA) (2004): www.eelgc.gov.uk/eelgc Docs/scannedlordrooker.doc (accessed 30 March 2004).

Lloyd, G. and Illsley, B. (1999), 'Planning and developed government in the United Kingdom', *Town Planning Review*, 70, 4: 409–432.

London Biodiversity Partnership (2005) *Action for Biodiversity*, LBP: London.

Long, D. (2000) *Key Issues for Sustainable Communities,* European Institute for Urban Affairs, Liverpool John Moores University: Liverpool.

Mace, A., Gallent, N., Hall, P., Porsch, L., Braun, R. and Pfeiffer, U. (2004) *Shrinking to Grow? The Urban Regeneration Challenge in Manchester and Leipzig*, Institute of Community Studies: London.

Malpass, P. and Murie, A. (1987) *Housing Policy and Practice*, Macmillan: Basingstoke.

—— and —— (1994) *Housing Policy and Practice* (4th edn), Macmillan: London.

—— and —— (1999) *Housing Policy and Practice* (5th edn), Macmillan: Basingstoke.

Martin, S. (1999) 'Picking winners or piloting best value? An analysis of English best value bids', *Local Government Studies* 25, 2: 102–118.

Marx, K. and Engels F. (1998) [1st edn 1848] *The Communist Manifesto*, Verso: London.

Mayor of London (2002) *The London Plan*, Greater London Assembly: London.

Mearns, A. (1885) [quoted from 1970 edn] *The Bitter Cry of Outcast London*, Leicester University Press: New York.

Meen, G. (2005) 'On the economics of the Barker Review of housing supply', *Housing Studies*, 20, 6: 949–971.

Mill, J.S. (1848) *Principle of Political Economy with some Applications to Social Philosophy*, J.W. Parker: London.

—— (1991 [1859]) *'On Liberty' in Focus* (annotated text edited by Gray, J. and Smith, G.W., 1991) Routledge: London.

Miller, M. (1989) *Letchworth: The First Garden City*, Phillimore & Co. Ltd: Chichester.

Mills, G. (2000) 'Sustainable Housing in Manchester: a Case Study of Hulme', in Edwards, B. and Turrent, D. (eds) *Sustainable Housing: Principles and Practice*, Spon Press: London: 96–105.

Mole Valley District Council (1996) *Local Development Plan* (Adopted), Mole Valley District Council: Dorking.

Monbiot, G. (1999) 'Hidden extras: homelessness and second homes', *Urban 75*, www.urban75.org/archive/news072.html (accessed 13 October 2002).

Monk, S. and Whitehead, C. (Eds) (2000) *Restructuring Housing Systems: From Social to Affordable Housing*, Joseph Rowntree Foundation: York.

Mumford, E. (2000) *The CIAM Discourse on Urbanism, 1928–1960*, MIT Press: Cambridge, MA.

Murdoch, J. and Abram, S. (2002) *Rationalities of Planning: Development versus Environment in Planning for Housing*, Ashgate: Aldershot.

Murray, K. and Evans, R, (2002) 'Winners and Losers', *Inside Housing*, 2 August: 18–19.

National Housing Federation and Chartered Institute of Housing (2003) *Draft Joint Response from the National Housing Federation and the Chartered Institute of Housing to the Consultation Leading to Regional Planning Guidance (RPG14) for the East of England*, National Housing Federation Midlands: Wellingborough.

Nettlefold, J.S. (1908) *Practical Housing*, Garden City Press: Letchworth.

—— (1914) *Practical Town Planning: A Land and Housing Policy*, The St Catherine Press: London.

Newchurch & Co. (2000) *Mapping Partnerships in Eleven Local Authorities*, DETR: London.

Norberg-Schulz, C. (1985) *The Concept of Dwelling: On the Way to A Figurative Architecture*, Rizzoli: New York.

North West Regional Assembly (2000) *People, Places and Prosperity: Draft Regional Planning Guidance for the North West*, NWRA: Wigan.

Office for National Statistics (1999) *National Population Projections 1996-based, Series PP2 no. 21*, Stationery Office: London.

Office of the Deputy Prime Minister (2002b) *Sustainable Communities – Delivering through Planning*, ODPM: London.

—— (2003a) *Sustainable Communities – Building for the Future*, ODPM: London.

—— (2003b) *Home Ownership Taskforce Gears up to Deliver Stronger Support to First-time Homeowners* – Press Release (March 18) ODPM: London.

—— (2003c) *Influencing the Size, Type and Affordability of Housing – Consultation Paper*, ODPM: London.

—— (2003d) *Planning and Sustainable Development*, ODPM: London.

—— (2003e) *Supporting the Delivery of New Housing – Consultation Paper*, ODPM: London.

—— (2003f) *Land-Use Change in England: No. 18* (May), ODPM: London.

—— (2003g) News Release 2003/0137: *Planning Must Deliver the Homes Needed in our Communities*, ODPM: London.

—— (2004a) *Consultation on Planning Policy Statement 1 Creating Sustainable Communities*, ODPM: London.

—— (2004b) *Housing and Planning in the Regions: Consultation*, (September), ODPM: London.

—— (2004c) *Planning Policy Statement 12: Local Development Frameworks*, ODPM: London.

—— (2005a) *Consultation Paper on New Planning Policy Statement 3 (PPS3): Housing*, ODPM: London.

—— (2005b) *Planning for Mixed Communities – Consultation Paper*, ODPM: London.

—— (2005c) *Planning for Housing Provision – Consultation Paper*, ODPM: London.

—— (2005d) *Planning for Housing Provision – Summary of Responses*, ODPM: London.

—— (2005e) *Affordability Targets – Implications for Housing Supply*, ODPM: London.

—— (2005f) *A Sustainability Impact Study of Additional Housing Scenarios in England*, ODPM: London.

—— (2005g) *Creating Sustainable Communities: Greening the Gateway*, ODPM: London.

—— (2005h) *Planning Policy Statement 1: Delivering Sustainable Development*, ODPM: London.

—— (2005i) *Local Strategic Partnerships: Shaping their Future – Consultation Paper*, ODPM: London.

—— (2005j) *Sustainable Communities: Homes for All*, ODPM: London.

—— (2005k) *Circular 5/2005: Planning Obligations*, ODPM: London.

—— (2006a) *Starting Out with Local Development Schemes*, ODPM: London.

—— (2006b) *A Framework for City Regions*, ODPM: London.

—— (2006c) *Household Projections to 2026*, ODPM: London.

—— (2006 websource) www.communities.gov.uk/pub/8/Table102_id1156008.xcs (accessed 06 September 2006).

Pahl, R. (1966), 'The social objectives of village planning', *Official Architecture and Planning*, 29: 1146–1450 (republished in Pahl, R. (1975) *Whose City? And Further Essays on Urban Society*, Penguin Books: London: 40–53).

—— and Spencer, L. (2004) 'Personal communities: not simply families of "fate" or "choice"', *Current Sociology*, 52, 2: 199–221.

Pembrokeshire Coast National Park Authority (2001) *Evidence for Housing Policy*, PCNPA: Haverfordwest.

Pembrokeshire County Council and Pembrokeshire Coast National Park Authority (2002) Joint Unitary Development Plan Deposit (2000–2016), PCNPA: Haverfordwest.

Phillips, D. and Williams, A., (1983) 'The social implications of rural housing policy: a review of developments in the past decade, *Countryside Planning Yearbook*, 4: 77–102.

Planning 1245 (1997) 'Minister defends brownfield targets', *Planning*, 21 November: 3.

Planning 1662 (2006a) 'Shadow cast on market bias', *Planning* 1662, 31 March: 8.

Planning 1663 (2006b) 'Committee casts doubt on infrastructure hopes', *Planning*, 7 April: 4.

Power, A. (1999) 'High-rise estates in Europe: is rescue possible?' *Journal of European Social Policy*, 9, 2: 139–162.

Prescott, J. (2002) *Sustainable Communities, Housing and Planning: Statement to the House of Commons*, 18.07.02, ODPM: London.

Priemus H., Rodenburg C. H. and Nijkamp, P. (2004) 'Multifunctional urban land-use: a new phenomenon? A new planning challenge?', *Built Environment*, 30, 4: 269–273.

Raco, M. (2005) 'Sustainable development, rolled-out neo-liberalism and sustainable communities, *Antipode*, 37, 2: 324–346.

—— (2006) *Building Sustainable Communities: Spatial Development, Citizenship, and Labour Market Engineering in Post-War Britain*, Policy Press: Bristol.

Ravetz, A. (2001) *Council Housing and Culture: The History of a Social Experiment*, Routledge: London.

Reade, E. (1987) *British Town and Country Planning*, Open University Press: Milton Keynes.

Regan, S. (2002) 'No longer right to buy: sales of council property worsen housing shortages in key areas', *Financial Times*, Wednesday, 7 August 2002.

Rhodes, R. (1988) *Beyond Westminster and Whitehall: The Sub-Central Governments of Britain*, Unwin Hyman: London.

Ricketts, S. (2006) 'Planning Gain Supplement . . . will it work?' *London Calling*, April: 2–3.

Robertson, M. and Walford, R, (2000) 'Views and visions of land-use in the United Kingdom', *Geographical Journal*, 166, 3: 239–254.

Rodenburg C.A. and Nijkamp, P. (2004) 'Multifunctional land-use in the city: a typological overview', *Built Environment*, 30, 4: 274–288.

Rogers, C.P. (1989) *Housing, The New Law: A Guide to the Housing Act 1988*, Butterworths: London.

Rogers, R. and Power, A. (2000) *Cities for a Small Country*, Faber & Faber: London.

Roger Tym & Partners (2004) *Costing the Infrastructure Needs of the South East Counties*, Roger Tym & Partners: London.

—— (2005) *South East Plan: Regional Assessment of Urban Potential – Stage Two*, Roger Tym & Partners: London.

Royal Town Planning Institute (2003) *Education Commission: Final Report*, RTPI: London.

—— (2005) *Planning Gain Supplement Consultation Exposes Folly of New Land Tax* (Press Notice), RTPI: London.

Schmied, D. (2002) *What Price Peace and Quiet? Rural Gentrification and Affordable Housing – The Example of Cotswold District, South West England*, Universität Bayreuth: Bayreuth.

Short, J.R., Fleming, S. and Witt, S. (1986) *Housebuilding, Planning and Community Action*, Routledge: London.

Shucksmith, M. (1981) *No Homes for Locals?* Gower: Aldershot.

—— (1990) *Housebuilding in Britain's Countryside*, Routledge: London.

Simmie, J. (ed.) (1994) *Planning London*, UCL Press: London.

Sims, G. (1889) [quoted edition 1984] *How the Poor Live in Horrible London*, Garland Publishing: New York and London.

Sitte, C. (1889) [translated and reprinted, 1965] *City Planning According to Artistic Principles*, Random House: New York.

South East England Development Agency (2005) *Review of Regional Economic Strategy for South East England 2006–2016* – Consultation Document, SEEDA: Guildford.

South East England Regional Assembly (2005a) *A Clear Vision for the South East: The South East Plan Core Document*, SEERA: Guildford.

—— (2005b) *Consultation Draft South East Plan: Technical Note 2: Spatial Options*, SEERA: Guildford.

—— (2005c) *Consultation Draft South East Plan: Technical Note 5 (Revised): Demography*, SEERA: Guildford.

—— (2005d) *South East Municipal Solid Waste and South East Plan Housing Projection Scenarios: Background Note*, SEERA: Guildford.

Statistical Society (1848) 'The state of the inhabitants and their dwellings in Church Lane, St. Giles', J*ournal of the Statistical Society of London*, vol. 11, 1–18.

Stead, D., Williams, J. and Titheridge, H. (2000) 'Land-use Change and the People – Identifying the Connections', in Williams, K, Burton, E. and Jenks, M. (eds) *Achieving Sustainable Urban Form*, Spon Press: London: pp. 174–184.

Steinberg, E. (2000) 'An integrative theory of urban design', *Journal of the American Planning Association*, 66, 3: 265–278.

Stoker, G. (1991) *The Politics of Local Government* (2nd edn), Macmillan: London.

Sutcliffe A. (1981) *Towards the Planned City: Germany, Britain, the United States and France, 1780–1914*, Blackwell Publishers: London.

Syms, P. (1997) *The Redevelopment of Contaminated Land for Housing*, ISVA: London.

Taylor, M. (1997) *The Best of Both Worlds: The Voluntary Sector and Local Government*, York Publishing Services: York.

Tewdwr-Jones, M. (1999) 'Discretion, flexibility, and certainty in British spatial planning: emerging ideological conflicts and inherent political tensions', *Journal of Planning Education and Research* 18, 2: 244–256.

—— (2002) *The Planning Polity: Planning, Government and the Policy Process*, Routledge: London.

—— (2004) 'Spatial planning: principles, practice and culture', *Journal of Planning and Environment Law*, 57, 5: 560–569.

—— and Williams, R.H. (2001) T*he European Dimension of British Planning*, Spon Press: London.

—— and Allmendinger, P. (eds) (2006), *Territory, Identity and Spatial Planning: Spatial Governance in a Fragmented Nation*, Routledge: London.

——, Gallent, N. and Mace, A. (2002) *Second Homes and Holiday Homes and the Land use Planning System*, Welsh Assembly Government: Cardiff.

——, Morphet, J. and Allmendinger, P. (2006) 'The contested strategies of local governance: community strategies, development plans, and local government modernization', *Environment and Planning A*, 38: 533–551.

Thatcher, M. (1987) 'AIDS, Education and the Year 2000', *Woman's Own*, 3 October, 8–10.

—— (1993) *The Downing Street Years*, HarperCollins: London.

Thornley, A. (1993) *Urban Planning under Thatcherism* (2nd edn), Routledge: London.

Town and Country Planning Association (1996) *The People: Where Will They Go? The Report of the TCPA Inquiry into Housing Need Provision in England*, TCPA: London.

—— (2000) *Housing Policy Statement*, TCPA, London.

Toynbee, P. (2003) *Hard Work: Life in Low-pay Britain*, London: Bloomsbury.

Unwin, R, (1912) *Nothing Gained by Overcrowding! How the Garden City Type of Development May Benefit Both Owner and Occupier*, Garden Cities and Town Planning Association: London.

Urban Task Force (1999) *Towards an Urban Renaissance*, Spon Press, London.

Wallace, A., Bevan, M., Croucher, K., Jackson, K., O'Malley, L. and Orton, V. (2005) *The Impact of Empty, Second and Holiday Homes on the Sustainability of Rural Communities: A Systematic Literature Review*, Centre for Housing Policy: York.

Ward, S.V. (2004) *Planning and Urban Change* (2nd edn), Sage Publication: London.

Welsh Assembly Government (2002) *Objections to the Joint Pembrokeshire Unitary Development Plan (to 2016)*, Welsh Assembly Government: Cardiff.

—— (2003) *People, Places and Prosperity: Wales Spatial Plan*, Stationery Office: London.

West Stevenage Consortium (2001) *West of the A1(M) at Stevenage: Development Principles and Design Guide*, Barton Willmore Master Planning: Reading.

Whelan, R. (1998) Editor's introduction to Octavia Hill and the Social Housing Debate: Essays and letters by Octavia Hill, IEA Health and Welfare Unit, St Edmundsbury Press: Suffolk.

Whitehead, C. (2002) 'The provision of affordable housing through the planning system', Paper presented at ERES Conference: Glasgow, June.

Williams, G., Bell, P. and Russell, L. (1991) *Evaluating the Low Cost Rural Housing Initiative*, DoE: London.

Williams, K. (2000) 'Does Intensifying Cities Make Them More Sustainable?' in Williams, K., Burton, E. and Jenks, M. (eds) *Achieving Sustainable Urban Form*, Spon Press: London: 30–45.

WSP (2005) *Journey to Work Analysis: Part 1, Regional*, WSP Group plc: London.

Index

Numbers in *italics* indicate plates, tables and boxes.

Related titles from Routledge

Planning on The Edge

Nick Gallent, Johan Andersson and Marco Bianconi

More than a tenth of the land mass of the UK comprises 'urban fringe': the countryside around towns that has been called 'planning's last frontier'. One of the key challenges facing spatial planners is the land-use management of this area, regarded by many as fit only for locating sewage works, essential service functions and other un-neighbourly uses. To others however, it is seen as a dynamic area where a range of urban and rural uses collide.

Planning on the Edge fills an important gap in the literature, examining in detail the challenges that planning faces in this no-man's land. It presents both problems and solutions, and builds a vision for the urban fringe that is concerned with maximising its potential and with bridging the physical and cultural rift between town and country.

Students, professionals and researchers alike will benefit from the book's structured approach, while the global and transferable nature of the principles and ideas underpinning the study will appeal to an international audience

ISBN: 978–0-415–37571–9 (Hb)
978–0–415–40290–3 (Pb)

Available at all good bookshops
For ordering and further information please visit:
www.routledge.com/builtenvironment

Related titles from Routledge

Territory, Identity and Spatial Planning

Edited by Mark Tewdwr-Jones
and Philip Allmendinger

This book provides a multi-disciplinary study of territory, identity and space in a devolved UK, through the lens of spatial planning. It draws together leading internationally renowned researchers from a variety of disciplines to address the implications of devolution upon spatial planning and the rescaling of UK politics. Each contributor offers a different perspective on core issues in planning today in the context of New Labour's regional project. Themes are illustrated throughout with significant case studies and key topics cover issues relating to:

■ Theoretical Contexts for Territory, Identity and Spatial Planning

■ Studies of Territorial and Spatial Planning

■ Institutions of Governance and Substantive Policy Roles

■ Complexities and Interdependencies in Spatial Governance

ISBN   978–0–415–36034–0 (Hb)
          978–0–415–36035–7 (Pb)
          978–0–203–00800–3 (eBook)

Available at all good bookshops
For ordering and further information please visit:
www.routledge.com/builtenvironment